Law in Eastern Europe

A series published in cooperation with
Leiden University, the Universities of Tartu and
Graz and the European Academy of Bozen/Bolzano

General Editor

William Simons

VOLUME 62

The titles published in this series are listed at brill.com/laee

The Legal Dimension in Cold-War Interactions

The Legal Dimension in Cold-War Interactions

Some Notes from the Field

Edited by

Tatiana Borisova
William Simons

MARTINUS
NIJHOFF
PUBLISHERS

LEIDEN • BOSTON
2012

Library of Congress Control Number: 2012952886

ISSN 0075-823X
ISBN 978-90-04-20332-7 (hardback)
ISBN 978-90-04-20333-4 (e-book)

Koninklijke Brill NV incorporates the imprints Brill, Global Oriental, Hotei Publishing, IDC Publishers and Martinus Nijhoff Publishers.

This book is printed on acid-free paper.

TABLE OF CONTENTS

Preface

Unlike the hot war of WWII which preceded it, the end of the Cold War was not marked by an official document of capitulation nor followed by a universal blaming of those adjudged guilty, by a legal tribunal, of having started and pursued the war or by reconciling the alleged perpetrators and the victims by a truth commission.[1] It seems that different rules governed this cold conflict.

Thus, while there is a multitude of materials dealing with the end of the CW,[2] on the one hand, on the other, remnants of unfinished business litter the byways of the path forward. So, the 1974 amendment to the US Trade Act—named after its two major co-sponsors in the US Congress, the late US Senator Henry "Scoop' Jackson and the late Representative Charles Vanik, imposing sanctions on nations restricting emigration so as to "assure the continued dedication of the United States to fundamental human rights"[3]—is still US law 'in books'. Most recently in 2011 and again in 2012, however, senior US politicians have called for the setting aside of this Cold-War milestone … two decades after the end of the USSR.[4]

1 "[…] only Germany, the Baltic states of Estonia, Latvia and Lithuania, and Romania have employed truth commissions as methods to reckon with communist crimes." Lavinia Stan, "Truth Commissions in Post-Communism: The Overlooked Solution?", T*he Open Political Science Journal* (2009) No.2, 1-13, reproduced at <http://www.academia.edu/183362/Truth_Commissions_in_Post-Communism_The_Overlooked_Solution>. See, also, Liviu Damsa, "Lustration (Administrative Justice) and Closure in Post-Communist East Central Europe", 1(4) *International Journal of Public Law and Policy* (2011), 335ff.

2 Reflected, for example. in historian Nathan Vigil's 'endofcoldwar' course (and website at the University of Georgia: <http://endofcoldwar.com/>) and the *'okonchanie kholodnoi voiny'* page of <http://www.coldwar.ru/bases/bases7.php>. And it is but a short hop from history, law, and politics to art:

> "[…] there are no grand monuments to the American victory [in the Cold War]. All this raises the question, did the Cold War ever end? Maybe not. Now, artists Yevgeniy Fiks and Stamatina Gregory have released a call for proposals for a 'Monument to Cold War Victory'."

The winning work of art which would become this 'Monument to CW Victory' is selected by a panel "[…] that includes artist Vito Acconci, philosopher and professor Susan Buck-Morss, theorist and professor Boris Groys, artist Vitaly Komar, curator Viktor Misiano and Creative Time curator Nato Thompson". See Hrag Vartanian (interview with Evgenii Fiks), "Did the Cold War Ever End?" (3 August 2012), at <http://hyperallergic.com/55171/monument-to-cold-war-victory/>.

3 19 *US Code*, Chapter 12, subchapter IV, part 1, §2432: Freedom of Emigration in East-West Trade.

4 Steven Lee Myers and David M. Herszenhorn, "Clinton Tells Russia That Sanctions Will Soon End", *The New York Times* (8 September 2012); and "Biden Urges Repeal of Jackson-Vanik Amendment" (14 March 2011), *Voice of Russia*, available at <http://english.ruvr.ru/2011/03/14/47359712.html>.

Tatiana Borisova and William Simons, eds.
The Legal Dimension in Cold-War Interactions: Some Notes from the Field vii-ix

Yet, there are those in the US (and elsewhere) who continue to pursue the (old) enemy on the trail of human rights—giving one pause to wonder about 'ends':

> "Sergei Magnitsky Rule of Law Accountability Act, named for a Russian lawyer who was arrested and died in prison after investigating official corruption. The Magnitsky measure requires that those responsible for human rights violations be denied visas and have their assets frozen. The State Department has already denied visas for some officials implicated in Mr. Magnitsky's death."[5]

The contributors to this sixty-second volume of the *Law in Eastern Europe* series (*LEE*) will enlighten the reader about several key aspects of the legal dimension in Cold-War interactions. While the chapters in this collection are not intended to exhaustively deal with this complex patchwork, they surely will stimulate the reader to appreciate—with clarity—the topics dealt with by our authors' collective.

Much has been done to consider the history of, and to analyze developments in, the field of East European law in particular—and in the comparative-law field more in general—and is reflected (albeit, of course, only in part) in this series. But there is more work to be done to further demystify the past as well as to consider the trends in current thinking and the possible course(s) of future developments. Science-citation and other such useful indices notwithstanding, there are no tools to measure—with any precision—the impact of writings, academic or otherwise, on policymakers or on the public at large (or which one is more important). But we hope that the sixty-one previous *LEE* volumes will have played a modest role in broadening an understanding among specialists and generalists of developments in law in Eastern Europe; of the interactions of law with other parts of society; of how these developments and interactions proceed in their own exceptional way (the '*spetsifika*' to which reference often is made in discussions about law reform in the region) and how they relate to debates in other parts of the region and the world.

This volume marks the fifty-fifth year of publication of the series, and the works in this collection are a fine addition to its traditions in offering to its readers the thinking of senior and, also, of up-and-coming scholars and practitioners.

First of all, I offer heartfelt thanks to the authors of this volume. In addition, several others also have made invaluable contributions to this work; we also are grateful to them for their many efforts in bringing this work to print: Ms. Alice Engl, at the European Academy (Bozen/Bolzano), Ms. Ingeborg van der Laan at Brill Publishers (Leiden), and Ms. Kärt Pormeister at the University of Tartu (a Master of Law candidate in the Faculty of Law in Tartu, Estonia, who *inter alia* compiled and refined the index with skill and verve). Thanks also to Keith Ewing, Jane Henderson, Albert J. Schmidt, and Peter Slinn for generously allowing us to reproduce the images which they made available for use in this volume.

5 Peter Baker, "Senate Panel Advances Trade Bill with Russia" (18 July 2012), at <http://thecaucus.blogs.nytimes.com/2012/07/18/senate-panel-advances-trade-bill-with-russia>.

This is also the first volume in the *LEE* series which bears the University of Tartu's name. Support for and encouragement of further work on the series was expanded, several years ago, to include the University of Graz and the European Academy of Bozen/Bolzano. The close involvement of these institutions has been invaluable and is something for which I am most grateful. For a few years, this also included the University of Trento in Northern Italy; another contribution to our work for which I have similar sentiments. Now, the University of Tartu and Estonia's Centre for EU Russian Studies in Tartu—along with the Tartu Faculty of Law—are generously adding, to this effort, their many intellectual and administrative resources.

The contributions to this work which have made by my Tartu colleagues already have proven, likewise, to be invaluable. A refreshing sense of vision for the future is reflected in this Tartu team—something which has not always been as visible in the field as one might expect after the 'end' of the Cold War.

This collective intellectual input and administrative drive from these institutions represent a welcome strengthening of the platform for this *LEE* series (and for the quarterly law journal *Review of Central and East European Law*) so as to continue sharing the work of interested and interesting scholars and practitioners with our readers. *Suur aitäh*!

The General Editor
Tartu, October 2012

Introduction
Legal Front of the Cold War: Why?

Tatiana Iu. Borisova and William B. Simons[1]

"Had the atomic bomb turned out to be something
as cheap and easily manufactured as a bicycle
or an alarm clock, it might well have plunged us
back into barbarism, but it might, on the other hand,
have meant the end of national sovereignty
and of the highly-centralised police state.
If, as seems to be the case, it is a rare and costly object
as difficult to produce as a battleship,
it is likelier to put an end to large-scale wars
at the cost of prolonging indefinitely a 'peace that is no peace'."
George Orwell, *You and the Atomic Bomb* (1945)[2]

This monograph is the result of two legal panels which we organized in Helsinki as part of the annual Aleksanteri Institute's Conferences; this one was "Cold-War Interactions Reconsidered" (29-31 October 2009).[3] First of all, we would like to extend our heartfelt thanks to the visionaries of the Aleksanteri Cold-War project—Professors Sari Autio-Sarasmo and Katalin Miklóssy—for their interest and support in our 'legal' input and, also, to all our colleagues who encouraged us to proceed in this endeavor.

The organization of these two panels on the legal dimension of Cold-War (CW) interactions included a certain degree of self-education as a motive, and we are grateful to the speakers who have shared our interest in the topic; one which has not been an 'established field' either in legal history or in Cold-War studies.

1 The authors would like to express their gratitude to the visionaries and organizers of the 2009 Aleksanteri Conference as well as to the participants of "The Development of Russian Law", a research seminar at the Institute of International Economic Law (KATTI) of the University of Helsinki's Faculty of Law for a stimulating discussion on a presentation of an earlier version of this work in September 2012. Our colleagues and friends posed a number of helpful questions and suggestions; a special word of thanks to Anna-Liisa Heusala, Sari Autio-Sarasmo, Heikki Mattila, Matti Mikkola, Marianna Muravyeva, Merja Norros, and Pia Letto-Vanamo. Any omissions or errors in this work, naturally, are solely of the authors. This project has received support from the Center of Fundamental Research, National Research University Higher School of Economics, as part of the "Circulation of Knowledge through the Iron Curtain" project, from the Helsinki Collegium for Advanced Studies and from the Centre for EU-Russian Studies of the University of Tartu.

2 Originally published in *Tribune* (19 October 1945) reproduced at <http://georgeorwellnovels.com/essays/tribune-and-the-atom-bomb-letters/>. This work is generally acknowledged to be the first to use the term 'cold war'.

3 Some conference papers already have been published; see Sari Autio-Sarasmo and Brendan Humphreys (eds.), *Winter Kept Us Warm: Cold War Interactions Reconsidered* in the *Aleksanteri Cold War Series* (Aleksanteri Institute, Helsinki, 2010).

Tatiana Borisova and William Simons, eds.
The Legal Dimension in Cold-War Interactions: Some Notes from the Field xi-xxiv

Both of us working in the field of Russian/Soviet/post-Soviet legal reforms—at some point in our studies or/and life experience—have come across the CW framework. What we both knew from our own experiences is that the Cold War certainly has influenced knowledge production and transmission in the area of Soviet law. However, problematizing and even verbalizing this experience was something with which one needed to come to terms in a more general context. What we both have been eager to discuss is the issue of the contextualization of law—and, more broadly, the legal sphere in general—in CW history. In short: how did the Cold War matter for law and jurisprudence?

The 2009 Aleksanteri Conference became our first attempt to stimulate an academic discussion on this issue. We suggested to our panelists that they offer the conference attendees (and, now, the readers of this volume) their perspectives on: (a) what the legal field of the Cold War was; and (b) how it might be studied. The presentations and resulting discussions provided us all with a number of challenges in going further with this publication project. *E.g.*, while the field is an interdisciplinary one and politically controversial, in terms of research, the surface appears barely to have been scratched. Over the past years, this situation has not changed radically although some materials have appeared in print.[4]

Our main message in taking this volume to publication—both for legal scholars and legal historians—is the following: notwithstanding the challenges of the field, we believe that it can be studied systematically, rather than situationally. Having said that, some of the chapters in this collection give the reader a precise situational perspective—especially of the Post-Cold-War period. Practicing lawyers and legal scholars—along with policymakers—should find insightful the efforts of our authors to research the genealogy of modern perceptions of 'ours'-'theirs' in the legal field and, also, manipulations with this division. The issue of the interrelatedness of law with a particular historical context, such as the Cold War, seems to be important for all since war(like) discourse—and, even worse, war(like) actions—have not remained locked in the Cold-War period. However, approaching this issue in as scholarly a fashion as possible implies certain methodological challenges, upon which we will comment later in this introduction.

4 *E.g.*, Harwell Wells, "'Corporation Law is Dead': Heroic Managerialism, the Cold War, and the Puzzle of Corporation Law at the Height of the American Century", *Temple University Legal Studies Research Paper*, 15 *University of Pennsylvania Journal of Business Law* (forthcoming 2013); Nathan Guttman, "Russia Seeks Exemption from Cold War-Era Law Aimed at Soviet Repression", *Forward* (10 June 2011), and (albeit from a slightly different perspective) Kamari M. Clarke and Mark Goodale (eds.), *Mirrors of Justice: Law and Power in the Post-Cold War Era* (Cambridge University Press, Cambridge, 2009).

Was There a 'Legal Front' At All? Did Law Really Matter in the Cold War?

At first glance, both questions can be answered with a resounding 'No'. Indeed, the 'real' front of the Cold War was hard science—physics being the hardest one—and technology. It is no exaggeration to remark that developments in science and technology provided the primary material 'checks and balances' throughout the Cold War, at least for the superpowers. It is the history of physics, during the Cold War, which has been the most researched field.[5]

Contrary to hard science, competition in the fields of social science and humanities—including jurisprudence—in the Cold War seems to be rather rhetorical at best, hardly substantial. Yet, soon after the end of the Cold War, American intellectuals and historians of science addressed the issue of the Cold-War impact on the institutional development of American social science.[6] Recent research claims that development of the social sciences in the Cold War (or even 'Cold-War social science')[7] was a function of the entanglement of the social sciences with Cold-War politics.[8]

The latter certainly played an important role in shaping area studies, behavioral sciences, human relations, development studies, American studies, and a host of other disciplinary and interdisciplinary fields. At the same time, as the Brandeis historian Professor David Engerman asserts, the agency of social scientists should not be overlooked.[9] He presents "a view of social science in the Cold War in which national security concerns were relevant, but with varied and often unexpected impacts on intellectual life".[10]

An important accomplishment of historical accounts of the development of the history of science has been an understanding that the politics of representing *science* as a *neutral* and *apolitical* affair was very much developed in the Cold

5 See, for instance, Helmuth Trischler and Mark Walker (eds.), *Physics and Politics: Research and Research Support in Twentieth Century Germany in International Perspective. Beiträge zur Geschichte der Deutschen Forschungsgemeinschaft* (Steiner, Stuttgart, 2010). The Trischler and Walker volume provides an important account of the Cold-War impact on developments in physics in countries, some of them far removed from the front-lines of the CW.

6 Francis Stonor Saunder, *The Cultural Cold War: The CIA and the World of Arts and Letters* (New Press, New York, NY, 2000); Christopher Simpson (ed.), *Universities and Empire: Money and Politics in the Social Sciences in the Cold War* (New Press, New York, NY, 1998); and Noam Chomsky *et al.*, *The Cold War and the University: Toward an Intellectual History of the Postwar Years* (New Press, New York, NY, 1997).

7 Mark Solovey and Hamilton Cravens (eds.), *Cold War Social Science: Knowledge Production, Liberal Democracy, and Human Nature* (Palgrave Macmillan, New York, NY, 2012).

8 Joel Isaac, "The Human Sciences in Cold War America," 50 *Historical Journal* (2007), 725-746.

9 David C. Engerman, "Social Science in the Cold War", 101 *Isis* (2010), 393-400, at 393.

10 *Ibid.*

War.[11] Dr. Elena Aronova, a historian at the Department of History and the Science Studies Program at the University of California (San Diego) even describes claims of science neutrality as a part of the 'cultural narrative' of the Cold War.[12]

Twentieth-century jurisprudence would find this policy of *neutrality* to be the most complicated. Being very close to power, the state, its institutions, and to politics, the tasks of jurisprudence went further than serving national interest; they implied extremely sensitive and responsible issues of legality and legitimacy. It is important to underline this aspect before we embark upon our examination of what could be studied and has been studied on the legal front of the Cold War.[13]

Developments in jurisprudence during the Cold-War era, obviously, should have been studied in the social-science general path. 'Cold-War jurisprudence' certainly was part of the general trends mentioned above; for instance, area studies generally (and of necessity) included studies of new developments in the law of a particular region. Unfortunately, contrary to social science in general, there has been a remarkable lack of interest in studying the legal dimension of the educational and scientific infrastructure shaped by Cold-War politics. By 'Cold-War politics' we have in mind here the politics of competition and co-operation of antagonistic socialist and capitalist camps between the end of WWII and the demise of the Soviet Union.

In searching for explanations of the lack of research interest in the legal field of the Cold War as a general theme, there are several key concepts we should not overlook: legitimacy, continuity, and responsibility. We will consider these concepts in detail later; for now, it should suffice to remark that research of the Cold War has been hindered because it may question the legitimacy of continuities of Cold-War legal practices and urges the legal community to adopt a more responsible attitude to political input. This message has been pioneered by Professor Mary L. Dudziak's research of the impact of (Cold) War on the development of civil rights in the USA (or the restrictions thereupon).[14] We should notice, in passing, that Dudziak's approach remains an exceptional one

11 Vidar Enebakk, "Lilley Revisited: Or Science and Society in the Twentieth Century", 42(4) *British Journal for the History of Science* (2009), 563-593, and Roy Porter, "The History of Science and the History of Society", in Robert C. Olby *et al.* (eds.), *Companion to the History of Modern Science* (Routledge, London, New York, NY, 1990), 33-45.

12 Elena Aronova, "The Congress for Cultural Freedom, Minerva, and the Quest for Instituting, 'Science Studies' in the Age of Cold War", *Minerva* (2012).

13 We acknowledge that some sources may have been overlooked; rather than a claim of comprehensiveness, a general picture is presented here.

14 Mary L. Dudziak, *Cold War Civil Rights: Race and the Image of American Democracy* (Princeton University Press, Princeton, NJ, 2000), 12-13. See, also, *id.*, "Unlimited War and Social Change: Unpacking the Cold War's Impact", 69 *University of Southern California Law School Legal Studies Working Paper Series* (2010). Professor Dudziak is Director of Emory University's new, interdisciplinary Project on War and Security in Law, Culture and Society.

for the present and has not been without criticism.[15] Nevertheless, her work has an important insight of bringing the discourse of responsibility into the legal field of Cold-War studies.[16]

However, in general, even in the field of international law—the sphere in which influence of the Cold-War factor was the most obvious—has not been sufficiently studied within the Cold-War perspective. Most likely, the reason for this is that the Cold War has been perceived as something which is just there; evident for all actors, embedded in institutions and practices. Yet, this 'understanding of the evident' can be misleading since it presents a superficial and static (rather than a dynamic) picture of the Cold War, which lasted (more than) half a century. The duration of this conflict presents a challenge to such an argument of 'understandable' or even 'evident'. An example of such a realist and pragmatic approach can be an understanding that international legal co-operation of the USSR differed according to whether the other party was a socialist or a capitalist state.[17] However, articulation of this difference as a problem or as a separate subject of research could give rise to political speculation possibly undermining legal co-operation in general. Here, we come across an issue of political sensitivity and continuity which we address in greater detail later.

Recent research by the international-law scholars Mamlyuk and Mattei pioneer focuses on political inclinations in comparative-international law at the theoretical level.[18] At the level of empirical research, there have been few attempts—as far as we are aware—to study the international system and its institutions through the prism of CW politics. The reason, as Western University's historian Professor Francine McKenzie has written, is that: "Literature in this field has been written by lawyers, economists, and political scientists whose work is primarily prescriptive or theoretical."[19] Her own research of the US trade policies surrounding GATT in the 1950s has demonstrated that the Cold War was the interplay of ideological factors (the goal of winning the Cold War as articulated by the State Department) and calls for a narrower economic agenda from other

15 See, for instance, Paul B. Stephan's contribution in this volume (at 147). We should acknowledge here that American scholars seem to champion a willingness to explore the Cold-War field in general, and its legal field, also in sensitive terms of responsibilities.

16 See, on this, Autio-Sarasmo and Humphreys, *op.cit.* note 3.

17 See Merja Norros, "What's New in Legal Cooperation in Criminal Matters with Russia since 2004?", 36(2) *Review of Central and East European Law* (2011), 91-125(35), a follow-up to her earlier work: "The System of International Legal Cooperation in Criminal Matters in Russia: Council of Europe Conventions in the Field of Penal Law and Their Implementation in Russia", 29(4) *Review of Central and East European Law* (2004), 497-525.

18 Boris N. Mamlyuk and Ugo A. Mattei, "Comparative International Law", 36(2) *Brooklyn Journal of International Law* (2011), 385-452.

19 See her reflections in Francine McKenzie, "GATT and the Cold War: Accession Debates, Institutional Development, and the Western Alliance, 1947–1959", 10(3) *Journal of Cold War Studies* (2008), 78-109.

policymaking agencies.[20] This has helped to shape the legal framework of GATT and legal interactions with other states within it; but, in turn, this has had its own nexus of pragmatic and ideological interests, and some of them certainly can be studied as part of the 'Cold-War factor'.

Still, the legal dimension was not the main focus because policymaking was supposed to be the main driving force of international development.[21] Did the formal legal rules on international institutions influence the decision-making of politicians? If there would be reliable empirical research focusing on this major question, then probably the primacy of the political will would be questioned and the role of law, not politics, would be discovered and rehabilitated from political primacy, if you will. Professor Boris Mamlyuk's chapter in this volume represents a first and remarkable step in addressing the indeterminacy of international-law doctrines as a result of the Cold-War agenda.

Problem of Continuity in the Legal Field

Our volume peculiarly represents the general trends within the development of CW studies as they can be observed in the stimulating reflection of Autio-Sarasmo and Miklóssy from their 2010 volume *Reassessing Cold War Europe.*[22]

The first trend is *bipolarity*: an overwhelming focus on the United States and the Soviet Union as main agents in the Cold War and their confrontation. Within our volume, only Jane Henderson's contribution is not focused on the superpowers: she writes on Cold-War legal co-operation in education and scholarship in Europe, namely between the United Kingdom and Poland. It is also remarkable that majority of the authors are Americans, and the main geographic focus of the book is Russia. A bipolar focus views the struggle as something which lies on the surface and provides a very superficial picture of the CW, which does not include the multi-level of Cold-War interactions and inner constraints within the opposing political blocks. Eastern Europe and other geographical CW fronts are just beginning to be explored by CW scholars; one also can expect the legal field to be approached from these vantage points in the not-too-distant future.

The second trend actually stems from the bipolar angle: chronologically, previous research has been focused on the start and the end of the CW. Logically the first dominated before 1991; the later—after the end of the CW, during the

20 *Ibid.*, 107-108.

21 *E.g.*, see the innovative research on policy within Council for Mutual Economic Assistance (CMEA), a now defunct international organization with Cold-War origins. Alas, this work does not include a legal perspective: Suvi Kansiakas, "Room to Manouevre? National Interest and Coalition-Building in the CMEA", in Sari Autio-Sarasmo and Katalin Miklóssy (eds.), *Reassessing Cold War Europe* in *Routledge Studies in the History of Russia and Eastern Europe* (Routledge, Abingdon, UK, 2010), 193-210.

22 Sari Autio-Sarasmo and Katalin Miklóssy, "Introduction: The Cold War from a New Perspective", in Autio-Sarasmo and Miklóssy, *op.cit.* note 21, 1-2.

current era of CW studies. What we face in our volume is the dominance of the end-of the CW and even of a post-Cold-War perspective. The 'narratives of the winners' are certainly a special type as Auto-Sarasmo and Miklossy put it.[23] It is not necessary that it is "depicting the triumph of the victorious West";[24] rather, as one can see, it is focused on the East-West mismatch—especially in present-day Russia.

The focus on the current situation—and, in particular, on the remnants of the Cold War in Russia—originates in more of a legal than an historical perspective of our authors.[25] Their interest in the CW history seems to be not in history *per se* but, rather, in the CW as a period of the past that limited the scope of today's choices—or even determined our choices, if you will.

Addressing the issue of the remnants of the Cold-War era in contemporary Russian jurisprudence and politics, our authors have a broad perspective which actually unifies the Cold-War era and Soviet law. The relevance of such a generalization is questioned in Dr. Leena Lehtinen's chapter. She starts with a very complex question: "Where is the boundary between past and present in developing new law?" And she continues: "Is it the CW or some much earlier period?"[26]

In doing so, she highlights some aspects of what she argues can be seen as remnants of the Cold-War era—actually, Soviet law—for contemporary Russian civil law and jurisprudence. Such a remnant can be seen in the institute of ownership; *i.e.*, no clear definition of private ownership and different forms of ownership according to subjects, the owners of the property (private persons, or other entity: the state or a municipality).

The main elements here are *continuity* and *discontinuity* in Russian (legal) history. In the case of ownership, Lehtinen takes into account the continuity with pre-revolutionary period. At the same time, she mentions that a remarkable switch in references has taken place in current Russian legal literature: from pre-revolutionary to Soviet legal literature.

Obviously, references usually have been used as a means to legitimize a particular position. Citation of Soviet legal literature is rather new as compared to the revolutionary times of 1990s when Soviet law and its legacy were heavily criticized and could not be used in order to legitimize policies or practices. It is a specific phenomenon which can be explained historically as almost an inevitable reaction after a revolution, but why the CW?

23 *Ibid.*, 3.

24 *Ibid.*

25 See, in this volume, *e.g.*, the chapters by Zlata Benevolenskaya, Leena Lehtinen, Boris N. Mamlyuk, and William Partlett.

26 Lehtinen (at 73).

Can all the institutes and practices—in the broad meaning of social sciences, not law—which were to be seen in the CW era be characterized as products of the CW?

In his chapter on the impact of the CW on the development of law in the US and the USSR, Professor Paul Stephan is skeptical about exaggerating any CW influence. He argues that especially for the USSR, domestic factors played the key role in legal development.[27] But did not the CW become a factor in the domestic politics of the states involved in the confrontation? Frankly, this is a substantial—and as far as we are aware—under-researched empirical issue: the problem of measuring the Cold-War factor in domestic legal reforms. Let us take, for example, Kosygin's economic reforms in Khrushchev's time; surely they had their roots in domestic economic inefficiency. But the necessity of the reform also was articulated with the slogan "Let us catch up and exceed America" (*Dogonim i peregonim Ameriku*). Competition of economies was certainly a part of the CW confrontation. Thus, economic reforms likewise had a CW *raison d'être*. Simultaneously, one should take into account the manipulative usage of propaganda—at least in the superpowers.[28] Indeed, the rhetoric of a struggle with a monstrous enemy was overused and became a kind of meta-narrative. Those who lived in the CW era probably have this narrative as a part of a cognitive framework for their past experiences. Problematizing perceptional patterns is something of which researchers and practitioners need to be aware.[29]

Legacy of the CW 'Impact'

What is the legacy of legal history of the very close past if we cannot answer challenges that legal scholarship impose on us? Namely, challenges of transferring to others the knowledge of the context of certain legal phenomena.

Indeed, an understanding of legal institutions and, also, of the development of specific legal practice needs to be contextualized. As Professor William Butler put it in 1985:

> "The historical experience of a state in coming into being and in the patterns and mode of diplomatic relations with others; its geopolitical frontiers; its cultural, political, economic and ancestral links with foreign entities; its sense of political, religious, or ideological mission; its capacity to exert military, economic, or political influence over other States either

27 See the chapter of Paul B. Stephan in this volume.

28 See visual examples of this in Susan Buck-Morss, *Dreamworld and Catastrophe: The Passing of Mass Utopia in East and West* (MIT Press, Cambridge, MA, 2000). The authors are grateful to Professor Alexei Yurchack (Department of Anthropology and a core-faculty-member with the Department of Performance Studies, University of California (Berkeley)) for introducing to us to the research of Susan Buck-Morss, Professor of Political Philosophy and Social Theory with the Department of Government, and Professor of Visual Culture with the Department of Art History, Cornell University.

29 See the reflection on this in Autio-Sarasmo and Humphreys, *op.cit.* note 3, 2-3.

> directly or through emulation and inspiration; its techniques of formulating and executing foreign policy; together with its political, administrative, economic and legal institutions, concepts of law and methods of legal reasoning and discourse are all components, amongst others, of a national style in international law; [...] a comparative perspective [is] essential."[30]

One can assume that this contextualization is an extremely difficult task. Think, for example, about the "famous invocation" of Rabel early in the twentieth century—offered to us later by Zweigert and Kötz—that the "future comparativist compare all possible factors affecting the law".[31] Mention of this in 2011 by Professors Mamlyuk and Mattei probably is meant to remind us that the task remains an almost impossible one even in the new century.[32] And while the brightest and the best may try to go for this challenge, they certainly will be perplexed as are Mamlyuk and Mattei when they ask: "Is there a rank, an order of importance, or method for including everything?"[33]

It appears that using broad concepts such as 'CW impact' can give the necessary *broad contextualization.* Yet on the other hand, the Cold-War factor may include everything while explaining nothing. At least however, efforts to deal with this impression have given us some recent research highlighting the CW impact in law.[34] In the present volume, we also have some examples of the broad perspective of the CW factor.

The Russian scholar and practitioner, Dr. Zlata Benevolenskaya, depicts rejection of the legal construct of trust in Russian civil law as the continuation of Soviet-law institutions and of Cold-War legal thinking. The same logic can be seen in Dr. William Parlett's very close and interesting analysis of the drafting the 1993 RF Constitution. For him, the Cold-War factor is a continuity of the supremacy of one particular political authority in Russian political system. He shows how the guiding role of the Communist Party was designed for the Russian president; that Western commentators failed to notice such a fact suggests that they were blind with the triumphalism of the 'victory' over communism and the associated illusions of transitions. While Parlett does not explicitly make this link, one should take into account that many of the transition illusions seem to

30 W.E. Butler, "Comparative Approaches to International Law", 190 *Recueil des Cours* (1985), 58-61.

31 The phrase "future comparativist" is from Mamlyuk and Mattei, *op.cit.* note 18, 416. The original piece from Konrad Zweigert and Hein Kötz is in their classic: *An Introduction to Comparative Law* (Oxford University Press, Oxford, 3rd rev. ed. 1998), 35.

32 Mamlyuk and Mattei, *op.cit.* note 18, 416.

33 *Ibid.*

34 One recent example is the work by Justice Zdeněk Kühn, *The Judiciary in Central and Eastern Europe: Mechanical Jurisprudence in Transformation?*, in William B. Simons (ed.), *Law in Eastern Europe*, No.61 (Martinus Nijhoff Publishers, Leiden, Boston, 2011).

have been cultivated by transitologists—former Sovietologists who finally had a chance to act and, also, to earn from actions.[35]

What is really meant when the Cold-War factor is introduced in an explanation model? A continuity which is extremely difficult to study precisely because it is represents continuity. In order to deal with this challenging issue, stimulating (but highly debatable) comparisons can be made with another ambiguous field: the study of the impact of Nazism and Fascism on (European) jurisprudence.

The editors of a most ambitious attempt to grapple with this subject—Professor Christian Joerges and Navraj Singh Ghaleigh (scholars in economic law and public law from the Universität Bremen Faculty of Law and the University of Edinburgh School of Law respectively)—have found an appropriate word to describe the object of their research: 'shadow'.[36] Indeed, it seems impossible to use adequately the methodology of historical research in order to devise some general criteria for defining—as National Socialist or as Fascist—particular features of Spanish, German, and Italian law, legal thinking, practice, and jurisprudence. In terms of a pure historical approach, *everything* was National Socialist or Fascist at particular time in particular states. This is exactly how it is put in a historical framework: 'Nazi Germany', 'Mussolini's Italy', etc.

The same logic works with Cold-War studies which historians understand in very broad—actually, primarily in chronological—terms. Broad understanding is probably a part of the limitations upon the CW as a research object; there seem to be no methodologically or politically 'innocent' approach to studying such a close past. The other limitation of the CW as a phenomenon is its multilevelness in the sense of time, geography and function. In trying to grasp the legal front-lines of the Cold War, situationalism becomes almost inevitable—as is the case with such complex phenomena as Fascism and National Socialism.[37]

There are remarkable differences, however, among these fields. Unlike WWII, the Cold War has not been blamed upon a particular agent (actor, nation, state, or regime). Also, it has not been the subject of any wide scale, direct public condemnation.[38] At least, there has not been anything like the *Vergangen-*

35 *E.g.*, the narratives in Janine R. Wedel, *Collision and Collusion. The Strange Case of Western Aid to Eastern Europe* (Macmillan, London, 1998).

36 Christian Joerges and Navraj Singh Ghaleigh (eds.), *Darker Legacies of Law in Europe. The Shadow of National Socialism and Fascism over Europe and Its Legal Traditions* (Hart Publshing, Oxford, 2003).

37 As Martti Koskenniemi observed in his stimulating review of the Joerges and Singh Ghaleigh volume at 15(4) *European Journal of International Law* (2004), 839-851.

38 There have been works which come close to this however; see, *e.g.*, the following:

> "Violation of human rights 20 years ago is not an issue that can be treated by the justice system today. Thus it can only be an object of moral condemnation. Some people benefited from membership in the communist party or simply from sincere cooperation with the communist authorities at the expense of people who did not do so. Some people used the human rights violations committed by the authorities for their own good. However, even this explanation is too simplified."

heitsbewältigung undertaken by German society, including the legal profession.[39] Although a strong moral drive gave this a specific framework, yet this kind of 'working on the past' has assisted in conceptualizing the 'Nazi impact'. Certainly, the *Vergangenheitsbewältigung* has been an important means for rejecting the past, and this also has been essential in writing its history.

The Cold War, on the contrary, has not been condemned in such a way; thus, even its end has not been something about which all have been sure.[40] To make things more complicated, the Cold War 'ended' along with the demise of the USSR, and thus may seem to be a distinctive part of the USSR's existence. At least this kind of narrative may be recognized in today's accounts, especially those of the 'winner's camp'. For instance, the argument of Professor Stephan in this volume that the Cold War was a greater challenge for the US legal system than it was for that of the USSR could be seen as a part of this cognitive scheme.

> "Peacetime international engagement in the role of a superpower was an entirely new task for the United States and required investment in new institutions and legal strategies. The Soviet Union, in contrast, experienced its struggle with the United States more as a continuation of the existential crisis that the Soviet state had faced since its inception."[41]

Here, we also can trace a general trend in studies of the political dimension of the CW which traditionally has been focused precisely on confrontation and contest; in fact, on *War*. In this sense, ideologically, indeed the Soviet Union was in a state of confrontation with the 'capitalist' states for a number of years before the 'outbreak' of the CW. However, the 'constructive' potential of the CW period for the totally new status of the USSR as a powerful leader of the world communist movement is not considered in this argument. This new status was a specific challenge which shaped both regimes of international relations as Dr. Boris Mamlyuk demonstrates in this volume and, to a certain, extent domestic institutions. Unfortunately, there has been much less research in the latter

Toomas Hiio, "About the Crimes Committed by the Totalitarian Regimes in Estonia", report delivered at the Conference "Crimes of the Communist Regimes: An Assessment by Historians and Legal Experts", Prague (24 February 2010), reproduced at <http://www.ustrcr.cz/data/pdf/konference/zlociny-komunismu/COUNTRY%20REPORT%20ESTONIA.pdf>. Or the Estonian Institute of Historical Memory: "[...] established by President Toomas Hendrik Ilves in 2008 in order to provide the citizens of Estonia with a thorough and objective account of the status of human rights during the Soviet occupation of Estonia". But: "The Institute is not a judicial body. No legal consequences follow from its findings. Rather, its goal is to establish facts and circumstances that represent violations of human rights during the period under review." See <http://www.mnemosyne.ee/>.

39 Michael Stolleis, "Prologue: Reluctance to Glance in the Mirror. The Changing Face of German Jurisprudence after 1933 and Post-1945" in Joerges and Singh Ghaleigh, *op.cit.* note 36, 1ff.

40 For some examples of the discussion on this issue in Russian literature, see Dr. Benevolenskaya's chapter in this volume (at 60-62).

41 See the chapter of Paul B. Stephan in this volume (at 141).

field—partly, because there is no discernible public interest in the issue, which is still very sensitive politically.

CW as a Personal Story

The two autobiographical narratives of Professors Jane Henderson and Albert Schmidt provide us with superb examples of the Cold-War legal front involving life experiences. Both of them are wonderful resources for grasping the images, perceptions, and mentalities of the period. What is important here is that such life stories are the optimal evidence of the dynamics of interactions during the CW through the narratives of changing attitudes and roles of the opposing systems. Furthermore, contrary to a simplified black-or-white, good-or-bad picture of CW attitudes and the emotional picture usually depicted by propaganda—one of fear and mistrust—Henderson and Schmidt illustrate their narrative with positive emotions. Although some might see this as a constraint in making an 'objective analysis'—as rectitude intruding upon our efforts to approach interactions involving the 'Iron Curtain'—our view is that such emotional scope certainly should be taken into account.

These multipolar interactions depicted by Henderson (she witnessed co-operation of the European West-East parties (the British and the Polish)) and Schmidt depict the end of the CW, partly caused by the interaction. As Professors Sari Autio-Sarasmo and Katalin Miklóssy have put it: "interaction was dysfunctional in terms of how the structures were supposed to work".[42]

But did the Soviet-law specialist actually undermine the CW boundaries? Considered as a part of the group of 'Sovietologists', they could be accused of keeping the boundaries; or, in other words 'watching the fence'.[43] Indeed, compared to other actors involved in CW interactions, the role of Sovietologists was much more complex and probably even controversial. If in hard science, physics, for instance, there were no inner boundaries within the very field of research, studying the 'other's' law implied both existence of the boundary and a necessity to examine it—observed by the authorities in the field.

Acting as 'knowledge-media' between 'we' and 'they', they actually articulated the difference and, as a by-product, to a certain extent even produced it. Take for instance, reception of the theory of peaceful co-existence promoted by Soviet international lawyers in the West. A leading Soviet-law specialist, the late Professor Leon Lipson, found it necessary to 'decode' it to introduce the concept to a Western audience: he named it PCX in order to underline his view that it had

42 Autio-Sarasmo and Miklóssy, *op.cit.* note 21.

43 *E.g.*, Ferdinand Feldbrugge, *The Perestroika Jig-Saw Puzzle: Observations of NATO's Sovietologist-in-Residence 1987–1989* (Institute of East European Law and Russian Studies, Leiden, The Netherlands), 2003.

nothing to do with 'peace' or with 'co-existence'.[44] The decoding procedure can be explored here as a process of the symbolic remapping of the legal concepts from 'their law' to 'our law'. By 'our law' of course, we understand here the sphere of expertise in Soviet law—not the domestic law of the former USSR.[45] Naturally, this is a very preliminary observation, asking for further empirical research; but it should make the point clear.

However, being at the very front line of the Cold War, their own perceptions of 'theirs-ours' could be transformed.[46] When and how did Soviet law become the domain of 'ours' for Henderson and Schmidt? What was still 'their Soviet law' for them and for other Soviet-law specialists? Accounts of these East-West encounters can be approached insightfully by a mental mapping or by using mental geographies.[47] In this sense, practices of the exchange of knowledge, of its transmission through the ideological border, are of a great importance. The article by Professor Schmidt provides the reader with a grand narrative of such an encounter of Soviet specialists with the western field of Soviet law through their groundbreaking participation in the 1987 Soviet Law Symposium at the University of Bridgeport. As an organizer, Schmidt did not expect much from his initiative to "travel to Moscow to urge Soviet inclusion" in Christmas/New Year break 1986-1987. [48] The very term which he uses—"inclusion"—speaks for itself as remarkable in the perception of the divided Soviet law field. The other striking fact to which Professor Schmidt refers is the refusal of the eminent former Soviet scholar (at that time expatriate), the late Olimpiad S. Ioffe, Professor at the University of Connecticut School of Law, to participate in the Soviet Law Symposium with Soviet scholars.

This episode echoes the boycott idea of members of the Law Department of the University College London; they had objected to negotiations on co-operation of departmental Soviet law specialists with Polish colleagues. Probably, they shared the same rationale as Professor Ioffe: to cut off any co-operation so as to avoid

44 See the chapter of Paul B. Stephan in this volume (at 148).

45 At a certain point, people in area studies (such as Soviet law) may begin to have difficulties with what is 'our' and 'their' law. Soviet law, as a field of expertise, may actually start to become 'our Soviet law'—or 'Soviet law' as we (specialists in the Soviet law field) understand it and present it to others.

46 On the interrelatedness of the 'our'-'their' in the Post-Cold War period, see inspiring research in the field of cultural anthropology: Domenic Boyer and Alexey Yurchack, "American Stiob: Or, What Late Socialist Aesthetics of Parody Reveal about Contemporary Political Culture in the West", 25(2) *Cultural Anthropology* (2010), 179–221, and in political theory: Susan Buck-Morss "Theorizing Today: The Post-Soviet Condition", reproduced at <http://falcon.arts.cornell.edu/sbm5/documents/theorizing%20today.pdf>.

47 György Péteri, "The Occident Within: Or the Drive for Exceptionalism and Modernity", 9(4) *Kritika: Explorations in Russian and Eurasian History* (2008), 929-937.

48 See the chapter of Albert J. Schmidt in this volume (at 51).

recognizing any academic legacy of Soviet jurisprudence.[49] The co-operation and recognition would mean legitimization of the legal structure of the Soviet rule. William Butler, who promoted the interactions with the University of Warsaw, was of different view—both realistic and pragmatic.

The realism of personal stories, in which ideology could be manipulated, is something which we dearly need. Essays focusing on actors—particularly on individuals, their careers and writings—would greatly benefit the field. They also would provide us with some understanding why the complex Cold-War practices have not (yet) been widely condemned. Although historians have made attempts to study some of the mechanisms of making 'Ideologically Correct Science', there remains a lot to be done: During the Cold War, there were politicians in the super-powers who denounced 'international' science and, instead, demanded an 'anti-communist' or '*anti-burzhua*' one.[50] For all-too-long, legal science has not been the subject of rigorous research from this perspective. Fortunately, it is not too late—although, as people pass away, the whole specter of the Cold-War story gradually is slipping from our grasp.

Many questions, upon which we have touched in this introduction, are still unanswered. We hope that this will stimulate a broader discussion and empirical research to shed more light on the Cold-War shadows. It is especially important nowadays when legal scholarship seems to be undergoing a turn to history as a part of a general shift to politics so as to 'reset' both direction and purpose. History will not provide ready-to-use answers for reasoning or justification but may provide a better understanding of our questions.

49 Unfortunately, the authors of this introduction are unaware of any published accounts of such a rationale, except those which are set forth in Jane Henderson's chapter. Interestingly, Professor Ioffe made no mention in his several memoirs about the episode of the 1987 Soviet Law Symposium. See, *e.g.*, O.S. Ioffe, "Pravo chastnoe i pravo publichnoe" and "O khoziaistvennom prave" in Anatolii Didenko (ed.), *Grazhdanskoe zakonodatel'stvo. Stat'i. Kommentarii. Praktika*, No.20 (Iurist, Almaty, 2004), 16-35 and 36-69, respectively, also containing an interview with Professor Ioffe (254-259); and O.S. Ioffe, *Grazhdanskoe zakonodatel'stvo Respubliki Kazakhstana. Razmyshleniia o prave. Nauchnoe izdanie*, Anatolii Didenko (ed.), (Institute for the Legislation of Kazakhstan, Astana, 2002). The authors are grateful to Professor Farkhad S. Karagussov for his kind assistance in reconstructing the sources cited in this footnote.

50 Mark Walker, "'Ideologically-Correct' Science: The French Revolution", 3 *HOST* (Journal of History of Science and Technology) (2009) reproduced at <http://johost.eu/?oid=91&act=&area=7&ri=2&itid=3#_edn2>. See, also, Michael Gordin, Walter Grunden, Mark Walker, and Zuoyue Wang, "'Ideologically Correct' Science", in Mark Walker (ed.), *Science and Ideology: A Comparative History* (Routledge, London, 2003), 35-65.

Talking Across the Fence: Cold-War Academic Cooperation in the Legal Sphere

Jane Henderson

Introduction

Walk down the main road in most English cities nowadays, and you may well hear Polish spoken. Visit European and Middle Eastern holiday resorts, and you will see Russian translations of the restaurant menus. Major sporting events include Russians and others from former Soviet states or the East European bloc. Where would the English football team Chelsea be without the investment from oligarch owner Roman Abramovich? We have become so completely accustomed to the easy liaison between the old East and West that it grows harder to remember that for the best part of the twentieth century the situation was very different.

I am a child of the Cold-War era. Born in the early 1950s, I was brought up with the USSR as a superpower, winning the space race with Sputnik, Laika the first space dog, and Iurii Gagarin the first man in space. My early memories include news of the Cuban missile crisis, Khrushchev beating the table with his shoe at the United Nations, and construction of the Berlin Wall. The practical impact of the Soviet threat did not seriously impinge; for example, there was no equivalent in my primary school of the routine nuclear bomb drill described in Bill Bryson's autobiographical *The Life and Times of the Thunderbolt Kid.*[1] In his Greenwood Elementary School in Des Moines, Iowa:

> "Once a month we had a civil defence drill at school. A siren would sound—a special urgent siren that denoted that this was not a fire drill or storm alert but a nuclear attack by agents of the dark forces of Communism—and everyone would scramble out of their seats and get under their desks with hands folded over heads in the nuclear attack brace position. I must have missed a few of these, for the first time one occurred in my presence I had no idea what was going on and sat fascinated as everyone around me dropped to the floor and parked themselves like little cars under their desks.
>
> 'What is this?' I asked Buddy Doberman's butt, for that was the only part of him still visible.
>
> 'Atomic bomb attack,' came his voice, slightly muffled. 'But it's OK. It's only a practice, I think'."[2]

But the impact on the psychological landscape was unquestionable. The Soviet contribution to the Allies' Victory in World War II (for the Soviets, the 'Great Patriotic War') was downplayed. Our fear of nuclear Armageddon was ramped up by films such as Stanley Kubrick's *Dr. Strangelove*, first released in 1964, and the BBC documentary *The War Game* deemed too shocking to be broadcast at

1 Bill Bryson, *The Life and Times of the Thunderbolt Kid: Travels through my Childhood* (Transworld Black Swan paperback edition, London, 2007) chapter 8 "Schooldays" esp. 216-219. See, also, photo of children taking part in a nuclear drill, *id.* 198, and chapter 7, "Boom!".

2 *Ibid.*, 216-217.

Tatiana Borisova and William Simons, eds.
The Legal Dimension in Cold-War Interactions: Some Notes from the Field 1-40

its intended release date in 1966. Various media—fact and fiction—presented Soviets as the baddies,[3] perhaps most famously Ian Fleming's *James Bond* books and most of the films loosely based on them, although both TV and film Russians had inappropriate accents and few of us knew what English spoken with a Russian accent would sound like.

I might have been an exception to this general rule, as I was lucky enough to learn Russian at secondary school from a native speaker. However my second-generation émigré teacher had a peerless English accent, as well as an English husband and children. For me, learning the Russian language was an amusing sideline. In keeping with English educational practice at the time, I had specialized during my final two years of school, and was learning more maths and physics than may have been good for me. I therefore seized the opportunity to sacrifice part of my lunch break on a daily basis to extracurricular Russian lessons. The teacher, Mrs. Davies, was wonderful, well organized, inspirational, and in the fortunate position that she was teaching for the joy of the language to a very self-selecting group of enthusiasts. My home town at that time was in North-West England; Birkenhead, a seaport on the River Mersey, the other side of the river to Liverpool. It was visited on one occasion by a Soviet merchant vessel. I cannot now recall its name, and we were never told what brought it to our somewhat undistinguished local dock. However, Mrs. Davies clearly received news of its arrival, and arranged for our Russian class to go on a visit. Picture the event. We were a group of English schoolgirls aged 16 or 17, brought up in a coastal town to be slightly wary of sailors at the best of times, and now we were to set foot on 'enemy territory'. Such a thrill! It was almost anticlimactic to find that both the ship and its crew were immaculately scrubbed and polished and impeccably turned out for their young visitors. We were treated to black tea with spoonfuls of jam and Russian sweeties, and given pictures and lapel badges as souvenirs. They were the most genteel and polite sailors we had ever encountered. Hence how even more inappropriate was the complete consternation of certain schoolmistresses when a couple of the crew members turned up the next day at our school for an impromptu return visit.

I now fast forward a few years to law school. I was both an undergraduate and postgraduate at University College London (UCL), where luckily for me Soviet Law was an option available for study in my final undergraduate year. In my masters degree, I specialized in socialist legal systems. In 1974 King's College London established a Centre of European Law and sought to recruit a specialist in East European Law. I was appointed, and have remained in post ever since. From 1976 I ran an undergraduate optional module on Soviet law,

3 One notable exception is Illya Kuryakin, the Russian sidekick to American Napoleon Solo in the TV series *The Man from UNCLE* (originally broadcast 1964-1968). The two fought to thwart the dastardly organization THRUSH in its aim to conquer the world. Kuryakin was played by David McCallum and Solo by Robert Vaughn.

and each year up to a couple of dozen interested students explored the contrasts of the Soviet legal system to their own English one. I was also involved with the Centre for the Study of Socialist Legal Systems based at UCL and established in 1981 by my former lecturer, William Elliott Butler, Reader and later Professor of Comparative Law in the University of London. He became the Director of the Centre, which was renamed the Vinogradoff Institute in 1993. It now operates as a unit of Penn State Dickinson School of Law where Butler is currently the John Edward Fowler Distinguished Professor of Law.

It is the fruits of Butler's endeavors at UCL, once he had become Director of the Centre for the Study of Socialist Legal Systems and earlier, to facilitate academic exchanges with socialist states which are the subject of this chapter. Two arrangements are particularly recalled, one with the Faculty of Law and Administration of Warsaw University, and one with the Institute of State and Law of the USSR Academy of Sciences, also known by its Russian acronym of *IGPAN*.[4] Both led to delegations of scholars visiting each others' institutions for meetings, usually labelled Colloquia or Symposia, from which papers were published. Some visits by individual scholars were also fostered by the Anglo-Soviet agreement. We will trace the establishment of both joint links, and gather some views from those who participated in the consequent visits and meetings.

Forging the Links

In many ways the Cold-War era was a golden period for the study by Western scholars of Soviet Law. Soviet and Eastern European legal materials were cheap, if somewhat erratic to obtain, but they were supplemented by a wealth of material in translation, funded by 'Kremlin watchers' and others. All the major Soviet legal reforms were covered by accessible media, which greatly facilitated teaching Soviet Law to my English speaking students. The group of Western academics who took the study of the Soviet and other socialist legal systems seriously was small, but as with many who pursue minority interests, the individuals who comprised that group were generally good-humoured and friendly.

What was missing, however, was the possibility of discussing Soviet and East European law with Soviet and East European legal academics. The innovative links instituted by William E. Butler with Warsaw University and *IGPAN* helped to fill this lacuna.

The Link with Warsaw University

The first of Butler's regular exchanges to bring scholars together across the divide of the Iron Curtain was an informal Anglo-Polish exchange relationship dating from 1977 followed by a formal inter-faculty Agreement signed at Budapest on 23 August 1978 between the Faculty of Laws, University College London and

4 From its Russian name: *Institut gosudarstva i prava akademii nauk.*

the Faculty of Law and Administration of Warsaw University.[5] The aim of this was to:

> "[...] facilitate mutual contacts between staff and students from the law faculties of both universities and enable them to participate in lectures, seminars, visits, and tours of or relating to legal institutions in the United Kingdom and the People's Republic of Poland, as well as appropriate sightseeing and cultural activities." (Section 1; see Appendix 1)

An initial exchange visit of one week each for ten students from each side was planned for academic year 1978-1979, and further exchanges followed in successive years. This link arose because:

> "The Institute of State and Law of the Polish Academy of Sciences acceded to Professor Butler's request that his Field Course for 'Introduction to Socialist Legal Systems' offered as an option in the LLB degree to visit Poland in order to see something of Polish legal institutions first hand."[6]

As well as the student visits, there were colloquia with presentations by staff on both sides, which led to publications such as *Anglo-Polish Legal Essays* edited and introduced by W.E. Butler and published in 1982.[7] We will see later that members of the UCL staff and others who participated in these meetings hold warm memories of them, and, in individual cases, friendships were established which lasted decades.

Poland may have presented an exceptional case. As Lech (Leszek) Garlicki, then a 'docent' (the youngest grade of full professor) at the Warsaw School of Law, now a judge at the European Court of Human Rights, explained in relation to trips abroad:

> "Poland was a quite special country in this respect, because—from the beginnings of détente with Germany and the US in the early 70s—foreign contacts for academics were allowed on a quite developed basis. In effect, most of professors from my age group have already spent at least one year abroad as research scholars or visiting professors."[8]

An experience of openness in the other direction was recorded by Roger Cotterrell,[9] a leading pioneer in the study of sociology of law. He explained:[10]

5 The text of the agreement is in the "Second Annual Report of the Centre for the Study of Socialist Legal Systems" (Faculty of Laws, University College London, 1983), 15, on file with the author, and in William E. Butler (ed.), *Yearbook on Socialist Legal Systems 1987* (Transnational Publishers, Dobbs Ferry, NY, 1988), 387-388. It is reproduced in Appendix 1 to this chapter.

6 First Annual Report of the Centre for the Study of Socialist Legal Systems, (Faculty of Laws, University College London, 1982), on file with the author.

7 (Transnational Publishers Inc, Dobbs Ferry, NY, 1982). Number 128 in William E. Butler, *International and Comparative Law. A Bibliography* (Wildy, Simmonds & Hill, London, 2005).

8 Personal information (31 August 2009).

9 Professor Roger Cotterrell, FBA, LLD MSc(Soc) (Lond), Anniversary Professor of Legal Theory at Queen Mary University of London School of Law.

10 Personal information (22 July 2009).

> "In the late 1970s I had visited Poland solely because of musical contacts and found a lively 'underground' arts community in Warsaw with ways of life well adapted to survival despite official restrictions and economic difficulties. I developed an enduring affection for Poland from that time. In October 1985 I went back to Warsaw, and also Cracow, and this time I met academics—one or two law teachers but mainly legal sociologists. [...] I met very able intellectuals, including people who became, over the years, valued colleagues in my research field and whom I still meet at conferences.
>
> Those meetings [...] came about by entirely independent means, through my visits to Poland as an individual originally through musical contacts in the 1970s and then later (in the mid-1980s) through academic contacts I made myself (I wrote to Polish law faculties and received some invitations to visit; in other cases I was introduced to academics by mutual friends in Warsaw). [...] By 1978 I had many non-academic contacts in Poland.
>
> It may be of interest to your readers, however, that it was quite easy for me to make some of my Polish academic links just by getting in touch directly, person-to-person, with scholars in the universities. My Polish contacts were only too ready to reach out to the West. No formal institutional arrangements were needed in order to begin to co-operate. But then sociology of law is an inherently international research field."[11]

If the link between UCL and Warsaw University was not so unusual in the context of the time, the same cannot be said for the second collaboration agreement brokered by Butler. This was the groundbreaking "Protocol on Scientific Co-operation between the Faculty of Laws, University College London (Great Britain) and the Institute of State and Law of the USSR Academy of Sciences [*IGPAN*]".

Establishing the Link with the USSR

Establishing the link with a Soviet institution was not uncontroversial, even for a law faculty such as that of University College London, with its tradition of tolerance and inclusiveness.[12] Jeffrey Jowell, then Dean and Head of Department of the Faculty of Laws, UCL, recollects the internal struggle:[13]

> "During my first tenure as Dean of the UCL's Law Faculty Bill Butler brought to me a proposed agreement between us and the Institute of State and Law. He had previously pioneered a similar agreement with Poland and I knew that some members of the Faculty would object to further links with socialist countries. During that time there were fierce debates about whether or not we should join the academic boycott of South Africa. I told Bill that I was opposed to such boycotts for two main reasons. First, on an academic level, provided we were free to speak and to see whom and what we wished (within practical limits), contact could only be beneficial. Secondly (at least in the South African context) it was important

11 Personal information (28 August 2009).

12 As the UCL website asserts at <http://www.ucl.ac.uk/about-ucl/history>:

> "Just 180 years ago, the benefits of a university education in England were restricted to men who were members of the Church of England; UCL was founded to challenge that discrimination. UCL was the first university to be established in England after Oxford and Cambridge, providing a progressive alternative to those institutions' social exclusivity, religious restrictions and academic constraints."

13 Personal information (5 September 2009).

> to show our solidarity with an isolated opposition. But I warned him that there were members of the Faculty who, when the matter came to be discussed, would not take that view.
>
> When the matter reached the Faculty agenda I was approached by some members who were concerned that Bill's access to the Soviet Union could disguise, knowingly or unknowingly, the hand of the KGB. Others named the CIA rather than the *KGB*. I was impatient with this speculation and warned that I would not like the Faculty discussion to be polluted by unsubstantiated innuendos and smears.
>
> I have not checked the minutes of the Faculty meeting in 1983 when the matter came to be discussed. There was a strong view expressed that we should boycott the Soviet Union, but that view did not prevail. The pro-boycott argument was not helped when it was revealed that its chief advocate had himself recently lectured in apartheid South Africa!"

Good sense having prevailed, the Protocol between UCL and *IGPAN* was signed on 24 October 1983, with effect from 1 January 1984.[14] It established a cooperation agreement which lead to a series of academic visits, and colloquia on a range of important legal topics. The Protocol was possible because of an umbrella inter-Academy agreement, between The British Academy and the Academy of Sciences of the USSR, which entered into force from 1 April 1977. This created the framework within which academic collaboration agreements could be concluded.

The British Academy's current website describes its role:

> "The British Academy is the UK's national academy for the humanities and social sciences. Its purpose is to inspire, recognise and support excellence and high achievement in the humanities and social sciences, throughout the UK and internationally, and to champion their role and value.
>
> As a *funding body*, in receipt of Government grant-in-aid, it supports excellent ideas, individuals and intellectual resources in the humanities and social sciences, enables UK researchers to work with scholars and resources in other countries, sustains a British research presence in various parts of the world and helps attract overseas scholars to the UK."[15]

The British Academy has a long tradition of International Engagement[16] including "Partnerships: working with key UK and overseas partners and international organisations to support and stimulate policy formation, research collaboration and international exchanges and networks".[17] It has a specific "Agreement with the Russian Academy of Sciences, providing the opportunity for individual research visits to Russia, and joint projects between British and Russian scholars".[18]

14 *Op.cit.* note 5, 13. The text of the Protocol is reproduced in the Second Annual Report *id.* 17-20, and in the *Yearbook on Socialist Legal Systems 1987*, *op.cit.* note 5, 388-392. It is reproduced in Appendix 2 to this chapter.

15 "About the Academy" available at <http://www.britac.ac.uk/misc/index.cfm>.

16 "International Engagement" available at <http://www.britac.ac.uk/intl/index.cfm>.

17 *Ibid.*

18 "Funding opportunities - countries list" available at <http://www.britac.ac.uk/intl/funding3.cfm>.

The Second Annual Report of the Centre for the Study of Socialist Legal Systems tells us that the Protocol between UCL and *IGPAN* was:

> "[...] the second such 'Direct Link' between a university institution in Britain and an Institute of the Soviet Academy which has been signed within the framework of the 1977 inter-Academy agreement on cooperation in the social sciences, and so far as we are aware, the very first of its kind in the field of law involving any Anglo-American law faculty or school."[19]

The two academicians inspired to make the link were Butler, by then Professor of Comparative Law in the University of London, and Director of the Centre for the Study of Socialist Legal Systems, and Vladimir Nikolaevich Kudriavtsev,[20] Academician (and Vice President) of the USSR Academy of Sciences, and Director of the Institute of State and Law of the USSR Academy of Sciences.[21] Kudriavtsev had drawn Butler's attention to the Direct Link possibility and suggested that he verify this with The British Academy and consider the possibility of establishing such a link.[22] Kudriavtsev was clearly a farsighted man. Some years later in 1991 he was instrumental in enshrining the principle of inalienable and inviolable human rights into Soviet law by introducing the draft USSR Declaration of the Rights of Man to the USSR Congress of Peoples' Deputies (CPD). It was passed on 5 September 1991 as the CPD's last act before it dissolved itself. William Butler wrote of Kudriavtsev: "He was the most senior Russian jurist during his lifetime."[23] We will see below that Kudriavtsev's eminence and his association with the UCL-*IGPAN* link may have had historic consequences.

Butler noted:

> "The willingness to assertively seek out comparative legal dialogue with Western lawyers in a constructive spirit originated in [this] Protocol. [...] The Protocol itself, unprecedented in Soviet practice, was a hopeful sign, but the subject-matter to be pursued under the Protocol—comparative law—was chosen by the Soviet side and happily accepted by ours."[24]

Other research topics of mutual interest were listed in point two of the Protocol as: Law, policy, and state administration; criminal law and the system of justice;

19 *Op.cit.* note 5, 14. See, also, William E. Butler, Editorial Introduction, *Justice and Comparative Law; Anglo Soviet Perspectives on Criminal Law, Evidence, Procedure and Sentencing Policy* (Martinus Nijhoff Publishers, Dordrecht, The Netherlands, 1987), saying that it was the "first 'Direct Link' of its kind between an Academy institute and Western law faculty".

20 1923-2007. He was Vice-President of the Russian Academy of Sciences from 1988-2001, a sometime member of the Central Committee of the Communist Party of the Soviet Union, a member of the USSR Congress of Peoples' Deputies (the highest legislative body at the time), and of the Presidential Council on Questions of Improving Justice. There is a photo of him available at <http://www.ras.ru/win/db/show_per.asp?P=.id-17.ln-ru>.

21 Ascriptions from the title page of William E. Butler and Vladimir N. Kudriavtsev (eds.), *Comparative Law and Legal System: Historical and Socio-Legal Perspectives* (Oceana Publications, New York, NY, 1985).

22 Personal information from William E. Butler (22 April 2009).

23 Personal information from William E. Butler (2 February 2009).

24 Butler, *op.cit.* note 31, 31-32.

contemporary problems of international law; and history of law and political theory (see the list in the Protocol in Appendix 2.)

Another factor in the background which must have encouraged high-level institutional agreement to the Protocol was the Helsinki Final Act. This Final Act was signed on 1 August 1975 at the First Conference on Security and Co-operation in Europe (CSCE) Summit of Heads of State or Government, Helsinki, by the High Representatives of 35 states, including Poland, the Union of Soviet Socialist Republics and the United Kingdom.[25] It "embodied more than two and half years of arduous negotiation".[26] The Helsinki Final Act provides for "4. Co-operation and Exchanges in the Field of Education"[27] and commitment that the signatory states will:

> "[...] endeavour in developing their co-operation as equals, to promote mutual understanding and confidence, friendly and good-neighbourly relations among themselves, international peace, security and justice."[28]

This must have strengthened the hand of those negotiating cooperation agreements. The timing of the umbrella inter-Academy agreement from 1977 creates a strong implication—unverified at the time of writing this chapter—that it resulted from the agreement for cooperation in the academic sphere included in the Helsinki Final Act. Certainly, the Protocol between UCL and *IGPAN* directly refers in paragraph two of its Preamble to the "purposes of that Agreement which arise from the provisions of the Final Act of the CSCE".[29] The Helsinki Final Act is perhaps better known for its result that human rights became subject to monitoring within the signatory states. The Group to Assist in the Implementation of the Helsinki Agreements in the USSR, soon known as the Moscow Helsinki Group, was formed on 12 May 1976. The work of it and other internal grassroots pressure groups arguably had a regime changing impact on the Eastern European states that had signed up to the provisions of the Final Act.[30]

Financial support for the academic exchanges between UCL and *IGPAN* was given on an *ad hoc* year to year basis by the British Council.[31] The British Council (originally known as 'The British Committee for Relations with Other Countries') is "The United Kingdom's international organisation for cultural

25 Text available at the Organization for Security and Co-operation in Europe (OSCE) website at <http://www.osce.org/documents/mcs/1975/08/4044_en.pdf>.

26 Daniel C. Thomas, *The Helsinki Effect: International Norms, Human Rights, and the Demise of Communism* (Princeton University Press, Princeton, NJ, 2001), 86.

27 *Op.cit.* note 25, 55.

28 Principle IX, *op.cit.* note 25, 62.

29 See *op.cit.* note 5 and Appendix 2.

30 This is a summary of Thomas' overall thesis, *op.cit.* note 26.

31 W.E. Butler, "Techniques of Law Reform in the CIS", 1(1) *Sudebnik* (1996), 30.

relations and educational opportunities".[32] It was incorporated by Royal Charter in 1940. It is an executive non-departmental public body, a public corporation (in accounting terms) and a charity. It celebrated its 75th anniversary in 2009. It began work in the USSR in 1945, and in 1955 a Soviet Relations Committee was formed. The British Council has a long history of fostering links across the Iron Curtain even during the challenging Cold-War period.[33] It contributed financially to many of the meetings arranged under the Protocol, as well as individual scholars' visits.[34]

The Protocol was formally signed at the then new premises of The British Academy. A grant of £100 had been received from the Metcalfe Trust "to assist in local administrative expenses incurred when co-ordinating the Direct Link."[35] The signatories were William Butler; Konstantin Filippovich Sheremet, Deputy Director of the Institute of State and Law of the USSR Academy of Sciences;[36] Jeffrey Jowell; and Sir James Lighthill, the Provost of UCL.[37] Also present were the Vice President of the British Academy, Professor J Trapp; the Foreign Secretary of the British Academy, Professor E.W. Handley; and Peter W.H. Brown, the Secretary of the British Academy.

> "Attending the luncheon given by the British Academy, in addition to the above, were representatives from The Royal Society, the Presidium of the USSR Academy of Sciences, and the Scientific Attaché of the Soviet Embassy in London."[38]

Of these luminaries, a few words should be said about the extraordinary Sir James Lighthill (1924-1998). He had succeeded Paul Dirac as Lucasian professor of Mathematics at the University of Cambridge, a post he held for ten years before becoming Provost of UCL, 1979-1989. "Considered by his peers to be one of the great mathematicians of the century, perhaps even a genius, Lighthill was a pioneer in supersonic aeronautics, in oceanographic studies and astrophysics".[39] He died

32 "Who we are" available at < http://www.britishcouncil.org/new/about-us/who-we-are/>.

33 Unfortunately from late 2007 there have been some difficulties in the British Council's relations with Russia, possibly in retaliation for British authorities' moves in the dispute over the 2006 murder in London of former Russian security agent Aleksandr Litvinenko; see Patrick Moore, "Russia Admits Move Against British Council is 'Retaliation'", 11 (230) *Radio Free Europe/Radio Liberty Newsline* (13 December 2007).

34 Jeffrey Jowell recalls an incident where there was "dissatisfaction [among some of the Soviet delegates visiting London] at being on the *per diem* rates of the British Academy (as I recall about £27) whereas some of their colleagues in other disciplines were on British Council rates (as I recall about £28.50)". *Op.cit.* note 13.

35 *Op.cit.* note 5, 1.

36 1923-2001.

37 Personal information from William E. Butler (2 February 2009).

38 *Op.cit.* note 5, 14.

39 Obituary, *The Times* (20 July 1998), available at <http://www-groups.dcs.st-and.ac.uk/~history/Obits/Lighthill.html>.

on 17 July 1998, aged 74, while attempting to swim around the Channel Island of Sark. He had successfully completed the nine-mile swim six times preciously.

The first Anglo-Soviet Symposium held under the Protocol was in London on 9-11 March 1984.[40] The Soviet delegation was headed by Academician Kudriavtsev, and included Professors V.V. Pustogarov and Vladimir Aleksandrovich Tumanov. The Symposium theme was "National Systems of Law and Comparative Law". The theme of comparative law was not as uncontroversial as it might sound. At that time Soviet theory dictated that socialist and bourgeois legal systems were predicated on such different ideological, economic and societal bases that they were incapable of anything but contrastive comparison that would demonstrate the superiority of the socialist system. At the symposium Professor Tumanov delivered a groundbreaking paper "On Comparing Various Types of Legal Systems".[41] In it he "pronounced the death knell of former Soviet attitudes towards comparative law and acknowledged that there could be useful and constructive comparison between socialist and bourgeois systems".[42]

> "The central theme of Tumanov's paper was that comparative law could legitimately be used by the USSR for law reform purposes, that bourgeois legal systems had something to teach the Soviet Union."[43]

Tumanov distinguished between micro and macro comparison; respectively looking at specific rules and at the overall societal stage of development. This gave a theoretical basis justifying fruitful discussion of the

> "[...] major and general issues of legal theory and legal system, the relationship between international and municipal legal systems, general approaches to comparative law and an examination of controversial new branches of law that cut across traditional classifications of the legal system."[44]

Papers from the Symposium were subsequently published in the jointly edited *Comparative Law and Legal System: Historical and Socio-Legal Perspectives*[45] and at least one paper, that by Roger Cotterrell (on sociology of law in the UK), was expanded later beyond the original Oceana book publication. Revised versions appeared in an Italian volume, and then in Cotterrell's own *Law's Community* book.[46]

40 An account of it appears in XXXIII *International and Comparative Law Quarterly* (1984), 777-778.

41 In Butler and Kudriavtsev, *op.cit.* note 21, 69-78.

42 Personal communication from William E. Butler (2 February 2009).

43 Butler, *op.cit.* note 31, 31.

44 Editorial Introduction, Butler, *op.cit.* note 19, 3.

45 Butler and Kudriavtsev, *op.cit.* note 21. Number 133 in Butler, *op.cit.* note 7.

46 Roger Cotterrell, *Law's Community: Legal Theory in Sociological Perspective* (Clarendon Press, Oxford, 1996). Personal information from Roger Cotterrell (22 July 2009).

Apart from the two-day Symposium, the Soviet delegation enjoyed other academic and cultural visits during their ten-day stay in Britain. They were shown legal information retrieval systems, visited Baker & McKenzie solicitors, had a day looking at civil and criminal courts and touring the Inns of Court, with luncheon at Lincoln's Inn, and visited the Parliamentary Ombudsman. They visited Edinburgh for a seminar on comparative law and other meetings as well as a city tour, and saw the Institute of Criminology at Cambridge University, dining as guests of Professor Peter Stein at Queens College, and also visiting Trinity College.[47]

A delegation of eight legal scholars and practitioners visited Moscow and Kiev during the period 5-16 September 1984 for the second symposium, devoted to "Justice and Comparative Law". The papers presented considered Criminal Law, Evidence, Procedure and Sentencing Policy. The symposium's timing was fortuitous as a Report from the Law Commission of England and Wales on a draft criminal code had recently been published for discussion. Also, a number of the Soviet participants had been working on a draft new Model All-Union Criminal Code. There were therefore ample issues within equivalent fields for the participants to make "constructive and useful contributions to original legal scholarship".[48] Papers from this Symposium were published both in a special edition of the journal *Coexistence* and as a book edited by Butler: *Justice and Comparative Law; Anglo Soviet Perspectives on Criminal Law, Evidence, Procedure and Sentencing Policy*.[49]

As well as participating in the symposium, the delegates visited the Supreme Court of the USSR and the RSFSR Ministry of Justice. In Kiev they saw the Institute of State and Law of the Ukrainian Academy of Sciences. An account of the Symposium written by Galina Nikolaevna Vetrova was published in Russian in the prestigious journal *Sovetskoe gosudarstvo i pravo* (Soviet State and Law) and a translation by W.E. Butler of the piece was reproduced in the 1984 Third Annual Report of the Centre for the Study of Socialist Legal Systems.[50]

That Report also notes individual visits by three research scholars from each side. Three scholars came from the Institute of State and Law: Dr. A. Lisitsyn-Svetlanov, researching export control regulations, Dr. N.S. Krylova, a specialist on British constitutional law, who, as well as conducting research, delivered a public lecture at UCL on 8 May, and Dr. William (Vil'iam) V. Smirnov, who

47 Details in "Third Annual Report of the Centre for the Study of Socialist Legal Systems" (Faculty of Laws, University College London, 1984), 14.

48 Butler, *op.cit.* note 19, 4.

49 *Op.cit.* note 19. Number 145 in Butler, *Bibliography*, *op.cit.* note 7. Also in XXXIII *Coexistence* 1-2 (1986), 1-188. Number 144 in Butler, *Bibliography*, *op.cit.* note 7.

50 G.N. Vetrova, 'Iustitsiia i sravnitel'noe pravovedenie', *Sovetskoe gosudarstvo i pravo* (1985) No.3, 145-146, noted Butler *op.cit.* note 19, 4, and appearing as translated by Butler in the Third Annual Report, *op.cit.* note 47, 17-20.

investigated the legal regulation of political participation in Britain. The first visit in the other direction was made by the law librarian from UCL, Mrs. Barbara Wells, who investigated systems for dissemination of legal information in the USSR and subsequently published a couple of papers on the topic.[51] Other visits were by William Butler, to Moscow and the University of Tartu to complete archival research for his study of the history of international law in Russia, and Dr. Richard Plender,[52] who visited the Institute of State and Law pursuing research on public international law and economic integration.

The third symposium was in Moscow in May 1985, on the theme of Labor Law and Comparative Law. An impressive array of labor law specialists from the United Kingdom formed the visiting team, and the symposium proceedings were the basis for the publication in 1987 of *Comparative Labour Law*, edited by William E. Butler, Bob A. Hepple and Alan C. Neal.[53]

The Anglo-Soviet Symposium on "The Right to Work under British and Soviet Law", held at UCL over three days in 1987, similarly resulted in the publication of a monograph under that title, edited by Butler, Hepple and Roger W. Rideout.[54]

The fourth symposium was in London, and dealt with aspects of public law and state administration. Its papers, edited by William E. Butler and Dawn Oliver, appeared in 1988 in *Law, Policy and Administration*.[55] Professor Oliver also subsequently published an article based on the papers entitled "Perestroika and Public Administration in the USSR".[56]

Overall—under the Protocol between 1984-1992—there were more than forty Anglo-Soviet symposia on various legal themes.[57] "More than 150 legal scholars took part in both directions and it was THE major conduit for collaboration in legal research and joint symposia."[58] Publications apart from those already mentioned, edited by William Butler and others, include:

51 Barbara Tearle, "The Dissemination of Legal Information in the Soviet Union", XV(1-2) *The Law Librarian* (1984), 3-6; and *id.*, "A Visit to Some Libraries in Moscow", XIX *Solanus* (1984), 1-16.

52 Now The Honourable Mr. Justice Richard Plender QC, MA, LLB, LLD (Cantab), PhD (Sheff), LLM JSD (Illinois), since he was appointed as a judge in the Queen's Bench Division of the High Court on 31 January 2008. See "List of the Senior Judiciary" available at <http://www.judiciary.gov.uk/keyfacts/list_judiciary/senior_judiciary_list.htm>. Further biographic details available at <http://www.20essexst.com/bar/pdf_cv_files/q_plender_r.pdf>.

53 (Gower, Aldershot, 1987). Number 132 in Butler, *Bibliography*, *op.cit.* note 7.

54 Published in 3(3) *International Journal of Comparative Labour Law and Industrial Relations*, (1987), 83-228. Number 152 in Butler, *Bibliography*, *op.cit.* note 7.

55 25(1) *Coexistence* (1988), 1-135. Number 146 in Butler, *Bibliography*, *op.cit.* note 7.

56 66 *Public Administration* (1988), 411-428.

57 Butler, *Bibliography*, *op.cit.* note 7, xxi.

58 Personal information from William E. Butler (2 February 2009).

(1987) *International Law and the International System* (based on papers delivered at an Anglo-Soviet symposium on public international law held with the Russian Association of International Law);[59]
(1988) IV Anglo-Soviet Symposium on the Law of the Sea and International Shipping;[60]
(1989) *The Rule of Law: Reports Presented to the I Anglo-Soviet Law Student Colloquium, in Moscow, 18-20 December 1989*, with I.P. Blishchenko;[61]
(1989) Symposium on Environmental Law in the USSR and United Kingdom, with M.J. Grant;[62]
(1989) *The Non-Use of Force in International Law* (papers delivered at an Anglo-Soviet Symposium on public international law held with the Russian Association of International Law);[63]
(1990) VI Anglo Soviet Symposium on the Law of the Sea and International Shipping;[64]
(1990) *Perestroika and International Law* (based on papers delivered at the III Anglo- Soviet Symposium on public international law held with the Soviet Association of International Law);[65]
(1991) *Control over Compliance with International Law* (based on papers delivered at the IV Anglo-Soviet Symposium on Public International Law, Moscow (14-16 May 1990));[66]
(1991) *Criminal Law Reform: Anglo Soviet Perspectives*, with Ian Dennis;[67]

59 (Martinus Nijhoff Publishers, Dordrecht, The Netherlands, 1987). Most of the papers were also published previously in Issues 1 and 2 of 24 *Coexistence* (1987). Number 683 in Butler, *Bibliography, op.cit.* note 7.

60 12(3) *Marine Policy* (July 1988), 178-324. Number 729 in Butler, *Bibliography, op.cit.* note 7.

61 (Centre for the Study of Socialist Legal Systems, London, 1990). Number 156 in Butler, *Bibliography, op.cit.* note 7.

62 4 *Connecticut Journal of International Law* (Winter 1989). Number 143 in Butler, *Bibliography, op.cit.* note 7.

63 26(1) *Coexistence* (1989), 1-111; and William E. Butler (ed.), *The Non-Use of Force in International Law* (Kluwer, Dordrecht, The Netherlands, 1989). Number 799 in Butler, *Bibliography, op.cit.* note 7.

64 14(2) *Marine Policy* (March 1990), 101-80. Number 730 in Butler, *Bibliography, op.cit.* note 7.

65 (Martinus Nijhoff Publishers, Dordrecht, The Netherlands, 1990). Number 690 in Butler, *Bibliography, op.cit.* note 7.

66 (Kluwer, Dordrecht, The Netherlands, 1991). Number 668 in Butler, *Bibliography, op.cit.* note 7.

67 28(1) *Coexistence* (1991), 1-200. Number 134 in Butler, *Bibliography, op.cit.* note 7.

(1991) *Perestroika and the Rule of Law: Anglo-American and Soviet Perspectives*;[68]
(1992) VIII Anglo Soviet Symposium on the Law of the Sea and International Shipping.[69]

In 'By Way of Introduction' to his bibliography, Butler says:[70]

> "Most notable was the International Symposium held at Moscow in October 1991 on 'Law and Co-Operation in Europe', attended by more than 2000 jurists from around the world."

In a personal communication (22 April 2009), he summarized:

> "The Direct Link itself served as an umbrella for others, including the Law Student symposium in Moscow (you refer to the publication of 1989); the Grand Symposium of 1991 attended by 2,000; and reciprocal symposia with the Soviet Association of Maritime Law (Kolodkin) and the Soviet Association of International Law (Tunkin). All of these last were self-funding, but the symposia were no less pathbreaking."

Overall, the symposia "were used as a sounding board for countless legal initiatives and policy debates, feeding in ways often invisible to us a larger policy debate in Soviet legal circles".[71] The impact, academically, politically, and socially, was incalculable but clearly significant.

Participants' Impressions

Collecting Responses

There was also a human dimension to the meetings, which is where I now wish to turn. My own view, as might be inferred from the autobiographical details in the Introduction, is that the opportunity for face-to-face meetings with people brought up under regimes regarded as our Cold-War enemies was invaluable. Our common humanity could shine through even where there were clear differences in both approach and opinion. I was interested to explore other participants' perceptions. It was easy to identify those who had given papers at the various symposia which were subsequently published. I therefore undertook to contact as many of these as I feasibly could to see if they were willing to share their reminiscences. A number agreed. I obtained appropriate clearance from the Ethics Committee for Law at King's College London, and sent my informants a simple questionnaire aimed at eliciting memories. In fact, I was agreeably surprised by the enthusiasm with which the informants responded, not only with memories and opinions, but, in a couple of cases, with photographs (see Appendix 4).

Unfortunately, the overwhelming majority of my target group are the Western participants. The more senior of the Soviet delegates have since passed

68 (Tauris, London, 1991). Number 148 in Butler, *Bibliography*, *op.cit.* note 7.

69 16(2) *Marine Policy* (1992), 73-129. Number 731 in Butler, *Bibliography*, *op.cit.* note 7.

70 *Op.cit.* note 7, xxi.

71 Butler, *op.cit.* note 31, 31.

away, and I have not been able to contact other Soviet scholars, with one major exception. I regained personal communication with one of the individual exchange participants, Dr. Vladimir Belykh, through his legal academic daughter-in-law who came on a recent academic exchange to London and with whom I formed a friendship.[72] Dr. Belykh kindly agreed to send me his thoughts and impressions from his research visit. Of the Polish delegates, Judge Lech Garlicki has also kindly responded. Together the collected reminiscences conjure up a picture of participants enthusiastically taking up the opportunity the meetings and visits offered to catch a glimpse of the other side of the Iron Curtain.

Who was Involved?

On the British side, Professor Butler invited his staff colleagues and other interested parties to volunteer for the trips. Sometimes colleagues assisted in rounding up suitable team members, for example, Roger Cotterrell recalls being recruited by William Twining for the first colloquium meeting in 1984.[73] For the Labor Law symposium, experts in the field known to Bob Hepple were invited by him to take part.[74] It is fair to say that very few of these had specific interest in socialist legal systems, but all were intellectually curious and pleased to be given the opportunity to see something of the different world. A list of known or recalled participants is in Appendix 3.

Vladimir Belykh, the Russian respondent who had not come under the Anglo-Soviet exchange agreement but on an individual placement, was asked if he knew how the selection process had worked for him. He replied:

> "I don't know how the process of selection worked. I know that at the institute, where I work up to the present day, authorisations (which during Soviet time were called letters from the superior authorities) arrived for a visit to England from the section of the Ministry of Education. The Pro-rector for scientific work made a proposal to me. I agreed. Then came the stage of learning the foreign language and assessment of the candidates for the trip to England. I passed this selection and was recommended by the Selection Commission."

The comparative freedom of the Poles to make academic links noted above also applied to the group trips under the Anglo-Polish agreement. Lech Garlicki reported:

> "The list of Polish participants could be reconstructed from the ensuing publications—the rule was that whoever wants to participate (and to travel abroad), he/she must present a paper. [...] I have no direct knowledge, how the personal composition of the Polish group was established. Usually, on such occasions, the organizer (*i.e.*, Professor Jerzy Jakubowski) would propose some names to the Dean and usually the Dean's approval would be a formal-

72 And co-authored a paper: Marina Lomovsteva and Jane Henderson, "Constitutional Justice in Russia", 34(1) *Review of Central and East European Law* (2009), 37-69.

73 William Twining, FBA, QC, DCL, JD, LLD, Quain Professor of Jurisprudence at UCL, now Emeritus.

74 Professor Sir Bob Hepple QC, FBA, LLD (Cambridge), BA, LLB and Hon LLD (Witwatersrand), Hon LLD (London), Hon LLD (Capetown).

ity. Other authorities were not directly involved: while all foreign trips and all invitations from abroad had to be accepted by the President of University, I do not think would make any practical problems."

Face-to-Face

For the majority of the British respondents the meetings were the first time they had met Soviet or Polish citizens who were not émigrés. The exceptions were Roger Cotterrell who had independently visited Poland in the 1970s because of musical contacts, and Peter Slinn and Bob Hepple, both of whom had had previous professional contact with scholars from Eastern Europe. Peter Slinn, then senior lecturer in law at the School of Oriental and African Studies, noted that during his time as Foreign and Commonwealth (FCO) Legal Adviser 1967-69, he had some official contacts with Romanian embassy officials, during the thaw with that country, and Bob Hepple had had quite extensive East-West experience in his field of labor law. He wrote:

> "I met Soviet and other scholars from the communist countries at several international conferences, particularly through the International Society for Labour Law and Social Legislation.. In particular I knew from these conferences the leader of the Soviet group, Professor Semion Ivanov, and Professor R.Z. Livshits. I had also undertaken trips to Czechoslovakia and been a visitor to Polish Universities (Wrocław, Łódź, Poznań, Warsaw) and the Institute of State and Law in Poland, and had been a consultant on the Polish Labor Code in the 1980s, which gave me an opportunity to meet many of the principal players in the dialogue between Solidarity and the Government. I had also met several Soviet and Eastern European lawyers on ILO [International Labour Organisation] committees and ILO officials, including Dr. V.V. Egorov, with whom I subsequently conducted an official ILO visit to the Soviet Union to advise on labor matters in 1992."

His wealth of experience was unusual compared with that of the other respondents, with the notable exception of Roger Cotterrell. For them, citizens of Eastern European states, either in London or on their own home ground, was a complete novelty. The importance of the availability through the exchange agreements of this opportunity to meet those from the other side in the Cold War cannot be underestimated. As was mentioned in the Introduction, the chance to assess the veracity of media presentation of 'the enemy' was rare and was an 'eye-opener'. To mention but one factor: it was apparent even amongst the obviously hand-picked Soviet teams that there were differences of opinion and something of a generation gap. Soviet academe was not monolithic.

The opportunity to meet specific Soviet scholars was noted by Peter Slinn:

> "It was fascinating to meet Gregorii Tunkin, the grand old man of Soviet international law, the editions of whose books reflected the doctrinal shift from confrontation to co-existence and finally *perestroika*."

That shift was also apparent in changes over the period of the meetings. Nicola Lacey, than a junior lecturer at UCL , had a vivid memory of "the second trip to Poland, when we got exactly the same tour as the first time, but with an entirely different, supplementary—and critical—commentary". Dawn Oliver recalled that in Moscow: "We had an invitation to dinner at the flat of [a particular official] in 1988, which Bill [Butler] said was a remarkable sign of change in that Soviet citizens would not have felt able to entertain foreigners privately before." Peter Slinn also noted:

> "There was a notable difference between 1988 and 1990. I vividly remember Galina S. [Shinkaretskaya] taking the microphone on a coach tour to the monasteries to announce that her husband had been elected in the first ever free election to the Russian *Duma*. In 1988, our trip to Riga showed straws in the wind. When we arrived at the Latvian SSR Academy, we were addressed in Latvian, our Russian colleagues having to listen to the English translation."

In London we also got a flavour of the *perestroika* changes in the Soviet Union:[75]

> " [...] in the spring of 1990, in the civilized setting of UCL Faculty of Laws Moot Court Room we were to enjoy the hitherto unseen spectacle of a leading Soviet academic—Professor V.M. Savitskii, heckling another—Professor A.M. Larin. The issue in dispute was what the latter as the main draftsman of the legislation had chosen to include as 'law' for the purposes of consideration of its constitutionality by the USSR Committee for Constitutional Supervision. Professor Larin, with almost British pragmatism, had included the binding guiding explanations of the Supreme Court. Professor Savitskii pointed out that these were mere interpretation, not law. Larin shrugged, and said that they had the effect of law so he had included them anyway. Nowadays we have grown used to such open debate, but then it was thrilling to see the taboo against public disagreement being broken so emphatically."

Jeffrey Jowell, the UCL Law Faculty Dean, did not participate in any of the academic sessions of the Institute either in London or the Soviet Union, but entertained some of the Soviet visitors to London from time to time. He recalls:

> "A professor of Labor Law who came frequently to London from Moscow over the years. In the early days he told me that he was resolutely against any right to strike. Under early Gorbachev he became converted to the idea of 'collective agreements to withdraw labor'. Finally, under late Gorbachev he seemed to favour the right to strike. However, when Yeltsin came to power he told me (perhaps jokingly) that he now believed that strikes interfered unduly with the workings of the free market."

In Poland with the rise of *Solidarność* (the Solidarity independent trade union) "the atmosphere was electric—excited but very tense" recalls Nicola Lacey. The Poles response to their own situation was instructive, as Dawn Oliver observed:

> "One evening we were all invited to the apartment of one of the professors, and had a delicious meal. The sideboard was covered in all sorts of hard spirits, but no wine. They used to put vodka in whisky barrels so that the vodka tasted of whisky. That evening the large TV was on all the time in the drawing room, and suddenly there was General Jaruzelski in uniform on screen being sworn in as President. It struck us as very sinister, but our Polish colleagues emphasized that the army was a people's army and there was nothing to fear. Not much later martial law was declared. But when the Poles came over to England for the return visit a few months later and we played a game in which someone draws something and you have to guess what it is, they drew 'martial law' as a large umbrella with tanks under it. The

75 Jane Henderson, "William E Butler – An Appreciation", in Natalia Iu. Erpyleva, Maryann E. Gashi-Butler and Jane E. Henderson, (eds.) *Forging a Common Legal Destiny: Liber Amicorum in Honour of William E Butler* (Wildy, Simmons & Hill, London, 2005), 5.

> point of martial law was to protect Poland from the fate of Czechoslovakia in the Prague Spring in 1968—to deter the Russians from invading it—to that extent it was successful."

From the Polish perspective, the impact of political developments was quite marked. Lech Garlicki recalled:

> "London was a nice city and I had quite favourable impression, but—particularly in 1981—the academic dimension of events was clearly overshadowed by the political situation that was very dynamic at this time. I remember that when the UK group was in Poland, we visited the Nazi Majdanek camp (close to Lublin) and, on the way, in the bus, we learned that Jaruzelski took the position of the Prime Minister. Then, in March, during our stay in London, there was a general strike under preparation in Poland and it seemed quite possible that it may lead to a confrontation with the Polish or Soviet army. We were, of course, quite concerned. The strike was called off on Friday, we were scheduled to leave on Sunday, but on Saturday evening, during a farewell dinner, the BBC informed that the air space over Poland had been temporarily closed. It could mean the beginning of a military intervention, so we were really frightened (and so were our hosts who suddenly realized that we may need to stay with them much longer than planned). Our flight finally left on time, but this is what I really remember now. The 1984 meeting was less dramatic—the martial law was over and there was a mixture of good and bad changes in Poland. So, again, we probably discussed more politics that law."

One very pleasant outcome of the meetings arranged under the interdepartmental agreement with the Poles and the Protocol with the Soviet scholars was personal contacts which have been maintained over years, in some cases decades. Links have even been forged by British academics with no direct professional interest in the Soviet (or Russian) or Polish legal systems. In one case, a British academic who made friends with a Soviet counterpart subsequently sent them food parcels. In another, reciprocal visits were later made with spouses, and one set of families became close enough to organize exchange schemes for their teenaged offspring. One or two overtures by scholars from the East of the Iron Curtain for assistance to emigrate did not mature; for example, one British academic was pressured (unsuccessfully) to write a joint textbook with a Polish expert in order to give the latter a better profile for a visa for the United States.

Impressions of 'The Other Side'

Some British respondents retain strong memories of their encounters with Soviet reality. Dawn Oliver remembers:

> "We stayed at the Rossiya Hotel, where we felt the *babushka* on each floor was watching us. The rooms were awful. I shared a room with another English academic who was on the exchange: poor soul suffered bites from bed bugs. There were cockroaches in the showers. There was very little food to eat and you had to queue at the little cafés at the corner of each floor for anything to eat. And it was only hard boiled eggs and cold chicken, and tea. [...] We were shocked at the fact that there were hard currency shops where only Westerners, or anyway no Russians could shop. There was nothing much to buy. The restaurants where we were taken for meals had very little choice."

The other side of the coin was the power of position. Roger Rideout recalled:

"The concierge on our floor was contacted by the organisation due to provide our taxi to depart from the airport and asked to confirm the booking. Since no one had told her she cancelled it. When nothing turned up Bill Butler contacted our Russian organizer. He got us to the airport just in time, waving his red card to get us through security and passport control on the nod. Even the security staff looked astounded, but at that time anyone who had authority in Russia really did get by without challenge.

This same chap, who was in charge of our visit, waved the same red card from the door of the bus that took us to the centre of Moscow on the day that the Italian prime minister and entourage were visiting. The centre of Moscow was closed to traffic that day. That evening he and his daughter took us to the top rated Georgian restaurant. (He was a Georgian, I think). The Italians were dining there in force and the restaurant was closed to everyone else—except us! The Italians had the main room to themselves but he insisted on taking us for a walk through it, allegedly to view the opulence of the decoration. We did not think we imagined that two or three men at the end of each table put their hands on their revolvers. Our host was delighted by this public demonstration of his influence."

Stephen Guest was surprised at:

"[...] how conservative they all were, both in Moscow and in Poland; they were impressed—very impressed—by the fact that Jack Jacob was 'Sir' Jack Jacob and his wife 'Lady' Jacob. They were exceedingly polite in Moscow, but I thought they were genuinely impressed by the titles. In Poland, informally, we were told time and again how Thatcher was a 'wonderful' leader who—at last—would be able to 'stand up' to the threat from the Soviet Union; at last we had a 'strong leader' and they were all aware of the name 'the Iron Lady'. On the question of trade unions, they were so in favour of 'closed shops', 'flying pickets' and various other monolithic attributes of trade unions that had been for a long time regarded by a majority in the UK as undesirably conservative, etc, that they didn't understand criticisms of them."

He was not the only respondent to remember the Poles' adulation of Margaret Thatcher. In his meetings with Polish academics outside the framework of the UCL agreement Roger Cotterrell was "told by one person how lucky I was to live in a country with Margaret Thatcher as its leader".

In the USSR a side visit to Ashkhabad in Turkmenistan was described by Dawn Oliver as "so exotic! Samarkand etc. etc.".

"In Ashkhabad we learned virtually nothing about the law, but we did have fascinating visits to, for instance, a stud farm, a place where prize stallions and other race horses were trained and sold, a state owned carpet factory, a government department dealing with environment. And we drove through the desert, including shifting sand dunes which many of us had not seen. There were shepherd boys looking after camels. We were quite struck by how 'private' farming and activity seemed to continue and the fact that the locals were very keen gamblers on horse racing, which seemed un-Soviet."

Even in Moscow there might be unusual visits, as Nicola Lacey discovered.

"I got on rather well with the senior chap who was meant to be replying to my paper. I don't think we really achieved much intellectual exchange, but through a translator, he told me that as a mark of his respect he would like to take me after the session to the mortuary!!! In fact this turned out to be hugely interesting, as what he meant was the cemetery where Khrushchev, Stalin's daughter and various other out-of-favour figures were buried. It was closed to foreigners and his wife was obviously nervous about his taking me."

The visit to Majdanek mentioned above by Lech Garlicki made a deep impression on Stephen Guest, not only for the place itself—originally planned to be the largest Nazi concentration camp in occupied Europe[76]—but also for the apparent disinterest of his fellow participants. It may be that the immediate political events of the time were overshadowing the memorial to the harrowing past, but that would not explain why "when we went to Kiev, as part of our later Moscow trip, I found the same lack of interest in going to Babi Iar,[77] although I managed to push this through".

At this point we can get a view 'from the other side' from Vladimir Belykh, who was in Great Britain on a scholarly internship for a period of six months from 2 December 1985 until 1 June 1986 in the Centre for Commercial Law Studies at the School of Law, Queen Mary, University of London. Professor Roy Goode was assigned to be his supervisor. Vladimir Belykh wrote: "This was my first trip abroad. I was 33 years old and, it seemed that the whole world lay at my feet." The internship was a great success and Belykh writes warmly of the help he received from Professor Goode and others (including William Butler and the author), and the friendship and assistance of Brian Bercusson. But to the young Soviet visitor, some aspects of London life were not so pleasant:

> "My first impression of London began with Heathrow, and then a trip on the electric train to Hyde Park. First of all, a dazzling spectacle. I arrived flying late in the evening from Moscow. So then it was on the train that my attention focused on the fact that some subgroups of Londoners talk loudly and drop litter. Moreover they do this publicly, and in a habitual manner. After some time I visited the cinema and encountered newly a similar example: after I had seen the film—grime. It is a typical problem of large metropolises: the collision of different cultures and religions. [...] I was temporarily placed in a hotel, near to Hyde Park. I left the hotel. I was surrounded by the lights from advertisements, the noise and the din of city at night. It proved to be something of a shock. The feeling was as though I came from another world. After the week I moved to the eastern part of London, not far from Queen Mary College. I lived with the college students. They were friendly and kind. London—it is a unique historical city. It is literally impregnated with history. It is majestic and is divided into zones with tightly-knit enclaves of the descendants from different countries. In a word, it is possible to live in London for one's entire life, but not to learn anything about Englishmen."

He did, however, learn something of British scholarly culture, which he saw as contrasting his own academic background:

> "From numerous encounters with English scholars I would focus attention on two particular instances. First, the equal relationship between scholars and teachers, independent of their academic rank or degree. At its most extreme, I did not notice any deference towards authorities. Secondly, scientific toleration towards the theories and views of opponents. For example: commercial law. In both the former USSR there were, and in modern Russia there

76 See the website of the State Museum at Majdanek, available at <http://majdanek.pl/articles.php?acid=45&mref=1>.

77 A ravine where mass extermination of Jews took place. In 1961, the Russian poet Evgenii Evtushenko wrote a poem entitled "Babi Iar" decrying antisemitism.

> are, even now, bitter disputes about the existence of economic (entrepreneurial) law. Even mentally it is difficult to imagine that anyone from amongst the English scholars could allow himself to doubt the existence of English commercial law, stating: 'Esteemed Professor Roy Goode, but there is no commercial law'. That would be ridiculous!"

Away from the academic milieu, Vladimir Belykh met both ignorance and tolerance.

> "I would like to give two examples of informal contact. The first—when I visited to the British Council, I was waiting for my moderator, Nina Battleday. One of her colleagues asked me: 'Where are you from?' I answered: 'From the USSR'. He did not understand and asked back: 'From the USA?'. Further refining the question: 'From Moscow?'. Answer: 'No. From Sverdlovsk'. He did not know the city. Then I said—'The Urals'. He still did not understand. When I specified: 'Siberia', he exclaimed with happiness: 'It is there cold, bears walk, and Russians drink vodka.' It was completely absurd! The second example: in the centre of London we were sitting with Ian Mathers and his associates in the Alexandria Restaurant, somewhere near Victoria Street. A group of men. One of the participants in this proceedings was somewhat drunk and unexpectedly asked me to accompany him to his workplace, at the DTI [Department for Trade and Industry]. I agreed. When we left the restaurant, he remembered about some documents, which he had allegedly left in the restaurant. I reassured him: 'Do not be disturbed. Your documents are with me. But I am a Soviet spy'. His face noticeably shot up in surprise and, for a moment he became sober: 'It is true!' I waited, and then said that I was joking. My English associate broke into a run into the restaurant, and when he returned with the documents, he was then again in a state of alcoholic intoxication. An absolute oil painting. We go along Victoria Street. A tall Russian and a diminutive, slender Englishman. When we approached the office of the DTI, the security man asked, looking at me: 'Who are you?' My friend reassured him: 'This is my friend; he is a Soviet spy!' You should have seen the tall, athletic, well-muscled security man, who whole-heartedly laughed out loud. He clapped me on the arm: 'Pass, sir'."

The Formal Symposia Sessions

There seemed to be a common opinion from the respondents that, despite the impressive level of expertise on both sides, the formal sessions did not give rise to high level academic debate. Logistically, the fact that papers and any comments needed to be translated somewhat inhibited spontaneous interaction. More profoundly, there were some serious dissonances in the academic approach to topics by the teams from each side. Roger Rideout noted that, "[...] the Russians were much more interested in legal procedures (which at that time did not figure much in British academic thought)". One British respondent commented of the Soviet academics, "Their papers were rather abstract and difficult to follow. I did not feel we engaged much intellectually. For us the law actually happens, for them it seemed to be an aspiration but not actually effective on the ground." Similarly: "We were continually told what the 'reality' was, without comment on whether this 'reality' was a good thing or not." Another commented:

> "The theoretical papers delivered to us did not make a lasting impression as far as detail is concerned. But I obtained insights into our own system and the deep cultural differences in attitude to the rule of law etc."

Stephen Guest, who has a deep and longstanding interest in jurisprudence (theory of law) found the dissonance between the two sets of scholars instructive in itself. It is worth quoting his assessment at length:

> "I found it enormously interesting from the legal theory perspective. I thought they had no legal theory at all, although they appeared to believe that they were applying 'Marxist theory'. But it was totally under-thought out; a pretty well meaningless doctrine utterly and hopelessly unanalyzed. I thought about this a lot: I think they had to follow the official line of Marxist doctrine and had more or less internalized this fuzzy way of thinking. The main difficulty they had was distinguishing the descriptive from the normative, and so we had in most seminars masses and masses of descriptive material without much comment on it; I found the very long sessions very long indeed. Facts, facts, facts. And when we got to an interesting point there was such intellectual constipation over what to us in the West would be fairly straightforwardly critical or would be a straightforward proposal for reform. [...] A lot of the time, in both the Soviet Union and Poland, there was a confusion of procedure with substance; we had to steer off substance I thought, and I could never work out quite whether this was intentional or whether this had become so embedded: I thought more likely it was embeddedness. So, for example, a question about the sense of certain trade union regulation was converted into a question about how regulations were made, how they were in accordance with the very general aims of the Constitution and then [...] back to questions which seemed unanswerable to them about the criteria for the interpretation of the Constitution. [...] I would say that practically all the academic lawyers I met in both countries were naturally legal positivists—they thought of law as identifiable through the 'black letters'—but didn't realize it. They weren't supposed to recognize it, of course, because law was supposed to be informed by the Marxist doctrines—that is, an ideology, not by a description of the 'black letters'."

Labor law was an interesting field where the dichotomy between ideology and practical implementation showed quite markedly. Bob Hepple wrote:

> "My main impression was the dogmatic and Party-dictated approach of the Soviet scholars and their reluctance to speak frankly about Soviet labor relations. For example, when Brian Bercusson asked why there was no right to strike in the USSR, the reply by the scholars was the Party line that 'this is the workers' state, why should workers strike against it?' Then we went to an oil refinery and met the legal director who, when asked whether they ever had strikes, responded: 'We have them all the time, and I spend a lot of my time sorting them out, making the management deal with the situation and persuading the workers to return to work!' The scholars were happy to talk about the black letter law, but avoided the reality, except occasionally in private."

And Roger Rideout, formerly Professor of Labor Law at UCL, commented:

> "I suspect that the Russians were pretty surprised by a paper by Keith Ewing on the qualifications required by an employee to make claims for such things as unfair dismissal. They could not understand why a worker needed to qualify for rights as a worker."

There was also a cultural divide: "The Russians at the seminars had by English standards rather bad manners—they would speak among themselves while a speaker was delivering a paper, they would come and go from the room." If the English were shocked by the Russians' manners, "[...] the Soviet team being a bit shocked by the youth of the team UCL fielded (I was only about 25 at the time)". In fact within the Soviet team there appeared to be a generation gap. Roger Rideout observed:

> "The gulf was rigidly maintained by the old guard and the younger people clearly attended more as observers than participators. I can illustrate this by an occurrence on the morning when I chaired the session. I was approached in the coffee break by a youngish woman who asked if I could fit in time for her to say something. I did so. What she said did not seem to me controversial but as soon as she had finished the Russian in overall charge said that we were running short of time and there were three more speakers to be fitted in before lunch. These three were then wheeled out, one by one, to deliver thoroughly boring factual accounts of things like safety regulation in Soviet factories, and they made sure they kept talking until the end of the session. I took particular note of the body language of the younger members, who kept together as a group. It was pretty obvious that they were used to being silenced."

He continued: "This was not apparent in Warsaw, where the younger people were lively participants who did not hesitate to meet with us in the sessions and even for a meal." This contrast between Soviet and Polish approaches was noted by another informant:

> "The scholars we met in Moscow were mostly dour and not very friendly to us. They were not very friendly to one another either—they would have private conversations during the presentations, come and go and not listen politely to each others' papers. No personal hospitality was offered. The scholars we met in Odessa were much more open and friendly.
>
> By comparison we did feel we were connecting with the Polish scholars and learning from one another. They were very friendly, offered us lots of personal hospitality, shared the same senses of humor. We were entertained in style. The British ambassador gave a reception for the British and Polish scholars and told a rather indiscrete anti Soviet joke which we all enjoyed a lot. When the Poles came to England we offered them personal hospitality too. We felt able to speak frankly about politics etc in Poland, Solidarity etc."

One example of Polish humor encountered by the author in 1986 was an academic in Warsaw saying with a wry smile that we should never trust a state whose emblem looks in two directions at once.[78]

Despite some doubts expressed about the depth of interaction possible at the formal sessions, they clearly had value for a number of reasons. We noted above Professor Tumanov articulating a major revision of the Soviet approach to comparative law, which was an important ideological shift. More prosaically, the symposia gave the Western scholars, who were mainly young lecturers fairly near the beginning of their academic careers, an opportunity to try out newly developing thoughts and theories in their papers. A couple of respondents noted that they found it as valuable to have the opportunity to discover what research topics their British colleagues were pursuing as to be presented with Soviet legal views. One respondent noted that a welcome side-effect of one of the Moscow symposia was the setting up on the UCL team's return of a system of regular staff lunchtime seminars to discuss work in progress and "I obtained important

78 Taken to be a reference to the two headed eagles of both the Habsburg and Russian coats of arms.

insights into the peculiarities of our own legal and constitutional system from the exchanges". There were discussions, even if not exclusively with the foreign visitors. Roger Cotterrell recounts his diary entry for the first Anglo-Soviet colloquium:

> "I noted that Graveson[79] came up to talk to me enthusiastically about my paper, which he liked as a view 'from the other side (*i.e.*, from the standpoint of sociology of law rather than sociological jurisprudence). He wanted to discuss Roscoe Pound, who had influenced him. Later in the day Tumanov engaged me in conversation and wanted to know what I thought of Jean Carbonnier's (French) sociology of law. So there were exchanges of views."

Bob Hepple was quite specific about the academic value to him of the Anglo-Soviet labor law symposium:

> "The experiences helped me by way of background when writing my piece on "Trade Unions and Democracy in Transitional Societies: Reflections on Russia and South Africa" in Keith D. Ewing, Conor Gearty and Bob A.Hepple (eds.), *Human Rights and Labour Law: Essays for Paul O'Higgins* (Mansell, New York, NY, 1994), 56-75."

Peter Slinn wonders if he might have helped spark an idea:

> "As far as my own contribution in 1988 was concerned, I thought I was on safely original ground in choosing to speak about the role of the (Formerly British) Commonwealth of Nations in the settlement of disputes. However, I arrived to discover that the Institute of State and Law had a research project on the Commonwealth led by Dr. N. Krylova who contributed a paper to the symposium. It was typical of Soviet scholarship that there was much interest in classifying the Commonwealth in the periodic table of organizations. However, Dr. K. took a very positive view, describing the Commonwealth as a 'brilliant example of the diversity of interlinkages of the modern world'. [Butler (ed.) at 149] I suspect that in an earlier era the Commonwealth would have been written off as a British neo-imperialist sham. Of course the Commonwealth of Independent States was to 'succeed' the old Soviet Empire as the Commonwealth emerged from the old British Empire. Did our discussions help to give birth to the idea of the CIS [Commonwealth of Independent States]?"

Opinions on Outcome

The individuals who were involved in these cross-cultural exchanges almost invariably went on to successful careers, if they did not already have renown in their field. The young British delegates have since achieved seniority, in academia, in legal practice, or indeed in both, and are too numerous to list here (see Appendix 3 for an incomplete list of participants). Three individuals from the Soviet team later achieved prestige as Russian Constitutional Court judges. Tamara Morshchakova (mentioned in the account by Vetrova in *Soviet State and Law*) was appointed when the Court was first established in 1994. Vladimir Tumanov, mentioned above for his paper on comparative law, and Marat Baglai (who gave a paper at the labor-law symposium) were appointed when the Court was re-established in 1996, and Tumanov then became its Chairman, serving from 24 December 1996 until 20 February 1997 when he achieved mandatory retirement age. He moved on to became the first Russian judge of the European

79 Ronald H. Graveson QC CBE (1911-1991), Professor of Law at King's College London.

Court of Human Rights (ECHR) from 1997 to 1998, and Marat Baglai succeeded him as Russian Constitutional Court Chairman from 20 February 1997 to 23 February 2003. Of the Polish delegates, Lech Garlicki also became a judge at the European Court of Human Rights in 2002, having previously worked in the Polish Constitutional Tribunal.

In response to a question as to what they thought was the most important outcome of the exchange agreements, the British respondents emphasized that they broke down barriers. Roger Rideout commented:

> "By far the most important outcome of the meeting with Soviet lawyers was the fostering of a spirit of cooperation. I would not presume to suggest that we contributed much to the ending of the Cold War. As I have said, I think that was on the way anyway; fostered, no doubt, by an increasing flow of information and contact from and with the West. It would have been surprising if most Russians had not noticed how much more profitable everything in the West was and to have asked why. They knew well that Russia had vast natural resources, far outstripping the rest of Europe. But our meetings contributed to this flow; not so much, in my view, as to knowledge of the law as to our general attitudes, particularly to free discussion."

Nicola Lacey saw intrinsic value in the meetings: "I guess I feel that any contact reduces mutual ignorance and hence hostility." Peter Slinn also took a broad view:

> "Improved mutual understanding and awareness of the transformation of Soviet thinking—the wide acceptance that there was only one world-wide science of international law and that the new global problems challenging humanity could only be countered by all States acting together."

Lech Garlicki also saw the opportunity for face-to-face discussion as the main benefit that came from the exchange scheme:

> "As I see it now, this was probably the main profit of those contacts—to get in touch and to discuss different problems. It would be difficult to describe them as historical—it was just one out of many exchanges our Law School was involved at this time. But, it was useful and interesting. Unfortunately, the exchange with the UK has never developed to a degree comparable to the German or US exchange."

He added, in response to a question: "Did you feel that you were being monitored during your visit(s), by either the Polish or the British authorities?"

> "I do not know whether we were monitored, by any of secret services. As far as the Polish side is concerned, I think that in 1981 our services had more acute problems to deal with. Even in 1984, I do not think that our visits were regarded as important enough to attract any attention. But, if you wish to try your luck, you may write to the *Instytut Pamieci Narodowej* in Warsaw.[80] Who knows? Perhaps they have something for you."

80 The Polish "Institute of National Remembrance" which maintains the archives of the state security authorities in the period from 22 July 1944 to 31 July 1990. English-language website available at <http://www.ipn.gov.pl/portal/en/>.

Historical Importance?

On this issue of whether the meetings had historical importance, Roger Rideout replied (so typically for a legal academic): "It depends what one thinks of as history." He continued:

> "[...] our meetings were no more than one of many factors in the thaw. That being so they would have significantly encouraged those moving in that direction. Since some of the Russians were significant intellectuals with more public influence than most UK academics these meetings would have assisted the underlying movement. This is particularly so since our meeting acknowledged, to a proud and nationalistic people, our belief that, in our field, they were as significant to us as any Western European country (or perhaps the whole lot put together since at the time there was no similar initiative even toward France and Germany). The Poles, who really only waited for the end of Russian imperialism, did not need so much stirring. They came as friends (although they were annoyed the Churchill had sold them to Russia at Potsdam). In both instances our cooperation was a cog (or perhaps oil on the cog) in a machine already beginning to turn."

Peter Slinn expressed a similar view of that the meetings might have assisted an existing process:

> "One certainly had a sense of being present while history in the making. The modest claim to historical importance would be that the meetings helped to strengthen the process whereby the old cold-war barriers were coming down and that soviet intellectuals felt free to express themselves in a forum now longer subject to rigid control. I remember one senior Soviet remarking calmly that the Stalinist regime was much worse than that the Tsars who exiled opponents rather than murdering them."

There is one historic and symbolic event for which some credit may be given to the Anglo-Soviet link. The fascinating story is told by Jeffrey Jowell:[81]

> "In 1986 Bill Butler told me that the triennial Work Programme agreed under [Article 7 of] the 1983 Protocol with the Institute was about to expire and that the Soviets were very keen that I as Dean sign the follow-up agreement in Moscow, where he and I had been invited for a week. I agreed and asked whether I could have some academic discussions with our hosts and Moscow University (and if possible hear some music in Moscow). [...]
>
> We had a number of negotiating sessions about the new agreement with the Institute, during which I tried to insist that we move from mere dry accounts of the law in our respective jurisdictions to an account of the practical implementation of the law. Words to that effect were written into the agreement, which Bill and I signed on the morning of Thursday 17th September. After the signing the Butlers left for Tblisi and I, by pre-arrangement, was entertained to lunch by one of the Institute's Directors, Professor Kudriavtsev (apparently one of Gorbachev's right hand men).
>
> *Lunch with Kudriavtsev*
>
> After the Butlers left, Kudriavtsev, I and another professor [...] walked to the Hotel Praga. We entered a private room all set for lunch. To my surprise, Kudriavtsev suddenly suggested that we leave that room and led the three of us up the back stairs to another room, and then to another, and then ordered the lunch to be brought there. It crossed my mind that he may have been trying to evade any bugs in the first room or, more likely given my

81 Personal information (5 September 2009).

London experience, that he was trying to reassure me that I could talk freely, despite the fact that we had no agenda.

Without any preliminaries, Kudriavtsev leant over to me and asked: 'How can we persuade the West that we are serious about radical change in this country?'

I was nonplussed. I had no experience in international diplomacy and was hardly in any position to comment. I wondered whether they had misunderstood my position or status. Nevertheless, I felt that somehow I should rise to the challenge and was rather surprised to hear myself blurt out: 'Free Sakharov!'[82]

Kudriavtsev also seemed surprised. 'Do you know that he broke many regulations?'

I asked for examples. 'He attacked the police.' I asked for details.

'After the Moscow explosion he gave a press conference in favour of violence. He also worked with strict nuclear secrets, so is a possible security risk. He has been used by Western journalists.'

I said rather awkwardly that I was unaware of these incidents but felt that in the eyes of the West Sakharov was a person of considerable distinction and freeing him would mark an important indication of intent.

Kudriavtsev then changed tack, saying that I should know the personal details of Sakharov. He had a very unhappy first marriage. His second wife had suddenly come out in favour of Zionism, although she was not Jewish. She attends some dubious doctor in Italy.

I said that was all interesting but, irrespective of his wife's behaviour, the widespread view abroad was that he was being persecuted for holding unorthodox scientific and/or political views.

Kudriavtsev denied this, and said that in fact Sakharov had never been expelled from the Academy.

'He still attends meetings there and gives papers. He was sent to the Gorkii Institute to work.'

I repeated that, whatever the reasons were for Sakharov's confinement, and rightly or wrongly, his detention was in my view a stumbling block to Western recognition of any real change in the Soviet Union.

During the rest of the lunch Kudriavtsev stressed the need for peace and disarmament and hoped that the forthcoming round of disarmament talks would bear fruit.

82 Andrei Dmitrievich Sakharov. As summarized in *Encyclopædia Britannica Online*, available at <http://www.britannica.com/EBchecked/topic/518715/Andrey-Dmitriyevich-Sakharov>: "Soviet nuclear theoretical physicist, an outspoken advocate of human rights, civil liberties, and reform in the Soviet Union as well as rapprochement with noncommunist nations. In 1975 he was awarded the Nobel Prize for Peace." See, also, his autobiography written at that time (with updated post-script) available at <http://nobelprize.org/nobel_prizes/peace/laureates/1975/sakharov-autobio.html>. From 1980 until 1986, Sakharov was forced to live in Gorkii (the name from 1932 to 1990 of the city now known again as Nizhnii Novgorod); his resident's permit for Moscow was revoked, although there was no judicial process. In December 1986, Mikhail Gorbachev—then General Secretary of the Communist Party of the Soviet Union—reportedly had telephoned Sakharov to invite him to return to Moscow.

> *Postscript*
>
> Not long after that lunch Sakharov was indeed freed. For some reason I never got round to reporting the lunch with Kudriavtsev to Bill Butler, but remember telling our Provost, Sir James Lighthill about it and, after Sakharov's release, joking with my wife that I had a hand in it, before forgetting the whole incident for over twenty years.
>
> At Bill Butler's retirement dinner just over a year ago I finally reminisced with Bill about our time together in Moscow in September 1986 and recounted the Kudriavtsev lunch (in scant detail—the account above results from my recently finding my comprehensive notes of the visit).
>
> I have not checked this again with Bill but after I told him about the lunch he exclaimed: "That explains something I have never understood!"

When this recently written account of Jeffrey Jowell's recollection was presented to William Butler, he responded:[83]

> "Whether we had any impact on Sakharov, I do not know, and I depend upon Jeffrey's recollection for luncheon at Praga, as I was not there. However, in support of his recollection, I was in Moscow on the day that Sakharov was released and heard the news from Professor A.L. Kolodkin, with whom I was having dinner. This was also the first occasion that I saw a Coca Cola bottle in a Moscow restaurant (Rossiia Hotel)—the more remarkable since Pepsi had a monopoly still in force. Kolodkin told me of Sakharov's release (which I was unaware of that day), and then said: 'I suppose you are very glad about this?' I was puzzled by the comment, but acknowledged that I was and that this removed a considerable source of tension with the West."

In his account, Jeffrey Jowell went on to say that: "Sakharov's release was no doubt the result of huge international pressure and deep forces within Gorbachev's Soviet Union. It is not likely that the UCL-Institute link could have played any part in it." But perhaps he undersells the possibility. Could his honest and heartfelt words, coming without obvious premeditation from an English academic with no political axe to grind, have been the pebble that started the avalanche of Andrei Sakharov's return from administrative exile?

End of the Era

The exchange schemes came to an end with the end of the Cold War. Professor Butler explained:

> "We competed each year with everyone else for British Council support, but the absence of longer term support always made it difficult and uncertain as to whether the Link would survive. When the USSR disappeared, this type of bilateralism was no longer in vogue, and we did lose our funding."[84]

One of the other respondents similarly noticed that: "Once Elt'sin took over and much Russian industry was privatized, etc., I believe that the funding for the protocol exchanges disappeared and so there were no more of them."

83 Personal information (9 September 2009).

84 Personal information (22 April 2009).

The impact of the new more open relationship between West and East was not uniformly positive. Peter Slinn noticed that: "There was perhaps more trust and openness to 'western ideas' than is evident now in the Putin era."

Vladimir Belykh comments from the Russian perspective that there now seems to be surprisingly little appetite for cooperation from Western institutions, even when there are clearly shared areas of interest and appropriate expertise.

> "With the aim of instigating collaboration with European associates in the field of entrepreneurial (commercial) law, stock exchange, bank, investment, and insurance law, I founded the scientific research centre of comparative jurisprudence and international entrepreneurial law, of which I have been appointed director. Information about the centre is located on the website/online periodical 'Business, Management and Law'.[85] We are ready for collaboration with analogous centres, schools, and colleges. Letters have been sent out inviting collaboration. But, so far, without success. In my department on entrepreneurial law work there are young lecturers, graduate students who cope well with foreign languages and are ready for trips abroad as probationers. But to obtain such an invitation—this is a very difficult thing. There is no Soviet Union, orders no longer exist. The decentralized system of control in the sphere of scientific research and exchange of experience has lead to failure.
>
> The main result of my internship [was] encounters with English associates—it is my firm opinion that nothing can be achieved in scholarly research without comparative jurisprudence. But if earlier there was the Iron Curtain between the USSR and the countries of the West, then, up until now, there still remains a curtain against the utilisation of foreign experience of scholarly researches. One example: recently the publishing house 'Prospekt' (Moscow) published my book *Transport Legislation of Russia, Foreign States, the European Union, the Shanghai Cooperation Organization (SCO)* [Russian acronym *SHOS*], and the *Eurasian Economic Community* [*EvrAzES*]. But it was improbably difficult to find appropriate literature and legal sources. There is no Berlin Wall. But there are still many obstacles in the path of free contact and exchange of opinions.
>
> I undertook the attempt to translate into Russian and publish Professor Roy Goode's book *Commercial Law*. But, unfortunately, the publishing house 'Pingvin' dragged out the process of agreement, although the elegant project might yet be realized. Generally I want to note, there is a great desire for collaboration with English associates in different spheres: participation in conferences, exchange of scientific articles, reading lectures and so forth. The main thing is the mutual interest."

Conclusions

Both the Inter-faculty Agreement between University College London and the Faculty of Law and Administration of Warsaw University, and the Protocol of Cooperation between UCL and the Institute of State and Law of the USSR Academy of Sciences (*IGPAN*) were pioneering ventures. The link with *IGPAN* was arguably more groundbreaking as at the time the Soviet Union was more isolated from the West than Poland, and it led to an impressive number of meetings, visits and exchanges during a period when otherwise contact with Soviet legal scholars was well nigh impossible. Poland had remained more open to

85 Available at <http://www.bmpravo.ru/>.

external links, and, as we have seen, the agreement with UCL was not the only forum for academic exchange for the Polish scholars.

We have also seen that an overwhelming number of those whose opinions have been canvassed about their experience of the interactions were extremely positive about the beneficial effect of such face-to-face contact, even when there were some reservations about the level of mutual understanding of each other's academic work. As Jeffrey Jowell said:

> "[...] my short week in Moscow convinced me that the kind of dialogue that exchanges such as ours promote can have unexpected and important value, which Bill Butler was so right to recognize through his pioneering efforts."

However, we are left with a paradox. During the Cold-War era, at a time of ideologically inspired mistrust between East and West, through the institutional arrangements of the academic exchange schemes there was access, albeit for limited numbers, which allowed scholars to meet, make links, exchange information, form friendships, and have materials published. The schemes were not the only opportunity for such contacts, but they allowed regular group meetings on an unprecedented scale. In the modern, 'freer' world, large-scale collaboration can be more difficult to achieve because the bureaucratic frameworks which support such ventures do not exist on all sides. Those who control the purse strings see little strategic value in fostering academic collaboration. In a world governed by the market, activities which may not have apparent scope for very immediate commercial exploitation are out of fashion. Short-term gains are the main focus, rather than the long view, which no doubt inspired the instigators of the exchange agreements we have been examining. This limited vision of our current age should not occlude our memories of the pioneering ventures that brought the two sides from a divided world together and established settings within which enhanced mutual understanding and regard could be fostered, and which may have gone at least a little way to creating a window in the Iron Curtain during the Cold-War era.

Appendix 1

AGREEMENT BETWEEN THE FACULTY OF LAWS, UNIVERSITY COLLEGE LONDON, AND THE FACULTY OF LAW AND ADMINISTRATION. WARSAW UNIVERSITY[86]

[Signed at Budapest, 23 August 1978]

Section 1. The purpose of the present Agreement is to facilitate mutual contacts between staff and students from the law faculties of both universities and enable them to participate in lectures, seminars, visits, and tours of or relating to legal institutions in the United Kingdom and the People's Republic of Poland, as well as appropriate sightseeing and cultural activities.

Both parties hope that the implementation of the present Agreement will strengthen scientific and personal contacts between the faculty members and students of these two Universities.

Section 2. Ten undergraduate and postgraduate students studying socialist legal systems at the Faculty of Laws, University College London, and ten Polish students and research workers shall take part in an exchange visit during the academic year 1978-79 to the Faculty of Law and Administration, Warsaw University, and the Faculty of Laws, University College London, respectively.

Section 3. The group from the United Kingdom will visit Poland for one week and the group from Poland will visit the United Kingdom for one week at dates to be arranged at the earliest possible convenience.

Section 4. Each party will be responsible for its own transportation expenses to and from the other party. The host party will be responsible for local transfers and for transport relating to the organised programme. Other transport on the territory of the host party will be at the expense of the individuals concerned.

Section 5. Both parties obliged themselves to provide free accommodation and meals in appropriate university housing or hostels.

Section 6. Medical care shall be provided to participants pursuant to the intergovernmental agreements in force between the United Kingdom and the People's Republic of Poland.

86 The text of the agreement is in the "Second Annual Report of the Centre for the Study of Socialist Legal Systems" (Faculty of Laws, University College London, 1983), 15; and in *Yearbook on Socialist Legal Systems 1987*, *op.cit.* note 5, 387-388.

Section 7. The organised programme in each country shall be prepared on the basis of suggestions and requests made by both parties, which shall be exchanged at the earliest possible convenience.

Section 8. Both parties guarantee the equivalence of this exchange.

Section 9. The present Agreement, together with the organised programme, shall constitute the basis of the exchange and shall enter into force from the moment it is signed by both parties. Thereafter, changes may be made only with the consent of both parties.

Section 10. Both parties are obliged to inform one another about the exact date and place of arrival of their respective groups within at least seven days before the arrival.

Section 11. The present Agreement has been drawn up in two identical copies in the English language.

[Signed]:
W.E. Butler
Dean of the Faculty of Laws
University College London

[Signed]:
J. Rajski
Prodziekan
Wydział Prawa i
Administracji UW

Appendix 2

PROTOCOL ON SCIENTIFIC CO-OPERATION BETWEEN THE FACULTY OF LAWS, UNIVERSITY COLLEGE LONDON (GREAT BRITAIN) AND THE INSTITUTE OF STATE AND LAW OF THE USSR ACADEMY OF SCIENCES[87]

[Signed at London, 24 October 1983]

On the basis of and within the framework of the Agreement on Scientific Co-operation in the Social Sciences between The British Academy and the Academy of Sciences of the USSR, which entered into force from 1 April 1977,

Being guided by the purposes of that Agreement which arise from the provisions of the Final Act of the Conference on Security and Co-operation in Europe,

Proceeding from an acknowledgement of the importance of international scientific co-operation,

And for the purpose of further strengthening mutual understanding between English and Soviet scholars,

the Faculty of Laws, University College London, of the University of London, Great Britain, and the Institute of State and Law of the USSR Academy of Sciences have agreed on the following:

1. To effectuate scientific co-operation in the field of State and law, each of the Parties having the right to involve, when necessary, scholars from other scientific institutions of their country.

2. To include as priority problems of scientific co-operation the following research topics which are of mutual interest:

— national systems of law and comparative law;
— law, policy, and state administration;
— criminal law and the system of justice;
— contemporary problems of international law;
— history of law and political theory.

Carrying out research with regard to the said problems shall be determined by the work programme drawn up every three years.

87 The text of the Protocol is reproduced in the "Second Annual Report of the Centre for the Study of Socialist Legal Systems" (Faculty of Laws, University College London, 1983), 17-20; and in *Yearbook on Socialist Legal Systems 1987*, *op.cit.* note 5, 388-392.

3. Scientific co-operation will be carried out in the following forms:

(a) exchange of scholarly publications and of experience in the organisation of legal information;

(b) holding symposia and other scholarly meetings in Great Britain and the USSR in accordance with the work programme;

(c) exchange of scholars on the basis of reciprocity in order to carry on individual or collective research on topics included in the programme for co-operation and the work programme.

4. The holding of symposia, other scholarly meetings, and the exchange of scholars in order to carry on research shall be effectuated above and beyond the quota established by the Agreement on the social sciences between The British Academy and the USSR Academy of Sciences and shall comprise as a whole up to 6 man-months per year for each Party.

The exchange of scholars to carry on research shall be effectuated in accordance with the proposal of the sending Party, within the framework of the afore-said quota, the duration of the sojourns of a scholar in the receiving country being from two weeks up to two months.

The length of symposia and other scholarly meetings, the number of participants therein, as well as the number of scholars in the exchange according to Article 3(c), will be determined by the work programme for co-operation within the framework of the total quota established by the present Protocol.

5. Each Party will receive scholars on the financial conditions provided for by the said Agreement between The British Academy and the USSR Academy of Sciences.

6. Both Parties consider desirable the publication by each Party of the materials of symposia and other results of scientific co-operation in the procedure established by national legislation and with observance of the principle of reciprocity.

7. In order to give effect to the present Protocol, the Parties have agreed to appoint co-ordinators: for the English side, W.E. Butler, LLD, Professor of Comparative Law in the University of London and Director of the Centre for the Study of Socialist Legal Systems, Faculty of Laws, University College London; for the Soviet side: Professor K.F. Sheremet, doctor of legal sciences, Deputy Director of the Institute of State and Law of the USSR Academy of Sciences.

The coordinators shall draw up the work programme for scientific co-operation for each three years, discuss the course of fulfilling this programme, and make changes therein by mutual arrangement. To this end, they shall meet once a year, in turn, in Great Britain and the USSR. These meetings may be effectuated within the framework of the symposia or the exchange of scholars.

8. The present Protocol, after signature by the Parties, shall enter into force from 1 January 1984 and be in effect unless and until one of the Parties informs the other Party of its desire to make changes therein or to terminate the effect thereof.

9. The present Protocol, and likewise changes therein agreed by the Parties, shall be subject to confirmation in the form of an exchange of letters between The British Academy and the Presidium of the Academy of Sciences of the USSR.

DONE at London 24th October 1983 in the English and Russian languages, both texts being equally authentic.

For University College London:	For the Institute of State and Law of the USSR Academy of Sciences:
The Provost of University College London	Deputy Director of the Institute of State and Law of the USSR Academy of Sciences
Sir James Lighthill, DSc, FRAES, FIMA, FRS	Professor K.F. Sheremet
Dean of the Faculty and Head of the Department of Laws, University College London, and Professor of Public Law in the University of London	
J.L. Jowell, MA, LLM, SJD	
Director of the Centre for the Study of Socialist Legal Systems, Faculty of Laws, University College London, and Professor of Comparative Law in the University of London	
W.E. Butler, MA, JD, PhD, LLD	

NOTE

In furtherance of Article 9 of the Protocol, the Council of The British Academy approved the Protocol at its session of 4 November 1983, the confirmation being notified to the USSR Academy of Sciences by a letter from the Foreign Secretary of The British Academy, Professor E.W. Handley, CBE, FBA, dated November 1983.

The Presidium of the USSR Academy of Sciences acknowledged receipt thereof and confirmed its assent to the Protocol in a Letter dated 7 December 1983, No. 672, from the Chief Learned Secretary of the Presidium of the USSR Academy of Sciences, Academician G.K. Skriabin.

The Protocol entered into force on 1 January 1984.

The Work Programme referred to in Article 7 of the Protocol was drawn up for the first three years by the Coordinators and signed at London on 26 October 1983.

Appendix 3: Indicative List of Participants in the Exchange Schemes

The following records mainly names of authors of papers subsequently published, although is incomplete as the periodical *Coexistence* was unavailable at the time of writing. Many other people, perhaps the same number again, attended the various Symposia meetings but are unrecorded.

Anglo-Polish Participants

Data from publications:[88]

Polish Academics		Academics from Great Britain	
Z	Czeczot	R C	Austin
T	Erecinski	W E	Butler
S	Frankowski	S F D	Guest
L	Garlicki	E R H	Ivamy
A	Gwizdz	N	Lacey
H	Izdebski	A D E	Lewis
J	Jakubowski	D	Oliver
A	Kojder	S	Oliver
K	Kubala	F	Parkinson
K	Lojewski	J	Richardson
W	Marek	R W	Rideout
J	Okolski	S	Saeed
E	Piontek	D J	Stephens
W	Suchecki	R C	Austin
M	Wierzbowski	S F D	Guest
W	Wolodkiewicz	E R H	Ivamy
		N	Lacey

Additional data from recollections:

Peter Birks, Dick Ivamy, Jack and Rose Jacob, Jane McGregor, David Nelken, Frank Rose, and Jim Stephens.

From personal communication from Lech Garlicki (31 August 2009):

The list of Polish participants could be reconstructed from the ensuing publications—the rule was that whoever wants to participate (and to travel abroad), he/she must present a paper. I can recall participation of some colleagues of my age group: Marek Wierzbowski—now professor of our Law School and a private lawyer; Tadeusz Ereciński—professor and one of the presidents of the Supreme Court; Michał Kulesza—professor and, on one occasion, undersecretary

88 William E. Butler (ed.), *Anglo-Polish Legal Essays* (Transnational Publishers Inc, Dobbs Ferry, NY, 1982); III Anglo-Polish Legal Colloquium, February-March 1985, papers in William E. Butler (ed.), *Yearbook on Socialist Legal Systems 1986* (Transnational Publishers, Dobbs Ferry, NY, 1986); and IV Anglo-Polish Legal Colloquium March 1986, papers in *Yearbook on Socialist Legal Systems 1987*, *op.cit.* note 5.

of state in the prime minister office; Eugeniusz Piontek—professor in Warsaw, now deceased; Stanisław Frankowski—left Poland in 1981, later professor at Saint Louis University, now retired. There were also some older colleagues, Andrzej Gwiżdż, professor and—later—director of the Library of Parliament). The Polish organizer was Professor Jerzy Jakubowski, an eminent expert in private international law. As far as I remember, he was behind the first exchange in 1981, but he was not in London in March 1981, unfortunately he died before the 1984 Colloquium.

Anglo-Soviet Participants

Data from publications:[89]

Soviet Academics		Academics from Great Britain	
A A	Abramova	M R	Anderson
L B	Alexeeva	B	Bercusson
G Z	Anashkin	P W	Birnie
M V	Baglai	V	Bogdanor
Iu Ia	Baskin	A E	Boyle
G I	Changuli	D	Brodie
L	Chikanova	W E	Butler
G M	Danilenko	J A	Carty
V V	Egorov	R	Cotterrell
V L	Entin	I	Delupis

89 "Third Annual Report of the Centre for the Study of Socialist Legal Systems" (Faculty of Laws, University College London, 1984); I Symposium on "National Systems of Law and Comparative Law" (March 1984), papers in William E. Butler and Vladimir N. Kudriavtsev (eds.), *Comparative Law and Legal System: Historical and Socio-Legal Perspectives* (Oceana Publications, New York, NY, 1985); II Symposium on "Justice and Comparative Law" (September 1984), papers in William E. Butler (ed.), *Justice and Comparative Law; Anglo Soviet Perspectives on Criminal Law, Evidence, Procedure and Sentencing Policy* (Martinus Nijhoff Publishers, Dordrecht, The Netherlands 1987); William E. Butler (ed.), *International Law and the International System* (Martinus Nijhoff Publishers, Dordrecht, The Netherlands, 1987); III Symposium on Labor Law and Comparative Law, Moscow (1985), papers in William E. Butler, Bob A. Hepple and Alan C. Neal (eds.), *Comparative Labour Law* (Gower, Aldershot, UK, 1987); 1986 Anglo-Soviet Symposium on "Law, Policy and State Administration", London (October 1986), papers from Soviet scholars in *Yearbook on Socialist Legal Systems 1987*, *op.cit.* note 5; "The Right to Work under British and Soviet Law", in William E. Butler, Bob A. Hepple and Roger W. Rideout (eds.), 3(3) *International Journal of Comparative Labour Law and Industrial Relations* (1987); William E. Butler (ed.), *The Non-Use of Force in International Law* (Kluwer, Dordrecht, The Netherlands,1989); III Anglo-Soviet Symposium on Public International Law, London (March 1989), papers in William E. Butler (ed.), *Perestroika and International Law* (Martinus Nijhoff Publishers, Dordrecht,The Netherlands, 1990); IV Anglo-Soviet Symposium on Public International Law, Moscow (May 1990), papers in William E. Butler (ed.), *Control over Compliance with International Law* (Kluwer, Dordrecht, The Netherlands, 1991); and William E. Butler (ed.), *Perestroika and the Rule of Law: Anglo-American and Soviet Perspectives* (Tauris, London, 1991).

D I	Feldman	I	Dennis
S A	Goloshchapov	G	Drewry
A M	Iakovlev	S	Evans
S A	Ivanov	K D	Ewing
E P	Kamenetskaia	S	Fredman
N	Kas'ian	J C	Freeman
V P	Kazimirchuk	M D A	Freeman
S G	Kelina	R K	Gardiner
I V	Khamenev	S F D	Guest
O N	Khlestov	J E	Henderson
I Ia	Kiselev	B A	Hepple
V	Kleptsov	R	Higgins
A S	Koblikov	J	Jacob
V M	Kogan	J L	Jowell
N P	Koldaeva	K R	Khan
L V	Korbut	N	Lacey
M I	Kovalve	R M	Lewis
N B	Krylov	A V	Loew
N S	Krylova	R A	McCreadie
V N	Kudriavtsev	M H	Mendelson
E V	Kumanin	J G	Merrills
A M	Kurennoi	B I	Mordsley
A M	Larin	G S	Morris
M I	Lazarev	B W	Napier
A	Lisitsyn-Svetlanov	A C	Neal
R Z	Livshits	A D H	Oliver
I I	Lukashuk	F	Parkinson
P A	Lupinskaia	G	Plant
E B	Mel'nikova	R	Plender
A A	Mel'nikov	C J	Redgwell
T G	Morshchakova	R W	Rideout
A P	Movchan	B	Rudden
R A	Müllerson	P J	Sands
I L	Petrukhin	K R	Simmonds
S V	Polenina	R C	Simpson
V V	Pustogarov	W L	Twining
N V	Radutnaia	J A	Usher
A A	Rubanov	C G	Veljanovski
V M	Savitskii	C J	Warbrick
A I	Shebanova	B	Wrobel
E A	Shein	A A	Zuckerman
KF	Sheremet		
G G	Shinkaretskaia		
Z K	Simorot		
M M	Slavin		
V	Smirnov		
I O	Snigireva		
P	Timofeev		
A S	Timoshenko		
V N	Tolkunova		

B N	Topornin		
V A	Tumanov		
G I	Tunkin		
E T	Usenko		
V S	Vereshchetin		
S V	Vinogradov		
A M	Iakovlev		

Additional data from recollections: Irena Mashlenko, Irina Reshetnikova, Peter Duffy, Malcolm Grant, Ronald Graveson, Patrick McAuslan, James Michael, Michael Palmer, Sybille Van der Sprenkel, Sir William Wade, and Michael Zander.

Research visits under British Council arrangements: V.S. Belykh, E.T. Rul'ko, N.A. Semiderkin, and A.Iu. Iakusheva.

Soviet Law and *Perestroika* Revisited

Albert J. Schmidt

Introduction

In the spring of 1982, when I taught Soviet law for the first time, the USSR was muddling through. Its political fulcrum, the Politburo, was a stumbling gerontocracy coping with a stagnant economy, a losing war in Afghanistan, and restless East European satellites. Brezhnev's death the same year did little to energize the leadership: both his successors, Iurii Andropov and Konstantin Chernenko, were dead by early 1985. Almost magically, an aged and ailing leadership devoid of ideas was removed from the seat of power in Moscow.

In March 1985, a comparatively youthful newcomer took center stage: he was the new Party General Secretary Mikhail Sergeevich Gorbachev. There were a few hopeful signs: the plain-spoken British Prime Minister Margaret Thatcher, who had met Gorbachev early on, was impressed, exclaiming that he was a "man with whom she could do business".

Gorbachev, like Lenin a lawyer, recognized the pressing need to reform the ailing economy. He spoke of restructuring it (*perestroika*) and eventually of more openness (*glasnost'*) in society and even democratization (*demokratizatsiia*). Whether such rhetoric, hitherto absent in this notoriously closed system, signaled a positive step toward East-West rapprochement remained to be seen. Western leaders eagerly awaited the Secretary's first moves.[1]

Perestroika Revisited

A quarter century has passed since Mikhail Sergeevich and his cohorts in 1986 launched a broad-based legislative agenda for invigorating or even reforming the lagging Soviet economy. The Party's upper echelon received the reforms with seemingly mixed feelings: so long as Gorbachev's reformist program showed promise of success, there were celebrants who welcomed an end to Brezhnev stagnation; staunch conservatives, on the other hand, seemed fearful of navigating uncharted waters.

1 See M. Gorbachev, *Perestroika: New Thinking for Our Country and the World* (1987), *passim*. For general accounts see Martin Malia, *The Soviet Tragedy: A History of Socialism in Russia, 1917-1991* (The Free Press, New York, NY, 1994) and Stephen Kotkin, *Armageddon Averted: The Soviet Collapse 1970-2000* (Oxford University Press, Oxford, 2008). For a brief discussion of the economy and Gorbachev's economic choices, see Svetlana Savranskaya, "The Logic of 1989" in Svetlana Savranskaya, Thomas Blanton, and Vladislav Zubok (eds.), *Masterpieces of History: The Peaceful End of the Cold War in Europe, 1989* (CEU Press, Budapest, New York, NY, 2010), 25-26 & *passim*; and Donald Barry, *Russian Politics: The Post-Soviet Phase* (Peter Lang, New York, NY, 2002), 30-33.

Tatiana Borisova and William Simons, eds.
The Legal Dimension in Cold-War Interactions: Some Notes from the Field 41-54

Western reaction was less critical. The media, however disbelieving they may have been, certainly applauded Soviet reformist pronouncements absent Cold-War rhetoric. Intrigued by mouthings of *glasnost'* and rule of law, Sovietologists organized to dissect whatever lawyer Gorbachev's *perestroika* had to offer. This chapter purports to track early *perestroika* (1986-1987), by scrutinizing both the Gorbachev approach and Western reactions to it. Critical to the latter was the unprecedented interaction between Western and Soviet scholars, the first instance in which Soviet legal scholars were invited and accepted an invitation to participate in an international conference. By doing so they may inadvertently have made *perestroika/glasnost'* a vehicle for lessening Cold-War tensions. This chronicle of scholarly interaction in the past, undeniably anecdotal and unabashedly subjective, seems a crucial link to theme of the Ninth Aleksanteri Conference—*'Cold War Interactions Reconsidered'*—and to this volume.[2]

The Gorbachev roadmap for modernizing Soviet society, originally packaged in thirty-eight legislative measures, began with the 10 September 1986 resolution of the Presidium of the USSR Supreme Soviet and the USSR Council of Ministers[3] and read as follows:

RESOLUTION OF THE PRESIDIUM OF THE USSR SUPREME SOVIET AND THE USSR

[...] *The Presidium of the USSR Supreme Soviet and the USSR Council of Ministers resolve: To confirm the plan for the preparation of USSR legislative acts, resolutions of the USSR government and proposals for improving USSR legislation in 1986-1990* [dated 28 Aug.1986]

Appendix: Plan for the Preparation of USSR Legislative Acts, Resolutions of the USSR Government and Proposals for Improving USSR Legislation in 1986-1990:

1. Legislation on the Further Development of Socialist Democracy, Socialist Self-Management and Citizens' Rights and Freedoms.

A USSR law on the procedure for public discussion and voting on major issues of national life and on the public discussion of draft decisions by local Soviets. 1987.

A USSR law on the press and information. Second quarter of 1986.

Normative acts on enhancing the role of workers' and office employees' meetings, expanding the range of issues on which labor collectives' decisions are final, creating labor collectives' councils at the enterprise level and gradually expanding the extent to which certain categories of enterprise managers are elected. Second quarter of 1987.

Normative acts on expanding the range of issues that can be decided by state agencies only with the participation or preliminary consent of appropriate public organization and on granting these organizations rights in a number of instances to halt the implementation of administrative decisions. 1986-1987.

2 This conference was held at the University of Helsinki, Finland, in late October 2009.

3 *Vedomosti Verkhovnovo Soveta SSSR i Soveta Ministrov SSSR,* as translated in 38 *Current Digest of the Soviet Press* (1986).

A USSR law on individual labor activity. Second half of 1986.

A USSR law on the procedure for protesting to the courts for relief from legal actions by officials, in violation of citizens' rights. First quarter of 1987.

Proposals for changing legislation with respect to housing allocation and to making rent contingent on the amount and quality of the space occupied. 1987.

2. Legislation on Improving the Economic Mechanism and Economic Management.

A USSR law on the socialist enterprise (association). Second half of 1986.

A USSR law on atomic energy. First half of 1987.

Proposals for changing legislation with a view to improving the system for supplying materials and equipment and increasing the role and responsibility of the USSR State Supply Committee and its local agencies for the uninterrupted supply of material resources to the economy and for their effective use. Fourth quarter of 1986.

Proposals for improving legislation on the utilization of recycled resources in the economy. First quarter of 1987.

Proposals for changing legislation with a view to improving statistics. First quarter of 1987.

Proposals for legislation proving for a systematic restructuring of the price system in light of the directives of the 27th CPSU Congress. Fourth quarter of 1986.

A general statute on USSR ministries. Fourth quarter of 1986.

A general statute on USSR state committees. Second half of 1987.

A statute on interbranch production association and production-and-trade association for the manufacture and sale of light-industry goods. Second half of 1986.

Proposals for improving legislation with a view to further introducing economic management methods, substantially expanding the independence of collective farms and state farms and enhancing their interest in and responsibility for economic results, and developing the collective contract on a broad scale, on the basis of true economic accountability, with the ultimate goal of putting all enterprises of the agro-industrial complex on a self-supporting and self-financing basis. 1986 and 1987.

A legislative act on amending and adding to the Basic Principles of Civil Legislation of the USSR and of the Union-republics. First half of 1990.

Normative acts specifying relations between consumer-service organizations and clients, industrial and trade enterprises and other branches of the economy. Second half of 1987.

3. Legislation on Accelerating Scientific and Technical Progress.

A USSR law on output quality. First quarter of 1987.

A statute on the USSR State Committee for Science and Technology. Fourth quarter of 1986.

4. Legislation on Capital Construction.

A USSR Council of Ministers resolution on the procedure for planning capital investments and confirming approved lists of construction projects. Fourth quarter of 1989.

Regulations governing construction financing and credit. First quarter of 1988.

Regulations governing contractual agreements on capital construction. Fourth quarter of 1986.

Regulations governing contractual agreements on capital repair of buildings and structures. Fourth quarter of 1988.

5. Legislation on Transport and Communications.

Proposals for changes in legislation aimed at improving management of the transport branches, improving the coordination of all types of transport and creating a uniform legal system and rate policy. Third quarter of 1986.

A USSR Statute on Communications. First half of 1988.

6. Legislation on Environmental Protection and the Rational Utilization of Natural Resources.

Proposals for improving legislation with a view to further strengthening environmental protection in the country. Third quarter of 1987.

7. Legislation on Social Development and Culture.

A normative act on the periodic certification of responsible officials of Soviet and public organizations and economic managers and specialists. 1986.

A USSR Council of Ministers resolution on holding more than one job. Fourth quarter of 1986.

A statute on liability for disciplinary action, based on lines of subordination. Second half of 1986.

A normative act on giving pensioners additional incentives for participating in social production. 1986.

A USSR law on the USSR State Archival Fund. Fourth quarter of 1987.

8. Legislation on Other Issues.

A USSR law on USSR state security. 1990.

A USSR Council of Ministers' resolution confirming the Statute on the USSR State Committee on Foreign Economic Relations. Fourth quarter of 1986.

A USSR Customs Code (updated version). Fourth quarter of 1987.

A decree of the Presidium of the USSR Supreme Soviet on enforcing decisions of foreign courts. First half of 1988.

The New York Times noted the plan nearly a month after this legislation action, but the article by Serge Schmemann was tucked away in the inner folds of the paper.[4] It called the proposed undertaking a five-year endeavor (through 1990) "to codify Gorbachev's blueprint for the reconstruction of Soviet society". To Schmemann, the laws and degrees to be drafted or revised "appeared to cover most of the fields in which Mr. Gorbachev has called for changes in his campaign to modernize and revitalize the economy and society". [Soviet] "sources could recall no previous instance when a full legislative program was announced in advance". Gorbachev, Schmemann wrote, "evidently wants to assure the nation that his blueprint will be the law of the land soon and he also wants to put responsible agencies on notice that they have a deadline to get on with the program". The account noted that "all these topics have figured in lively press debates since a

4 "Soviet to Codify Gorbachev Overhaul", *The New York Times* (7 October 1986), A21.

Communist Party convention in late February and early March endorsed Mr. Gorbachev's calls for a 'radical restructuring'". Finally, Schmemann wondered "how far Mr. Gorbachev is prepared to go on such sensitive issues as private enterprise, voting and access to courts". Such an assessment, he concluded, would "have to await publication of the actual laws and their application in practice".

Despite the humiliation surrounding Chernobyl' and the collapse of nuclear weapon talks with President Reagan at Reykjavik, Gorbachev spent most of 1986 engaged in less dramatic *perestroika* matters of the domestic economy. But Gorbachev was no Khrushchev, not a fighter who put his life on the line. Rather, he was much more the consensus-builder or even, according to some, a procrastinator who got caught up in bureaucratic morass.[5]

There were those far and near who were eying the new Party Secretary and his *modus operandi*. 'Enlightened *apparatchik*'[6] and foreign policy aide Anatoly Cherniaev, an inveterate diarist, offered insights on Gorbachev's manner and thought during this critical *perestroika*-making period: He marveled that despite the headlines garnered by foreign affairs, domestic matters consumed 95 per cent of the General Secretary's time.[7] Although the diarist doubted Gorbachev's economic reforms would "change the system's essentials", he thought his 'evolution' during critical 1986, was one of "exceptional courage in words and evaluation of problems and caution in action".[8] Yet Gorbachev did have moments of pique when matters did not go his way. Chernaev detailed a scene in the summer of 1987 when the General Secretary grew increasingly frustrated from the lack of progress on *perestroika*: Gorbachev furiously tossed a 'big stack' of letters on the table in front of his colleagues exclaiming:

> "They write many different things, but it all comes down to one and the same. What's this *perestroika*? How do we, ordinary people, benefit from it? We don't. [...] Here, in our Soviet state, big bosses enjoy every luxury and remodel their apartments at government expense.

5 Vladislav M. Zubok, *A Failed Empire, The Soviet Union in the Cold War from Stalin to Gorbachev* (The University of North Carolina Press, Chapel Hill, NC, 2007), 278; for a fuller appraisal of Gorbachev's operative mode, see 278-302.

6 The phenomenon of 'enlightened *apparatchiks*', employed as consultants, dates to the Khrushchev era. Besides Cherniaev, Georgii Arbatov, Fedor Burlatskii, Nikolai Inozemtsev, amd Georgii Shakhnazarov were among the 'New Thinkers' surrounding Gorbachev. See *ibid.*, 178.

7 Anatoly Chernyaev, *My Six Years with Gorbachev* (Svetlana Savranskaya (ed.), for the National Security Archive at The George Washington University in Washington, DC; this citation is from *The Diary of Anatoly Chernyaev, National Security Archive Electronic Briefing Book* (7 June 1986) No.220. Although Cherniaev was essentially a foreign policy aide, he is very reliable in describing the General Secretary's habits and energetic pursuit of early *perestroika*. As he noted regarding Gorbachev for 7 December 1986:

> "I see him every day candidly, with all of the ordinary nuances of his nature, his behavior, his education level—but all of this in no way lowers the greatness of this man in my 'intelligentsia' (snobbish) eyes."

8 *Ibid., Postscript for 1986.*

> They couldn't care less about the people. [...] I'm warning you—this is our last conversation about such issues. If nothing changes, the next time I'll be talking to different people."[9]

Archie Brown, another keen observer of early *perestroika,*[10] was initially unclear of what the General Secretary had in mind. He had spoken in 1986 not only of *restructuring* but also 'radical' reform;[11] then in another speech he appeared to equate *perestroika* with 'revolution', as he suggested increased power to factories and collective farms at the expense of the ministries.[12] Cherniaev believed *perestroika* peaked in 1987, but the famous January Plenum raised questions as to who or what would lead it. Both the Party and the Central Committee were unresponsive to the country's ailments; the Party appeared no longer in the vanguard of change.[13] Related was a growing resistance to *perestroika* among the General Secretary's conservative colleagues.

The unraveling of the so-called cohort of the 'founding fathers' revealed itself in the loss of support from Politburo members like Egor Ligachev and Gorbachev's increased reliance upon reformers like Aleksandr Nikolaevich Iakovlev, Eduard Shevardnadze, Nikolai Ryzhkov, and Vladimir Kudriavtsev (the latter director of the Institute of State and Law). Boris El'tsin's emergence proved especially galling. Cherniaev's characterization of him as 'loud, abrupt, and demagogically saturated' most likely mirrored Gorbachev's own view. Although El'tsin was banished from the inner circle before year's end, his presence had cast a long shadow over *perestroika* proceedings during the latter half of year 1987.[14]

Vladislav M. Zubok, a Russian-trained historian, worked as a junior researcher at the Soviet Institute of US and Canada Studies in Moscow during early *perestroika* and later at the National Security Archive in DC before he joined the Temple University faculty. Zubok observed that in the summer of 1987, Gorbachev revealed his intentions only to a narrow circle, which included Iakovlev and Cherniaev, that he intended overhauling 'the whole system—from economy to mentality'.[15] By that time, the General Secretary had few worries

9 *Ibid.*, Summer, 1987.

10 I am reliant here on the chapter entitled "The First Phase of Soviet Reform, 1985-6" in Archie Brown, *Seven Years that Changed the World: Perestroika in Perspective* (Oxford University Press, Oxford, 2007), 69-101. Written in late 1986, this chapter initially appeared in 4(1) *World Policy Journal* (Winter 1986-1987) No.1 under the title: 'Soviet Political Developments and Prospects".

11 *Ibid.,* 73.

12 *Ibid.*

13 Said Cherniaev: "The famous January Plenum was devoted to staff policies; here for the first time since Lenin the Party's and the CC's culpability for what had happened in the country, for the country's critical situation, was brought up. [...] From then on, the Party never found the wish nor the ability to be the vanguard of change." (*Diary, Postscript, 1987.*)

14 *Ibid., Postscript, 1987.* See, also, Herbert J. Ellison, *Boris Yeltsin and Russia's Democratic Transformation* (University of Washington Press, Seattle, WA, 2006), 14-21.

15 Zubok, *op.cit.* note 5, 301.

from conservatives in the Politburo and party *nomenklatura*; rather, complaints came from new men like El'tsin who, as Moscow Party head, grumbled at the slow pace of domestic reform.

While Gorbachev is treated here as one essentially focused on revamping the homeland economy, he was, of course, a savvy actor on the world stage. Cherniaev, whose expertise was foreign affairs, has been unrestrained in praising Gorbachev in this area:

> "The year 1987 is distinguished with a breakthrough into the outside world. Gorbachev's international recognition and fame are quickly growing. In the West people are slowly convinced that the 'Gorbachev phenomenon' in the USSR is not the Kremlin's tricky maneuver, that *perestroika* is for real A new and powerful factor arises in foreign policy—trust. This factor will later make possible the end of the Cold War. [...] Gorbachev's book, *Perestroika and New Thinking for Our Country and the World*, which became an international bestseller, played an enormous role in the formation of Gorbachev's and the Soviet Union's new image."[16]

Still 1987 fell short of expectations for Cherniaev:

> "As it were, when speaking of the year 1987 in the history of the country, one has to acknowledge: the year of the 70th anniversary of the Revolution did not gain enough potential for development that people had counted on in preparation for it."[17]

Not surprisingly, Gorbachev's view was different. Ignoring the original intent of his 1986 program and discounting evident failures, he observed:

> "It was during the years of *perestroika* and *glasnost'* that the foundation of the transition to democracy, rule of law, and a market economy was created. Anyone who knows our country will agree that if this was all we did, *i.e.*, just lay a foundation, this would have been sufficient to be recognized and praised by future generations, because it was very difficult to do."[18]

The Making of the Bridgeport Symposium

Having read the Schmemann article and the 38 measures in detail, I conceived organizing—in the autumn of 1986—an international symposium of law scholars to examine Gorbachev's proposed *perestroika* legislation. The late Dean Terence Benbow of the University of Bridgeport Law School (where I was professor) had promised funding. I conferred with two colleagues, Donald Barry and William Simons, both of whom offered valuable suggestions regarding symposium structure and participants.

16 Chernyaev, *op.cit.* note 7, *Postscript, 1987*.

17 *Ibid.*

18 F. Joseph Dresen and William E. Pomeranz (eds.), *The Russian Constitution at Fifteen: Assessments and Current Challenges to Russia's Legal Development, Kennan Institute Occasional Paper* (2009) No.304, 12.

The symposium would be of Soviet law experts from all parts of the globe.[19] Scheduled for the autumn of 1987, it would focus on *Soviet Restructuring through Law*. The program introduction, spells out this theme:

> "Soviet Restructuring Through Law. Just as the adoption of the USSR Constitution a decade ago required significant subsidiary legislation, so will the current Restructuring Program by Secretary Gorbachev. Such legislation has always been publicized well in advance of its approval. For example, a 'Plan of Organization on Bringing Legislation of the USSR into Correspondence with the USSR Constitution', adopted by the Presidium of the USSR Supreme Soviet in December, 1977, charted Soviet legislation into the 1980s. [...]"

The program continued with a description of *Change Through Law*:

> "This symposium will focus on change in the USSR today, change as facilitated by law. A key to understanding the Soviet system is 'Socialist Legality,' defined as the 'unwavering fulfillment of laws and related legal acts by the organs of the state, officials, citizens and public organization.' Although we may question whether this fulfillment occurs when matters of state security are at issue, for Soviet society (as for all societies) law is intended as a stabilizing factor: No Longer does on hear of legal nihilists, who, in the 1920s and early 1930s, demanded the 'withering away of state and law'."

Finally, the program touched on *Gorbachev as a Lawyer*:

> "'Socialist Legality', of course, did not originate with Mikhail Gorbachev; nevertheless, as the first lawyer since Lenin on the Politburo, he brings to the decision-making apparatus a legal perspective. It is instructive, perhaps crucially so, to analyze his blueprint for Restructuring, which projects fundamental change in Soviet society for the balance of this century."

The invited participants, their presentations, that part of the legislation to which they directed their remarks[20]—and a list of distinguished guests and other attendees—were as follows:

Gianmaria F. Ajani, Faculty of Law, University of Trento, Italy (*Perestroika* and Social Organization: Past Problems and Future Trends').

**George Armstrong*, Associate Professor of Law, Louisiana State University, Baton Rouge, LA ('Invention and Innovation').

Donald Barry, Distinguished Professor of Political Science, Lehigh University ('A Law on Atomic Energy: Preliminary Observations').

**Harold Berman*, Woodruff Professor of Law, Emory University and James Barr Ames Professor Emeritus of Law, Harvard ('Gorbachev's Law Reforms in Historical Perspective').

19 The Soviet Law symposium was sponsored by the University of Bridgeport (now Quinnipiac) Law School. See my own account of the Gorbachev program, in "Law and Perestroika", 9(2) *University of Bridgeport Law Review* (1988), 298-323 and the introduction to Albert J. Schmidt (ed.), *The Impact of Perestroika on Soviet Law* in F.J.M. Feldbrugge (ed.), *Law in Eastern Europe*, No.41 (Martinus Nijhoff Publishers, Dordrecht, The Netherlands, 1990), xxi-xxvii. This latter work is a full account of the symposium as of 1990.

20 I obtained from each a reasonable commitment to speak to an aspect of the Gorbachev blueprint. These participants appear here alphabetically with a short title of his/her presentation.

William E. Butler, Professor of Comparative Law in the University of London ('Modern Patterns of Law Reform in the USSR').

Vladimir Entin, Institute of State and Law, Moscow ('Lawmaking and Mass Media in the Period of Restructuring').

F.J.M. Feldbrugge, Professor of Law, University of Leyden, The Netherlands and Director of the Documentation Office for East European Law, Leyden ('The Legal Status of the KGB').

George Ginsburgs, Distinguished Professor of Law, The Rutgers University School of Law, Camden, NJ ('Execution of Foreign Arbitration Awards: the Heritage of Domestic Legislation, Bilateral Treaties, and Intro-COMECON Ententes').

Marshall Goldman, Class of 1919 Professor of Economics, Wellesley College and director of the Russian Research Center, Harvard University ('Economic Reform in the Soviet Union--Why a Need for Checks and Balances').

**John N. Hazard,* Nash Professor Emeritus of Law, Columbia University ('Gorbachev's Vision of the State Enterprise').

Susan Heuman, Visiting Assistant Professor of History, Pratt Institute, Brooklyn, NY ('Transforming Subjects into Citizens: A Historical Perspective on the Gorbachev Legal Reforms').

Thomas W. Hoya, Administrative Law Judge, US Department of Commerce, Washington, DC ('Soviet Foreign Trade Law: A Comment').

Peter H. Juviler, Professor of Political Science, Barnard College ('Law and Individual Rights').

**Serge L. Levitsky,* University of Leyden Faculty of Law ('Changes in the Fundamental Principles of USSR Civil Legislation Part IV, Copyright').

**Dietrich A. Loeber,* Professor of Law and Dean of the Faculty of Law, University of Kiel, Federal Republic of Germany ('*Glasnost*' as an Issue of Law: On the Future USSR Law on Press and Information').

Yuri Luryi, Professor of Law, University of Western Ontario and York University; Research Associate, Center of Russian and East European Studies, University of Toronto; Visiting Fellow, Center of Criminology, University of Toronto.

Peter Maggs, Professor of Law, University of Illinois ('The 1987 Decree on the USSR State Committee on Science and Technology').

Hiroshi Oda, Associate Professor of Law, Faculty of Law, University of Tokyo ('Judicial Review of Administration in the USSR').

Svetlana Polenina, Institute of State and Law, Moscow ('Development of Soviet Legislation Based on the 1977 Constitution: Tendencies and Prospects').

Stanislaw Pomorski, Distinguished Professor of Law, The Rutgers University School of Law, Camden, NJ ('Law on Individual Labor Activity').

John Quigley, Professor of Law, The Ohio State University College of Law ('The Soviet Bar as an Institutional Lobby for Rights').

Albert J. Schmidt, Arnold Bernhard Professor of History and Professor of Law, University of Bridgeport, CT ('Soviet Legislation for Protection of Architectural Monuments: Background').

Louise I. Shelley, Professor in the School of Justice and the School of International Service, The American University, Washington, DC ('Democratization and Law').

William Simons, Cole, Corette, and Abrutyn, Washington, DC and London; formerly of the University of Leyden Faculty of Law and presently in private law practice ('The Reform of Soviet Foreign Trade Through *Perestroika*: Decentralization Without Deregulation').

Peter Solomon, Professor of Government, University of Toronto ('Judicial Reform under Gorbachev and in Russian History').

Wim Timmermans, Research Officer, Documentation Office for East European Law, University of Leyden Faculty of Law (Article 37: A New USSR Customs Code').

**Ger van den Berg,* Senior Research Officer, Documentation Office for East European Law, University of Leyden Faculty of Law ('Developments in Soviet Labor Law under Gorbachev').

**Zigurds L. Zile,* Foley and Lardner-Bascom Professor of Law, University of Wisconsin Law School ('By Command, Bribe and Cajolery: Soviet Law on Output Quality').

*Deceased.

Distinguished (Invited) Guests

Martin Fincke, Professor of Law, University of Passau, Federal Republic of Germany.

**Olympiad S. Ioffe,* Professor of Law, University of Connecticut School of Law and formerly head of the Department,of Civil Law, Leningrad State University Faculty of Law.

**Leon Lipson,* Henry R. Luce Professor of Law, Yale University School of Law.

Henry Morton, Professor of Political Science, The Queens University of the City of New York.

Gabrielle Crespi Reghizzi, Professor of Comparative Law and Deputy Rector, University of Pavia, Italy.

Robert Sharlet, Professor of Political Science, Union College, Schenectady, NY.

Attendees

Randy Bregman, International Law Institute, Washington, DC and Adjunct Professor of Soviet Law, Georgetown University Law School.

Albert Boiter, Georgetown University Law School.

Susan Finder, East-Asian Legal Studies Program, Harvard Law School.

Christine Genis, US Embassy, Moscow.

Jane Giddings (now *Henderson*), Centre for European Law, King's College, University of London.

Malcolm L. Russell-Einhorn, Adjunct Professor of Soviet Law, Boston College of Law.

Christopher Senie, Senie, Stock and LaChance, Westport, CT.

Alan B. Sherr, Director of Project on Soviet Foreign Economic Policy and International Security, Brown University.

Stanisław Sołtysiński, Professor of Law, Universities of Cracow and Poznań, Poland and Visiting Professor of Law, University of Pennsylvania School of Law.

Lowry Wyman, Assistant Dean, DePaul University College of Law, Chicago.

This symposium became a Cold-War landmark in that it marked an end to the isolation of Soviet legal scholars from their counterparts in the West; their subsequent participation would provide such gatherings with a new intellectual and social dimension.[21]

Over the Christmas/New Year break in 1986-1987, I had this thought in mind as I traveled to Moscow to urge Soviet inclusion. I visited the Institute of State and Law on Frunze Street to explain the symposium and leave invitations for both Academician Vladimir Kudriavtsev, head of the Institute, and General Secretary Gorbachev himself. While I harbored no illusions about receiving acceptances from either, I thought it important to inform the Institute people of this international venture concerning *perestroika* hoping that it might generate a surprise response. That I had a friendly reception from a very curious front office *apparatchik* encouraged me, for I had a rich history of curt dismissals from such people.

This same official telephoned me shortly after I had returned to the US to say that Academician Kudriavtsev was honored but otherwise committed and therefore respectfully declined the invitation, as did Secretary Gorbachev. Kudriavtsev did, however, offer a counter proposal. He would nominate two colleagues, one a senior and former Brezhnev aide Dr. Svetlana Polenina, and the other English-speaking Dr. Vladimir Entin. Both he thought would be worthy participants in the symposium. The speed of this reaction was surprising if not unprecedented. This much accomplished, I had only to be sure that their visa applications would be approved.[22] Another flash point was the refusal by a Russian expatriate Olympiad S. Ioffe—who had originally accepted—to participate with Soviet scholars. Unable to reach a compromise in this matter, I refused to rescind the Soviet invitation.

The symposium came off well if one can judge from post conference comments. Entin wrote: "I join [Professor Svetlana Polenina] in expressing the gratitude for your hospitality and magnificent organizational effort."[23] Entin and Polenina had made the most of this trip, stopping off in Boston for the American Association for the Advancement of Slavic Studies meeting on 5-8

21 The timing *was* good, for since October 1985, scholars in the Soviet Union had increasingly been granted the hitherto rare privilege of traveling abroad and interacting with foreigners. Zubok, *op.cit.* note 5, 282.

22 I confirmed with Entin and Polenina the invitation to participate in the international "Soviet Law Symposium on Perestroika" (12-15 November 1987). Further, in order to avoid any problem with visas, I informed the State Department that their participation was "essential for international legal cooperation and success of symposium".

23 Letter (14 December 1987).

November, much shopping, and considerable socializing. Hal Berman thought: "The conference went splendidly. I learned a great deal from it."[24] André Loeber from the University of Kiel thought the conference 'stimulating and successful', and Henry Morton from Queens College offered the following: "You certainly know how to run an international conference. [...] It was truly a great privilege to be among an international galaxy of Soviet law experts. And you even succeeded in importing two Soviet legal beagles."[25] Louise Shelley's letter was one of thanks for "organizing such a wonderful conference. People all over Washington are eager to have a report".[26] Participant Yuri Luryi was effusive:

> "Please accept my heartfelt congratulations: It was fantastic! You managed to muster up and to run smoothly a really unique International Symposium. The flawless organization allowed you to cope with the agenda good enough for two ordinary conferences. The participation of two Soviet scholars attached some peculiar piquancy to the meeting and was both interesting and instructive as well. People familiarized themselves with the Soviet ways of arguing and reasoning."

He added that they even made jokes about the *KGB* and CIA.[27] Finally, participant Peter Maggs wrote thanking me for "your marvelous hospitality! It was the best Soviet law conference I ever attended, both in terms of content and organization!"[28]

The symposium also received recognition in Soviet scholarly circles. Polenina and Entin published a brief account in *Sovetskoe gosudarstvo i pravo* in which they observed that for the "first time Soviet attorneys participated together with their Western colleagues in an international symposium on Soviet law". Although they did not initially mention Gorbachev reform legislation which generated the program (rather they resorted to old clichés—the marking of the seventieth anniversary of the Soviet State and the tenth anniversary of the adoption of the 1977 USSR Constitution), they eventually did focus on *perestroika* legislation and participant analysis of it. They noted that participants included "prominent American, English, Dutch, Japanese, Italian, and West German Sovietologists, many of whom [had] visited the USSR and collaborated with the scholars of the Institute of State and Law of the Academy of Sciences of the USSR".[29]

Academician Kudriavtsev also wrote approvingly about both the symposium and the improved state of Soviet-US relations:

> "I share your satisfaction with the successful conclusion of the summit meeting between General Secretary Gorbachev and President Reagan and look forward to further developments. [...] It seems to me rather significant that you have the possibility to publish the

24 Letter (23 November 1987).

25 Letters (16 February 1988 and 18 November 1987 consecutively).

26 Letter (18 November 1987).

27 *Ibid.*

28 *Ibid.*

29 '*Sovetskoe pravo i perestroika*' (1988).

> reports and commentaries made by Professor S. Polenina and Doctor V. Entin during the symposium. I'll be glad to see you to discuss the possibilities of further cooperation in the field opened up by your efforts."[30]

The grandiose legislative plan projected in 1986 by General Secretary Gorbachev was variously received: some parts of it won approval; others were altered or never enacted.[31] Rarely did approval arrive as scheduled. There was no abandoning the notion that *perestroika* would and should follow a legislative route. That was lawyer Gorbachev's way.

Legislation on Improving the Economic Mechanism and Economic Management (Part II), proved especially troublesome to the reformers and was therefore significantly revised. The Law on State Enterprise (II.8)—which allowed for state enterprises to operate essentially as in a market economy—was slated for passage in 1986 but was not approved by the Supreme Soviet until July 1987. Delay also applied to the 1987 Law of Individual Labor Activity (*VII. Legislation on Social Development and Culture*).

The Law on Cooperatives, a remarkable piece of legislation, proved a deceptive if not dubious stimulus to a market economy. A throwback to Lenin's NEP, it was not included, as such, in the 38 pieces of projected legislation.[32] Whatever its ancestry, the Law on Cooperatives, enacted in May 1988, was arguably the most radical element in the *perestroika* package.[33] In allowing for private ownership of some businesses in areas of manufacturing, service, and foreign trade, the law effectively removed the economy from Party control and opened the floodgates to diverse capitalist ventures.[34] The unintended consequence was that it became a vehicle for free-wheeling post-Soviet capitalists. Oligarchs like Aleksandr Smolenskii and Mikhail Khodorkovskii proved especially adept in manipulating it for their own gain in the 1990s. While these people used their wealth to accumulate great power in El'tsin's Russia, they were largely undone in Putin's.[35]

30 Letter of V.N. Kudriavtsev (17 February 1988) responding to mine (11 December 1987).

31 For a detailed analysis of the economics of *perestroika* by a former Soviet scholar, see Vladimir Mau, "*Perestroika*: Theoretical and Political Problems of Economic Reforms in the USSR", 47(3) *Europe-Asia Studies* (1995), 387-411.

32 It became essentially an elaboration of II.10.

33 See Ulrich Weissenburger, 'The New Soviet Law on Cooperatives: Use of Private Initiative to Overcome Supply Bottlenecks", 25(4) *Economic Bulletin* (Sept. 1988), 6-9.

34 'Russia: Unforeseen Results of Reform' as re-published from the Library of Congress *Country Studies* and the *CIA World Factbook.*

35 See, especially, David E. Hoffman, *The Oligarchs: Wealth and Power in the New Russia* (Public Affairs, New York, NY, 2002), *passim.* Hoffman does cite oligarchs—besides Smolenskii and Khodorkovskii—Anatolii Chubais, Boris Berezovskii, and Vladimir Gusinskii.

That the Soviet Union would actually disappear at the end of 1991 was an outcome unforeseen by attendees, non-Soviet and Soviet alike, at the Bridgeport conference in 1987. They had come to scrutinize legislation and discuss reform in the USSR, not the Soviet state's dissolution.

From the vantage point of a quarter century, we can assess the goings on of 1986-1987 and the years following. We know that the Soviet Union reached a turning point; yet, in critical respects, it failed to turn. The question that haunts us: could it have ended differently and for the better? Could the old Soviet Union have achieved democratic reform, as seemed possible in 1986-1987, in accord with the rule of law?[36] Gorbachev in a recent writing, not surprisingly, thought that 'the breakthrough to freedom and democracy' was *perestroika*'s and *glasnost*'s enduring legacy. But that had hardly been his chief motive in early *perestroika*; nor has that legacy been as lasting as he suggests.

Stephen F. Cohen offers a more convincing analysis.[37] As does Citizen Gorbachev, Cohen believes that the removal of power from the 'hands of the Communist Party, which had monopolized it, to those to whom it should have belonged according to the Constitution—to the soviets through free elections—could have done the trick. There was the need only to buttress verbiage and structure with will.[38]

The scholars at Bridgeport were, however, wedded to law, not to power brokers and the law's manipulators; that being the case, they—like most others—misread the tea leaves.

36 See Stephen F. Cohen, "The Breakup of the Soviet Union Ended Russia's March to Democracy", *The Guardian* (13 December 2006). Calling the 'breakup' the most "consequential event of the second half of the 20th century", Cohen concludes this essay by observing that:

> "Political and economic alternatives still existed in Russia after 1991, and none of the factors contributing to the end of the Soviet Union were inexorable. But even if democratic and market aspirations were among them, so were cravings for power, political coups, elite avarice, extremist ideas and widespread perceptions of illegitimacy and betrayal. It should have been clear which would prevail."

Cohen has spoken frequently on 'end of Soviet Union' and 'end of Cold War' matters. See his remarks at the Woodrow Wilson Center (Kennan Institute) seminar in Washington, DC on "The Fifteenth Anniversary of the End of the Soviet Union: Recollections and Perspectives" (13 December 2006) on the internet. Cohen, making some of the same points, spoke to a Cold-War Conference at the Gorbachev Foundation in Moscow (1 March 2006); see H-Diplo Commentary on the internet.

37 "Was the Soviet System Reformable?", 63(3) *Slavic Review* (Autumn 2004), 488. The article has a superb bibliography interspersed in the footnotes.

38 Early in 2010, Gorbachev wrote an op-ed piece ("*Perestroika* Lost") in *The New York Times* (13 March 2010) in which he observed:

> "Our main mistake was acting too late to reform the Communist Party. The party initiated *perestroika*, but it soon became a hindrance to our moving forward. The party's top bureaucracy organized the attempted coup in August 1991, which scuttled the reforms."

The New Political Polarization of the World and the Reform of State Property Management in Russia[1]

Zlata E. Benevolenskaya

Introduction

The repeal of Article 6 to the USSR Constitution in 1990—which had proclaimed the leading and guiding role of the CPSU in Soviet society—was a milestone in Soviet and Russian jurisprudence, in the course of overcoming ideological opposition between the West and East. That event has radically changed Soviet and Russian jurisprudence.

In Soviet jurisprudence, this event was similar to the crash of the Berlin Wall. After the repeal of Article 6 from the Soviet Constitution, Soviet society became open for a multi-party political system as the country veered towards democracy and the protection of human rights—movement which has become irreversible.

The ideological defeat of communism in the Soviet Union has finally led to variety in the political spectrum inside the country and has led to the expansion of foreign trade outside the country. The rejection of the CPSU's guiding role in society gave rise to democratic civil legislation which we observe now in Russia and, also, in other states of the CIS.

At the same time, one can still observe the residue of the planned economy according to the principle of centralized management which was dictated by the militarization of the Soviet economy during the Cold War. On the legal horizon, this can be seen in the institutes of economic ownership (*khoziaistvennoe vedenie*) and operative management (*operativnoe upravlenie*) of state property in Russian legislation. These legal constructs have two characteristics which are important for our discussion: (a) they remain the primary forms of managing state property in Russia; and (b) they crowd out the development of the new legal model (for Russia) of trust management which arose as a competitive legal form to the two legal constructs of *khoziaistvennoe vedenie* and *operativnoe upravlenie.*

The legal model of trust management has its roots in Equity and has its basic features in the original trust. The latter proved to be unacceptable to the vast majority of Russian civil-law scholars. Witness to that is the short-lived fate

1 The ideas set forth in the present chapter, and in particular the interrelation which we are presenting of a new political polarization of the world on a 'North-South' rather than its 'East-West' axis—as well as the concept of reforming the management of the state property in Russia—are ones which we have not yet encountered in Russian (legal) literature. Of course, we realize that sources may exist of which we are unaware. A more recent presentation of fresh materials relating to political polarization 'North-East' are in a presentation delivered by Alexei Mordashov, General Director of the Severstal' Corporation, in which he expressed the concept of 'Northern Measurement' (*severnoe izmerenie*) during the 2010 Petersburg Economic Forum; see <http://www.forumspb.com/ru/programme/SPIEF_2010/programm_3#translation86|1276774768>.

Tatiana Borisova and William Simons, eds.
The Legal Dimension in Cold-War Interactions: Some Notes from the Field 55-71

of the December 1993 Edict of the RF President "On Trust".[2] The fire storm of criticism which it met from the Russian civil-law establishment[3] led to the quick replacement of the 1993 Edict by the 1994 Russian Civil Code.

By the way, there is a legal model of trust in Ukraine.[4] This is some evidence that the original concept of trust can be accepted by the legislator of a country which is from the continental legal system.

In our opinion, similar to the fashion in which the Soviet Union shed Article 6 of its Constitution, as Russia could stand down from an all-embracing system of state property during the process of privatization; thus, it is necessary for Russia to shed its all-embracing system for the state management of state property. As Russia has rejected ubiquitous planned management of its economy, it should likewise reject *khoziaistvennoe vedenie* and *operativnoe upravlenie* in favor of the form of the trust management of (state) property. As variety in everything is the basis of the new market-type economy, so too should there be flexibility of economic behavior in managing the affairs of legal persons.

Economic ownership and operative management should be surgically removed from Russian trade and commerce, indeed from economic activity in general in the new Russian Federation—and also from the legal horizon—in the course of globalization and economic integration in conditions of the emerging, new world political (multi-)polarization instead of the Cold-War opposition of two superpowers. Such political polarization has been termed the 'North-South' polarization, about which political commentators spoke during those times.[5]

2 *Sobranie Aktov RF* (1994) No.1 item 6.

3 *E.g.*, Evgenii Alekseevich Sukhanov, "Doveritel'noe upravlenie i trast", *Ekonomika i Zhizn'* (1995) No.6; *idem*, "Doveritel'noe upravlenie imuschestvom", *Kommentarii chasti vtoroi Grazhdanskogo Kodeksa RF* (Gardarika, Moscow, 1996), 311-312; *idem*, "Doveritel'noe upravlenie imuschestvom", in Mikhail Isaakievich Braginskii and Vladimir Dmitrievich Karpovich (eds.), *Kommentarii chasti vtoroi Grazhdanskogo Kodeksa RF dlia predprinimatelei* (Fond Pravovaia Kul'tura, Moscow, 1996), 237; Viktor Abramovich Dozortsev, "Doveritel'noe upravlenie imuschestvom", in Mikhail Isaakievich Braginskii, Vladimir Vladimirovich Vitrianskii, Iurii Khamzatovich Kalmykov, Oksana Mikhailovna Kozyr' (eds.), *Grazhdanskii Kodeks Rossii: Dogovory i drugie ob"iazatel'stva. Tekst proekta. Kommentarii. Problemy. Chast' vtoraia. kommentarii zakonov* (Issledovatel'skii Tsentr chastnogo prava. Mezhdunarodnyi Tsentr Finansovo-Ekonomicheskogo Razvitiia, Moscow, 1995), 340; *idem*, "Doveritel'noe upravlenie imuschestvom", in Oksana Mikhailovna Kozyr', Aleksandr L'vovich Makovskii, Stanislav Antonovich Khokhlov (eds.), *Grazhdanskii Kodeks RF. Chast' vtoraia. Tekst. Kommentarii. A'lfavitno-predmetnii ukazatel'* (Mezhdunarodnyi Tsentr Finansovo-Ekonomicheskogo Razvitiia, Moscow, 1996), 532; and Vadim Vital'evich Chubarov, "Doveritel'noe upravlenie imuschestvom", in Oleg Nikolaevich Sadikov (ed.), *Kommentarii chast vtoroi Grazhdanskogo Kodeksa RF (postateinii)* (Iuridicheskaia firma Kontrakt, Norma, Moscow, 1996), 595.

4 *Grazhdanskii Kodeks Ukrainy*, Chapter 31 (Folio, Khar'kiv, 2007).

5 Andrei Vladimirovich Kozyrev, "Vostok i Zapad. Ot konfrontatsii k sotvortchestvu i sorazvitiiu", *Mezhdunarodnaia Zhizn'* (1989) No.9, 3-14; and Andrei Vladimirovich Kozyrev and Andrei Iur'evich Shumikhin, "Vostok i Zapad v tret'em mire", *Mezhdunarodnaia Zhizn'* (1989) No.2, 71-72.

So, in 1989, Alexander Ianov—an observer of history and politics—wrote of terminating the competition of the superpowers in the Cold-War era:

> "There is a frontal attack on a rivalry paradigm before us, as a matter of fact there is an appeal to replace it with its new, alternative idea of cooperation in which the frameworks of national ideas are not irreconcilable, are not conducive to collisions as force ceases to be a determinative in world politics."[6]

Today, Ivanov argues that Russia is a "northern-European state".[7] I argue that in accepting the original trust, initially in the form of and the trust management of the state property, Russia will be integrated further into the community of 'northern' states, who make wide use of the experience of those states, where the legal model of trust has been extensively applied over a long period of time. A major part of the rationale for trust management to supersede the vestiges of the Cold-War planned economic system in Russia is the need for re-invigorating Russian law and the legal sense of Russian society. And: introducing trust management into Russian legislation—and more importantly into legal practice—should contribute further to the widespread mutual integration of the developed countries of the North (the USA, Canada, and Europe)—including Russia: since Russia in its geopolitical position belongs to the Northern States.

Russia and New Political Polarization of the World Which has Arisen Since the Cold War

The predecessor of the three main doctrines of new geopolitics was the conception of 'the new world order', which had developed after the end of the Cold War. During the War in the Persian Gulf, President George H.W. Bush frequently used the term 'a new world order' to describe the world after the Cold War. One political godfather of this idea is clearly Michael Gorbachev; in a sense, so is George Bush. The first steps directed to the establishment of trust, between the two nuclear super-states, have induced them to think that other fundamental divergences between the USSR and the USA can be quickly overcome. On 11 September 1990, President Bush said:

> "We stand today at a unique and extraordinary moment. The crisis in the Persian Gulf [...] also offers a rare opportunity to move toward an historic period of cooperation. Out of these troubled times, our first objective—a new world order—can emerge: a new era—free from the threat of terror, stronger in the pursuit of justice, and more secure in the quest for peace [...]."[8]

6 Alexander Ianov, "Novoe mishlenie i Amerikanskii 'brezhnevizm'", *Mezhdunarodnaia Zhizn'* (1989) No.1, 33. Unless otherwise noted, all the translations in this chapter from Russian to English have been made by the author of this chapter.

7 Available at <http://www.politstudies.ru/extratext/lm/flm007.htm#22ay>.

8 George H.W. Bush, "Address Before a Joint Session of the Congress on the Persian Gulf Crisis and the Federal Budget Deficit (1990-09-11)", reproduced at <http://bushlibrary.tamu.edu/research/public_papers.php?id=2217&year=1990&month=9>. See, also, "Bush's New World Order: The Meaning Behind The Words", Research Paper Presented to the Research

In the field of geopolitical concepts generated by the termination of the Cold War and the disappearance of the bi-polar political polarization 'West-East', the new characterizations include:

The 'uni-polar world', according to which the military, economy and cultural priority of the US has the predominant role. Professor Zbigniew Brzeziński is the bright representative of this conception[9] which puts upon the United States the responsibility for virtually everything that occurs in the world. From the point of view of the world's balance of forces, as well as culture and political influences, this position is not without danger for the US—to put it lightly—considering the fact that the US includes a large part of the world's intellectual elite. In other words, placing the responsibility for the major events in the world at the doorstep of a single country can obviously have negative repercussions for that country owing firstly to the magnitude of the responsibility. The acts of terrorism that have taken place in recent years are directed at a reality according to which the uni-polar world is not an all-embracing concept. The proposition that the world's intellectual elite is concentrated in the US clearly is in need of some qualifications (into which we will not enter now), but to a large degree I believe that it is true. It is enough to read the elite theories of such famous researchers as C. Wright Mills, Floyd Hunter, G. William Domhoff, James Burnham, Robert D. Putnam, and Thomas R. Dye. The developed and civilized countries cannot accept the uni-polar conception because the intellectual elite of the world concentrated in the US cannot be subjected to dangers. The exaggerated size of the responsibility of one country—the USA—within the limits of the concept of a uni-polar world threatens one of the main values of world culture: the American intellectual elite.

As to the problems of the Cold War, which we are considering here, Professor Brzeziński has seen the result of the juxtaposition 'East-West' as follows:

> "For America, the chief geopolitical prize is Eurasia. [...] Now a non-Eurasian power is preeminent in Eurasia, and America's global primacy is directly dependent on how long and how effectively its preponderance on the Eurasian continent is sustained."[10]

Adhering to the proposition of the prevalence of the Atlantic culture in Eurasia, we consider it necessary to indicate that the prevalence must be founded not on the uni-polar world conception but, rather, on the concept of the political polarization 'North-South', where international relations are built not on the subservience of Eurasia but on the flexible cooperation of northern states.

Department, Air Command and Staff College in Partial Fulfillment of the Graduation Requirements of ACSC by Maj. Bart R. Kessler (March 1997), reproduced at <http://www.dtic.mil/cgi-bin/GetTRDoc?Location=U2&doc=GetTRDoc.pdf&AD=ADA398504>.

9 Zbigniew Kazimierz Brzeziński, *The Grand Chessboard: American Primacy and Its Geostrategic Imperatives* (Basic Books, New York, NY, 1997) (subsequently translated and published in nineteen languages; see <http://www.takeoverworld.info/Grand_Chessboard.pdf. 30>); also, *id., Velikaia schakchmatnaia doska* (Mezhdunarodnye otnosheniia, Moscow, 1998, O.Iu. Ural'skaia, transl.), 20.

10 *Ibid.*

The 'multi-polar world' idea was repeatedly proclaimed by Russian President Boris El'tsin.[11] For example, in the spring of 1997, El'tsin and the Chairman of the People's Republic of China Tszjan Zemin signed a "Joint Declaration on a Multi-polar World and the Establishment of a New International Order" in Moscow.[12] This more successfully portrays a political reality and is accepted by most political figures. One can argue that the existence of large centralized states and communities of states—such as the United States, Russia, China, India, the European Union, the Muslim states—reflects diverse centers of politics and culture among which there are complex connections. But this multi-polarism can be viewed as being a temporal concept. According to history, the threat of violence forces countries to create blocks such as Entente, NATO, and the Great Powers Alliance during the period of the Second World War. Despite the popularity of the multi-polar world conception in Russia, two prominent commentators have asserted that: "the multi-polar world is a purely theoretical concept the realization which is possible by the way of developing the Shanghai Cooperation Organization".[13] The concept of a multi-polar world has been set forth *inter alia* in two Declarations of Heads of Member States of the Shanghai Cooperation Organization (of 7 June 2002[14] and of 5 July 2005[15] respectively).

The 'North-South' polarization has also arisen in place of the old 'West-East' confrontational paradigm and overcomes the former 'East-West' confrontation. Terrorist acts—of Muslim persons against citizens of Russia (Moscow, Beslan, Volgodonsk) and against the US (11 September 2001) and subsequent acts of the US against Iraq—testify to a general threat from the southern states for the North, and it is this threat which promotes cooperation between the states of North America and the Eurasian continent. Sergei Lavrov, RF Minister for Foreign Affairs, has opined:

> "We are open for co-operative, integrative processes both in Eurasia and, in a wider plan, in the Euro-Atlantic [...] in the presence of political will, it would be possible to build a strong design for interaction in a safety sphere in the Euro-Atlantic. [...] Clearly, [...] maintenance of safety in our region is possible only by involving all states and all corresponding organizations on the Euro-Atlantic space. [...] It is difficult to overestimate value of a religious-moral component at the present stage of world development. [...] Extremely pertinent is the ascertaining of late Patriarch of Russia Alexei the Second which he made in Strasbourg, that 'Christian ideas of advantage, freedom and morals interrelated create

11 Available at <http://old.polit.ru/documents/155121.html>.

12 Reproduced at <http://www.fas.org/news/russia/1997/a52--153en.htm>.

13 N.A. Nartov and V.N. Nartov, *Geopolitika* (Izdatel'stvo politicheskoi literatury, Moscow, 2007), 492.

14 See <http://www.sectsco.org/RU/show.asp?id=91>.

15 See <http://www.sectsco.org/RU/show.asp?id=98>.

> a unique code of European consciousness possessing an inexhaustible creative potential in personal and public life'."[16]

We agree with Minister Lavrov.

But the problems of imperial thinking still peculiar to Russia generate the following concepts:

> "The world at the beginning of the third millennium will be actually divided not into the West and the East or the North-South but into regions and countries which participate in globalization processes and countries that are unable to join in this process. [...] As a result of the evolution of relations between the North and the South, new conditions of cooperation for Russia with developing countries are formed. Irrespective of the traditional level of relations of all the great powers with the countries of the South, two-way communications in an increasing degree will be supplemented by interaction with regional and international institutes."[17]

To our mind, this view is unacceptable: on the one hand, nowadays the definition of Russia as a great power is no longer a valid one; on the other hand, the term 'developing countries' is the obsolete one dating back to the Cold-War era.

When it was clear that there was a move away from communist doctrine and from Soviet foreign policy in particular, various opinions could be noted among members of Soviet society at large—and among scholars in particular—about whether the Cold War had ended and about the crystallization of a 'North Pole' of the new political polarization and relations of two 'super-states' *vis-à-vis* the so-called 'Third World' (which can also be designated as the 'South Pole' within the new political polarization 'North-South'). For example, in 1989 Andrei Kozyrev, the former RF Minister for Foreign Affairs in the early 1990s, wrote:

> "On the whole in the social sphere in the East and in the West contains the important preconditions for crystallization, the statement and the transformation into a material force of the universal idea of preservation and maintenance of progress towards a uniform civilization."[18]

At the same time, Ivanov—whom we already have encountered above—stated that there was a group of persons in Soviet political society, which "was not afraid of competition either from the world market or from world culture. Peter Chaadaev who was standing up for Russia's joining to European family was the most remarkable herald during the new time. The irreversibility of this 'joining' means 'political modernization'."[19]

16 Sergei Victorovich Lavrov, "Kak okonchatel'no zavershit' kholodnuiu voinu?", *Mezhdunarodnaia Zhizn'* (2009) No.5, 3-12.

17 Anatolii Vasil'evich Torkunov, "Sovremennye mezhdunarodnye otnosheniia", reproduced at <http://www.gumer.info/bibliotek_Buks/Polit/tork/06.php>. Dr. Torkunov is rector of *MGIMO* (the Moscow State Institute of International Relations), a political scientist, and academician of the Russian Academy of Sciences.

18 Kozyrev, "Vostok i Zapad: Ot konfrontatsii [...]", *op.cit.* note 5.

19 Alexander Ivanov, "Sovetskaia vneshniia politika: na kriticheskoi stadii perestroiki", *Mezhdunarodnaia Zhizn'* (1989) No.9, 56.

During the formation of the bi-polar system 'North-South', there is important the role and the destiny of Eastern Europe, about which Dr. Brzeziński, in particular, has written the following:

> "In the process of the development of the crisis of the USSR, its control over Eastern Europe will weaken. [...] The term 'Eastern Europe' is a concept which is political, connected with 'Cold War' [...] Eastern Europe wishes to become again Central Europe [...] it wishes to be itself."[20]

The formation of the 'North Pole' simultaneously with the end of the Cold War can be illustrated by the following example:

> "One of the 'Burlington Northern' offers: the organization of an enterprise for transporting foreign cargoes on the Trans-Siberian highway (Pacific Ocean to Atlantic)."[21]

An important role in the formation of the 'North-South' political polarization has been played by the complex relations between the 'superpowers' and the so-called 'third world'. Andrei Kozyrev wrote in those days:

> "[...] backwardness preservation, permanent and growing backlog of many countries of 'the third world', and also irregularity of the conflicts in these countries and between them (at the residual involvement of great powers) have led to the further deepening of the rupture between the South and the North, to a ripening of the original ideology of the protest of the 'southerners', sharply worried about the unequal position [...] this protest [...] as a rule, takes an active form, first of all a national and religious-national one that does not give one high hopes of its fast cooling [...] 'The protest' is almost equally dangerous both for the USSR and for the USA as it is focused against a certain 'general enemy' in the person of rich 'North', and is directed against international law and order. [...] The sharp paradox is [...] that weapons of American or Soviet manufacture appear at times and are turned against the one who delivers them."[22]

And, also, there is the fact that countries of 'the third world' have (almost) reached the creation of nuclear weapons.[23] As former US Defense Secretary Robert C. McNamara wrote:

> "In a multi-polar world, the USA and the USSR cannot dominate completely, as now, in the spheres of influence. From here it follows that there is obviously a necessity for the development of a new type of relations between the North and the South. These relations should include, at least: guarantees of a military neutrality of 'the third world', the termination of conflicts among the countries of 'the third world' and conflicts among political parties resisting each other in these countries, the maintenance of system of collective safety for the South [...]".[24]

20 Zbigniew Kazimierz Brzeziński, "Okonchilas' li 'Xolodnaia voina'?", *Mezhdunarodnaia Zhizn'* (1989) No.10, 36 (originally published in Russian).

21 Iurii Vladimirovich Dubinin, "Predstavlaia perestroiku za rubezhom", *Mezhdunarodnaia Zhizn'* (1989) No.10, 85.

22 Kozyrev and Shumikhin, *op.cit.* note 5.

23 *Ibid.*

24 Robert C. McNamara, "Esli my otvaszhimsia razrushit' stereotipy", *Mezhdunarodnaia Zhizn'* (1989) No.3, 51 (originally published in Russian).

The integration of Russia into the community of 'northern states', the participation of Russia in G8 summits, the signing the Basic Act Russia-NATO in 1997, the creation of the Council of Russia-NATO, the joint struggle of the northern states against terrorism and, finally, the refusal of the US to disperse the Ballistic Missile Defense systems[25] in Eastern Europe are all links in the formation of the 'North Pole' in the political polarization 'North-South'. Ivanov argues that Russia is a 'Northern European state'.[26] Political observer Aleksei Pushkov has written: "It is the optimal position for Russia to keep an equilibrium position between the basic centers of forces."[27]

The Residual Elements of the Planned Economy Remained After the End of the Cold War and Their Competition with New Legal Forms of Managing Russian Strategic State Property

The integration of Russia into the community of the 'northern states' leads to integration of Russian jurisprudence into the legal field of the developed states of the northern world. In 1998, Professor V.M. Kulagin wrote:

> "The market model supersedes the last rudiments of a centrally planned economy and becomes universal. Simultaneously, there is a global process of liberalization of the system of the market economy. As a result of the increase of international trade the importance of the role of transnational corporations, of the strengthening and diversification of the investment streams, the mutual dependence of the national economies has increased tenfold. The world economic system turns into a uniform organism, where each national economy has its functional features, but all of them are connected in the unit's 'nervous system' and 'blood circulation system. The world economic system enters a new channel of global integration which has evolved over the course of centuries; an old breed of national egoism by incorporated Europe. [...] The economy becomes so interconnected that the interests of all its active participants demand their stability in economic, politic and military plans."[28]

It is thus that the paraphernalia of a planned economy—such as economic ownership and operative management[29]—have also become obsolete in Russian civil

25 See <http://www.regnum.ru/news/208541.html>. Today, the US position on BMD systems has changed.

26 See <http://www.politstudies.ru/extratext/lm/flm007.htm#22ay>.

27 Aleksei Konstantinovich Pushkov, "Dlia Rossii optimal'nim bilo by ravnovesnoe polozhenie mezhdu osnovnymi zentrami sily", *Mezhdunarodnaia Zhizn'* (1998) No.3 (reproduced at <http://www.mid.ru/mg.nsf/ab07679503c75b73c325747f004d0dc2/4380c504ed74504dc32565ca00314019?OpenDocument>). Dr. Pushkov is a Russian TV presenter as well professor at *MGIMO* (Moscow State Institute of International Relations).

28 Vladimir Mikhailovich Kulagin, "Sovremennye teorii mezdunarodnykh otnoshenii", *Mezhdunarodnaia Zhizn'* (1998) No.1, 81-91 (reproduced at <http://www.mid.ru/mg.nsf/ab07679503c75b73c325747f004d0dc2/df05b65dbbcf277dc32565c5004e3a51?OpenDocument>). Dr. Kulagin is a distinguished professor at *MGIMO* (Moscow State Institute of International Relations).

29 See Daniil Viktorovich Petrov, *Pravo khoziaistvennogo vedeniia i pravo operativnogo upravleniia*

legislation. These legal models arose in the 1960s (the operative management) and in the 1990s (the economic ownership); later, they were repeatedly modified within the framework of the market economy. From these constructs flow the following: the heads of state enterprises (based on the right of economic ownership) work within the regime of labor-law contracts and have no personal interest in the results of the state enterprise activity; they are deprived of any lawful commercial initiative whatsoever and, at the same time, are civil servants (state officials): the status of a civil servant does not allow them to display entrepreneurial initiative. The narrowed framework of the status of civil servants, as the result, encounters a situation where the goals of the activity of a state enterprise and the personal interests of the head of the state enterprise invariably will contradict each other.

Unitary state enterprises (*unitarnye gosudarstvennye predpriiatia*) are based on the right of economic ownership and distribute only their production; they are prohibited from independently managing their real estate, which is fixed on their balance sheet. They can engage in transactions involving their real estate only after receiving preliminary consent of the owner of the property—the Russian state—in the person of the Committee on the State Property Management. That means in practice, unitary state enterprises—based on the right of economic ownership—act according to the instructions of the property owner, *i.e.*, the Russian state.

Treasury state enterprises (*kazennye predpriiatia*) are based on the right of operative management and their rights are much narrower. The Civil Code provides that such enterprises may act only according to the precise instructions of the owner of the property which has been entrusted to the treasury state enterprise; in turn, such instructions need to be tailored to the purposes of the enterprise's activity, as set forth in its charter (*ustav*) and to the 'use' (*naznachenie*) of the property. As one can see from these provisions of the Civil Code, the authority of a treasury state enterprise *vis-à-vis* its property is quite restricted.

In principle, the Russian state—owing to its official function—has no authority to conduct business; furthermore, state enterprises (both unitary state enterprises and treasury state enterprises) cannot engage in business effective and efficiently because—at the end of the day—they are dependent upon the instructions of the state-owner, who is not a professional entrepreneur.

Direct instructions of the state-owner of property are not useful for the state, the purpose of which does not consist in engaging in commercial activity, and they are rudimentary from the point of view of foreign policy, because foreign investments are not permitted in state-owned enterprises. In addition, and perhaps most importantly, these legal forms of a planned economy retain

(Iuridicheskii Tsentr Press, St. Petersburg, 2002), 93; and K.P. Kriazhevskikh, *Pravo operativnogo upravleniia i pravo khoziaistvennogo vedeniia gosudarstvennym imushchestvom* (Iuridicheskii Tsentr Press, St. Petersburg, 2004), 207.

the constructs of a centralized military-orientated economy, alien for the open-market economy of the world.

Furthermore, direct instructions of the Russian state-owner for unitary state enterprises and treasury state enterprises lead to a situation where state enterprises are outside of a common legal field. The illustration of this thesis is to be seen in the absence of judicial practice concerning the disputes between the state and state enterprises, which are subordinated to its administrative superiors.

Economic ownership is the legal form of a planned economy. According to Article 294 of the 1994 RF Civil Code, a unitary state enterprise possesses and uses property freely and has the right to dispose of movables. But a unitary state enterprise has no right to dispose of real estate which has been allocated to it. Article 295 of the RF Civil Code provides that the owner of state property allocated to a state enterprise adopts decisions concerning the creation, reorganization and liquidation of the unitary state enterprise and of treasury state enterprises, appoints the directors thereof, defines the goals and purposes of the activities of such enterprises and supervises the use by these state enterprises of their property (including movables). The owner of the property verifies that the property is being used according to its 'destination', and—as we have noted above—engaging in transactions involving real estate, allocated to a state enterprise, requires the preliminary consent of the owner.

Trust Management as Testimony to the Acceptance by Russia of Western Values

The new legal form of the state property management is that of trust management. Prior to its introduction to RF Civil Code in 1994, this legal form briefly had been regulated by a 1993 RF Presidential Edict "On Trust".[30] As has been mentioned above, the Trust Edict encountered strong criticism from Russian scholars: Russian legal forms needed to be founded on continental legal traditions while the original trust was from outside continental legal traditions and, therefore, could not be accepted by Russian legislation. Commenting on the official opinion expressed by the Moscow-based Research Center for Private Law during the preparation of Part II of the Russian Civil Code (regulating trust management), Professor W.E. Butler wrote that Russian law lacked the system of Equity that was available to English courts; however, he added that this was not essential for the proposed construct which was based entirely on the law of contract.[31]

The roots of the modern trust management are in the legal form of the original trust. As a general rule, trust includes the following: the person who

30 *Sobranie Aktov RF* (1994) No.1 item 6.

31 William E. Butler, "Trust Ownership in Russia: Towards a Legislative History", 1 *The Parker School Journal of East European Law* (1994), 301-326 at 303.

established the trust (the founder) stipulates that the management of the property is to be carried out by one or several persons (trustees) who is/are to act in the interests of one or several persons (beneficiaries). The creation of the trust includes two separate moments:

(A) The founder signs the formal document—usually named the act of settling the trust—in which the trust is announced and the purposes of the trust and the structure of property are specified, and the beneficiary and trustee also are appointed; and

(B) The founder transfers the rights of the owner to the property, specified in the act, which is subordinate to the rules governing the law of ownership. The realization by the trustee of the rights and the performance of his duties give rise to the same legal consequences as those which have been elaborated by the founder of the trust.

The legal form of the trust is widely used in countries of the English-American system for a variety of practical purposes: familial (the management of property which has been inherited etc.), the protection of property of incapacitated persons, the realization of charities in the interests of specific subjects or of an indeterminate group of persons.

One of the characteristic features of the modern trust is its application in the commercial sphere. In ancient times, the trust existed primarily to preserve and redistribute property within the limits of the family; now, however, it frequently forms the legal basis of commercial activity directed toward the making of profit. Originally, the trust was applied in England as a way to bypass the rules of law concerning land.[32] For example, according to medieval English law, land could not be transferred according to a will and, as a rule, only could be passed after the death of the owner to his eldest son. Until the eldest son reached adult age, the land was transferred by the knight to the use of the family of the knight, and the knight's friends managed the land according to the use of the family of the knight. If the use was not settled, the land of the knight returned to the lord, whose rights were quite broad[33] (jurisdiction over the land).[34] According to the principle that all the lands belongs to the Crown, according to the principle of redistribution of feudal property and authorities and the principle of land grants by the Crown for service to the state, it can be said that the land returned to the

32 D.J. Hayton, *The Law of Trusts* (Sweet and Maxwell, London, third ed. 1998), 10; and T.E. Abova and A.U. Kabalkin (eds.), *Kommentarii Grazhdanskogo Kodeksa RF. Chast' vtoraia* (Urait, Moscow, 2003).

33 D.B. Parker and A.R. Mellows, *The Modern Law of Trusts* (Sweet and Maxwell, London, 1983), 1-2.

34 W.S. Holdsworth, *A History of English Law* (Methuen and Co Ltd., London, 1956), Chapter 1 "Origins", 19.

Crown in the person of the lord. "The lord who might gain advantage from a tenant dying, leaving an infant heir, was not necessarily the King, but could be one of the lords on a lower 'rung of the feudal ladder'."[35] According to Article 4 of the Magna Carta:

> "The guardian of the land of an heir who is thus under age, shall take from the land of the heir nothing but reasonable produce, reasonable customs, and reasonable services, and that without destruction or waste of men or goods; and if we have committed the wardship of the lands of any such minor to the sheriff, or to any other who is responsible to us for its issues, and he has made destruction or waster of what he holds in wardship, we will take of him amends, and the land shall be committed to two lawful and discreet men of that fee, who shall be responsible for the issues to us or to him to whom we shall assign them; and if we have given or sold the wardship of any such land to anyone and he has therein made destruction or waste, he shall lose that wardship, and it shall be transferred to two lawful and discreet men of that fief, who shall be responsible to us in like manner as aforesaid."[36]

So, in wide sense, the Crown owns all the land and takes care of the fulfillment by the guardians of their obligations. But use was the way in which land was freely distributed on temporary terms and conditions (trust, in later times).

This has been proven for the period of the XII-XIII centuries; but, later, the practice of transferring land to the use of closest friends of the knight was widely extended and the later acts of dishonest friends not returning the land to the knight had resulted in the necessity for the King to protect the knights' rights. Petitions were sent to the King and, then, were addressed by the King to the Chancellor, whose powers had gradually grown to the scale of the Courts of Equity.[37]

During the War of the Roses, use provided for belligerent parties a possibility to keep property from confiscation by the Crown as the penalty for hostile acts or disloyalty to the Crown. As Penner says:

> "Among nobles there was also the problem that the English Crown was bloodily contested over long periods of time, in particular during the War of Roses. If a landowner were in the position of having backed the wrong claimant to the Crown, not only would he lose his life, being condemned as a traitorous felon by the victor, but all his lands would be forfeit to the Crown ruining his family."[38]

However, if the owner had transferred property in trust, he had the right to nominate the beneficiary, who would own a property after his death. Later, the personal estate also began to be considered as a subject of trust.

The legal model of trust can be applied in commercial undertakings (rendering services to clients of banks and other credit organizations), prompting employee benefits (participating in corporate profits-sharing), and also dealing with bankruptcy proceedings (the assets of the bankrupt can be transferred to

35 J. Henderson, letter to the author (9 June 2010) on file with the author.

36 Reproduced at <http://www.constitution.org/eng/magnacar.htm>.

37 Hayton, *op.cit.* note 32, 10-11.

38 J.E. Penner, *The Law of Trusts* (Biddles, Ltd King's Lynn Ltd, Norfolk, 2005), 10.

a trust for the benefit of creditors for example). A trust can also be created to manage funds of a special-purpose designation, *e.g.*, in the interests of a wide circle of persons such as retirees.

The politico-legal sense of the appearance in Russian legislation of the trust management of the property should be seen in the competition which trust management can offer as an alternative legal model to the right of economic ownership and the right of operative management; as we have highlighted above, these latter two constructs traditionally have held near exclusive sway in the sphere of management of the state property during the era of the planned economy in the Soviet Union.

Trust management is regulated by Chapter 53 of the Civil Code of Russia. According to Article 1012:

> "Under an agreement for trust management, one party (the trust management founder) transfers the property into trust management to the other party (the trust manager) for a definite period, while the other party undertakes to manage this property in the interests of the trust management founder or a person indicated by him (the beneficiary). The transfer of property into trust management does not involve the assignment of the right of its ownership to the trust manager."

The founder of the trust management is the owner of the property. The trust manager (much like a trustee) has the right to administer the property vested in him but also has the obligation to administer the property as if it were his own. The purpose of activity of the parties of the trust management agreement is to increase the trust-fund property vested in the trust manager. The trust manager is obliged:

— to exploit (operate/use) the property with special care;
— to manage the property solely in the interests of the beneficiary(ies) (the founder of the trust management also may be a sole beneficiary);
— to carry out his duties as stipulated by law and by the trust management agreement;
— to include the rights, acquired by him, in structure of the property as a result of acts of trust management;
— to prepare and submit balance sheets, reflecting the transfer of property, to fiscal control agencies (this balance sheet must be separate and distinct from the trust manager's own balance sheet (report, declaration) on the one hand and, on the other, from the balance sheets of other participants in trust management relations).

Under a trust management agreement, the founder of the trust transfers the property in trust management to the trust manager; the latter administers this property in the interests of the founder of administration or of the person specified by her (a beneficiary). The transfer of property to a trust manager does not mean the transition of the title (ownership) to the trust manager however. As we have highlighted above, the trust manager must administer the trust in accordance with the trust management agreement in the interests of the beneficiaries. Limitations concerning specific acts of the trust management of property may be stipulated by a law or by the trust management agreement. The trust manager enters into transactions with property, transferred to trust management, on her own behalf specifying that she is a trust manager. This condition is to be considered observed, if upon the conclusion of transactions which do not require written registration, the counterparty is duly informed by the trust manager and the notation '*D.U.*' (trust manager) is entered in the relevant documents after the trustee's name.

If there is no evidence of the trust manager's activity in this capacity, she is personally responsible and compensation for damages can be claimed from property belonging to her/him where the trust manager cannot prove that such damages were due either to force majeure circumstances or resulted from acts of the beneficiary (or founder of the trust management).

Obligations involving transactions entered into by and acts of the trust manager during the term of the trust management which exceed the trust manager's powers or breach the limitations which have been established for her are borne by the trust manager personally.

Any debts under obligations which have arisen in connection with the trust management of property are repaid at the expense of this property. Where the trust management property is insufficient, execution may be levied upon property of the trust manager, and in the event that her own property is also insufficient, upon the property of the founder of the trust management which has not been transferred to the trust manager.

A trust management agreement may provide for the issuance of a security (*obespechenie*) by a trust manager to ensure the proper performance by the trust manager of her obligations; in particular, this security (bond) would be used to compensate losses caused by the improper management by the trust manager of the trust assets. If the trust manager has not shown the proper level of due care in managing the trust assets solely in the interests of the beneficiary (or the founder of the trust management), the trust manager must compensate beneficiary for any lost profit during the term of the trust management. Furthermore, the trust manager is liable for losses caused by the loss of or damage to trust property (except for it natural deterioration).

Essential conditions must be specified in a trust management agreement:

- the nature of property transmitted to trust management;
- the name of the legal or natural person in whose interests the trust management (founder or beneficiary) is to be carried out;

— the amount and the form of compensation payable to the trust manager where the payment of compensation is stipulated by the trust management agreement;
— the term of the agreement.

The term of a trust management agreement of property must not exceed five years. For various kinds of property transmitted to trust management, other limiting terms could be established by a law (but since the model has yet to be implemented, there are no other terms). Where neither of the parties has objected thereto, the trust management agreement is deemed to be extended for the same term and upon the same conditions originally stipulated by the agreement contract.

A trust management agreement of property must be made in writing while those involving real estate are to be concluded in the form stipulated for agreements for the purchase and sale of real estate. Furthermore, the transfer of real estate to trust management is subject to state registration in the same procedure as that for the transfer of the underlying property right (title).

Objects of trust management may be enterprises (or other property complexes), distinct objects of real estate, securities, rights certified as securities, as well as exclusive rights and other property. However, money cannot be an independent object of trust management except for the cases stipulated by a law; this is the 1990 Russian Law "On Banks and Banking Activity" which allows for the trust management of money.[39]

It bears repeating here that trust management is a new legal form of state property management in Russia and is not (yet) widely used. This notwithstanding, there have been some attempts to introduce it into the sphere of state property management (particularly strategic property) in Russia which will be described in the following part of this chapter.

Trust Management as a Concept of State Property Management in Russia

In November 1998, the Russian Government under the then-Prime Minister Evgenii Primakov proposed transferring important strategic property into trust management under professional trust managers. The following suggestions were contained in a Joint Declaration of the Russian Government and the RF Central Bank:

39 *Vedomosti S"ezda narodnykh deputatov RFSFR* (6 December 1990) No.27 item 357 (as amended), section 5.

> "State agencies of the executive branch of power should make decisions on the bankruptcy of the state enterprises and on the transfer of controlling blocks of shares of stock into state property with the subsequent transfer into trust management."[40]

In 1998, the Russian Government delegated to the RF Ministry for the Management of State Property and the Ministry of the Economy the right to verify the effectiveness of the management of state enterprises and blocks of shares of stock belonging to the state. This also included management of federal real estate as well as elaboration of a system for supervising and stimulating directors of state enterprises and, also, monitoring the activity of state representatives in joint-stock companies. Furthermore, it envisaged creation of a system of trust management of blocks of shares belonging to the state and trust management of state property in a broad sense. The Government deemed it necessary to raise incentives for trust managers and, at the same time, to tighten responsibility for the results of their actions in the interests of the state.[41]

In the fall of the next year, the Russian Government criticized the legal models of economic ownership and operative management (which we have outlined hereinabove) since the directors of state enterprises were deemed to be not duly responsible for the results of their activity.[42]

Those criticisms notwithstanding, economic ownership and operative management remained in place; questions concerning the problems of managing state property management were set aside and state property remained in state ownership.

The problem of creating new strata of professional trust managers for state property nevertheless remains an important issue. For example, a 2001 RF Governmental Decree[43] pointed out the necessity of preparing young professionals for work in enterprises and corporations of Russian Military-Industrial Complex. This Decree[44] went on to provide that "the participation of the state in the reform and development of Military-Industrial Complex will not only be in the form

40 Zaiavlenie Pravitel'stva Rossiiskoi Federatsii i Soveta direktorov Tsentral'nogo Banka Rossiiskoi Federatsii, "O merakh Pravitel'stva Rossiiskoi Federatsii i Tsentral'nogo Banka Rossiiskoi Federatsii po stabilizatsii sotsial'nogo i economicheskogo polozheniia v strane", *Rossiiskaia Gazeta* (17 November 1998).

41 *Ibid.*

42 Postanovleniie Pravitel'stva Rossiiskoi Federatsii (9 September 1999), "Konsteptsiia upravleniia gosudarstvennym imushchestvom", *Sobranie zakonodatel'stva RF* (1999) No.39 item 4626.

43 "O Programme sotsial'no-ekonomicheskogo razvitiia Rossiiskoi Federatsii", *Sobranie zakonodatel'stva RF* (2001) No.31 item 3295.

44 See, also, Ukaz Prezidenta Rossiiskoi Federatsii (23 July 1997) No.774, "O podgotovke upravliaiushchikh dlia organizatsii narodnogo khoziaistva Rossiiskoi Federatsii", *Sobranie zakonodatel'stva RF* (1997) No.30 item 3607; and Ukaz Prezidenta Rossiiskoi Federatsii (15 September 1997) No.1164, "O merakh po realizatsii Ukaza Prezidenta Rossiiskoi Federatsii ot 23 July 1997, No.774 'O podgotovke upravliaiuschikh dlia organizatsii narodnogo khoziaistva Rossiiskoi Federatsii'", *Rossiiskaia Gazeta* (7 October 1997).

of budget financing of the expenses thereof but, also, by way of transferring of blocks of shares of stock to holding companies of the integrated corporations in trust management".[45] To our mind, this is highly significant given the fact that Russian Military-Industrial Complex is made up of a plethora of state enterprises.

Thus, the Russian state repeatedly has attempted to resolve the problem of replacing the antiquated legal forms of economic ownership and operative management and creating the organic link of steps to (further) reform the management of state property. One can also observe these steps in the following: the accelerated bankruptcy of the unprofitable state enterprises, measures to monitor the effectiveness of the activity of state enterprises, and in particular in the creation of new strata of trust managers whose moral values are aligned with European ones. It is this group of fragmentary measures, which we have highlighted above, that constitute the reform of Russian strategic property management.

So, the accelerated bankruptcy of unprofitable state enterprises leads to the release of an enormous amount of the state property, free from any rights, except for the fact that it remains owned by the state. After the redemption of such state property, it should be transferred into trust management; this allows the state to keep the title to the property, but allows the property to be managed by professional businesspeople; this construction is distinguished from privatization because during the sale of state property, obviously the title to the state property is normally transferred *in toto* and no longer resides in the state. In either case, (the former) state property will be managed by the new strata of the professional young businesspeople, who one expects will follow the 'northern' and in particular 'northern European' values.

Conclusions

The necessity to replace the antiquated legal forms of state property management by the new form of trust management is confirmed by the reform of the Russian Military-Industrial Complex: among the other measures involved in reforming the management of strategic property in Russia, the transformation of the former organizational-technical structures of the Military-Industrial Complex into the modern product-specified structures and the attraction of out-of-budget investments into the structure of the Military-Industrial Complex are absolutely necessary to the effective functioning of the system.

The legal form of trust management is a new form of effective management of state property and state enterprises in Russia although it has its gnosiological roots in the Common-Law system. The acceptance of such form for managing Russian state property will mean that the Russian State is truly a northern-European state.

45 "O Programme", *op.cit.* note 43.

Relevance of the Cold War for Russian Jurisprudence: Private Law

Leena Lehtinen

Boundary between Past and Present in Russian Jurisprudence

Where is the boundary between past and present in developing new law, new private law, new civil law, and new civil procedure law in Russian jurisprudence? Is it the Cold War or some much earlier period?

In the first period of transition of the economy and social and cultural life in Russia, models for law-making were taken from Western countries, from the other side of the Cold-War border.[1] The rationale was the urgency of creating a market economy, which already existed in the Western countries. Russia adopted not only models for the regulation of the market economy directly from European and American states, but also rules and norms for society and human rights.[2]

The technical assistance given by European and American experts often consisted very simply of a transformation, or even translation, of laws for a new economy and society. When such transformation is very technical, mechanical or formal, the resulting legislation does not work for very long. In the early 1990s, when many statutes were adopted for the economy, everything associated with socialist-era legal conceptions was ignored.[3]

However, it is dangerous for a society to change its legal system too rapidly. Thus, the understandings and institutions used in the period 1917-1991 should not be forgotten.[4] This was understood in Russia in preparing the legal bases for a society based on the principle of the rule of law and can be seen in Russian legal doctrine in recent years.

More and more Russian scholars refer to legislation and jurisprudence from a more distant period, the period before the 1917 Revolution. This can be understood if one considers that a market economy was developing strongly in nineteenth-century Russia and that legislation and legal doctrine were also very active at that time.[5] The legal problems that must be solved today in Russia

1 Hiroshi Oda, *Russian Commercial Law* (Martinus Nijhoff Publishers, Leiden, 2007), 67; Wouter Snijders, "Lessons from St. Petersburg: Commerce and Civil Law", 34(2) *Review of Central and East European Law* (2009), 107-109; and Raymond Legeais, *Velikie pravovye sistemy sovremennosti* (Wolters Kluwer, Moscow, 2009, translated from *Les grands systèmes de droit contemporains: une approche comparative* (LexisNexic Litec, 2004)), 228.

2 Legeais, *op.cit.* note 1, 210-211.

3 Oda, *op.cit.* note 1, 69.

4 Legeais, *op.cit.* note 1, 3.

5 Sergei Sergeevich Alekseev, *Pravo sobstvennosti. Problemy teorii* (Institut chastnogo prava, Ekaterinburg, 2006), 60-61.

Tatiana Borisova and William Simons, eds.
The Legal Dimension in Cold-War Interactions: Some Notes from the Field 73-80

were very timely in that era as well; today's new legal institutions were also new at that time.

The first question that I would like to address in my paper is whether the relevant difference—the important dividing line—in the legal world has been the Iron Curtain, the border between East and West, or whether it might be more relevant for the long-term development of Russian law to examine the historical grounds of true Russian law.[6]

The second question to which I would like to draw the attention of the audience is as follows: In Russian legal doctrine today, one can encounter references to authors from the socialist period with increasing frequency. This means that the rationale for new Russian law—the modern legal society—is being sought not on the western side of the Iron Curtain, but on the eastern, within Russia, in the Soviet Union.

This second question is to some extent a second side of the problem. The reason for referring to Soviet-era legal doctrine and jurisprudence is perhaps not only that these represent Russian law, a Russian legal culture based on Russian philosophy and culture. The cultural background is very relevant,[7] very important, but probably it is not the only or even most important factor.

In this chapter, I would like to examine and present problems for discussion and explore whether this second phenomenon in Russian law today is connected with clarification of ordinary Russian law and authentic Russian legal institutions, or whether there are political or other tendencies to restore Eastern legal habits and even structures.

Private Ownership—Human Rights

The most important phenomenon in the new Russia is the existence of private ownership. It is crucial not only in the economy, but also for the development of human rights in society at large. The cultural and social function of ownership has been underscored by Russian scholars with reference to the legal and philosophical doctrine from the time long before the October Revolution.[8] Alekseev writes about "creative Russian traditions".[9] Referring to Russian legal doctrine from before the Revolution, Ikonitskaia emphasizes the importance of private ownership of land for the freedom of the human being.[10] She asserts that private ownership of land is one of the most important constitutional rights of a citizen.

6 Legeais, *op.cit.* note 1, 200-203.

7 *Ibid.*, 3.

8 Alekseev, *op.cit.* note 5, 5-7.

9 *Ibid.*, 14-15.

10 I.A. Ikonitskaia, "Pravo sobstvennosti na zemliu v Rossiiskoi Federatsii", in I.A. Ikonitskaia (ed.), *Pravo sobstvennosti na zemliu v Rossii i ES* (Wolters Kluwer, Moscow, 2009), 26.

The draft Russian Civil Code in the 1910s was based on European continental law.[11] Due to the Revolution and the total elimination of private ownership in the end of the 1920s,[12] Soviet doctrine cannot be used in creating the legal institution of ownership in the new Russia. That institution had no fundamental role in private law in the Soviet Union.[13]

In the USSR it was possible for citizens to own houses and cottages, and family members could acquire these later, but it was not really ownership. The piece of land on which a house stood was not the property of the owner of the house.[14] Soviet legislation accepted private ownership of land for the first time in the Constitution of 1978, but there was a ten-year moratorium in implementing that right.[15] Russian legislation adopted the private ownership of land in 1990.

However, even today ownership in Russia is not clearly defined, and the ownership that applies to the property of citizens is not unambiguously private. The legal status of ownership connected with the property of public and private legal entities is also unclear.[16]

The draft of the 1993 Constitution of the Russian Federation included a proposal that private ownership be defined as a natural right of any citizen.[17] This was not accepted, and there is now a definition of ownership according to which there are different forms of ownership depending on the subjects, the owners of the property: ownership by private persons and by other entities, such as the state or a municipality. With reference even to classical jurisprudence, Russian scholars have written that ownership as defined in Russian legislation today is not in fact ownership in the classical sense of the term.

One very difficult problem in Russian legislation and in court practice has been the definition of land as a piece of property, as the object of the right of ownership, and the legal connection to other immovables located on the parcel of land. The unity of real estate has been problematic in legislative work not only in the new Russia, but also in other former socialist countries; it also posed difficulties in Russia before the Revolution.[18]

11 Alekseev, *op.cit.* note 5, 61-62.

12 *Ibid.*, 63.

13 Legeais, *op.cit.* note 1, 208.

14 *Ibid.*, 209.

15 Ikonitskaia, *op.cit.* note 10, 16-17.

16 Alekseev, *op.cit.* note 5,16-19.

17 *Ibid.*, 25.

18 S.I. Gerasin, "Problema formirovaniia edinogo ob"ekta nedvizhimosti v Rossiiskoi Federatsii", in IIkonitskaia, *op.cit.* note 10, 160.

Quasi-Ownership—State Influence

The Russian Civil Code provides for not only right of ownership, but also other rights to thing,[19] which could be called 'quasi-ownership'. They were created in the Soviet economy, and they have been important in the privatization process. These special rights to thing continue to exist. In order to understand the meaning and legal character of these rights, Russian lawyers refer to Soviet legislation and legal practices.[20]

This is very relevant, for example, in the privatization of industrial enterprises, because property in quasi-ownership should be changed into private ownership in the legal sense. A large industrial complex can have goods under different forms of quasi-ownership as well as property that must not be privatized at all but must remain state- or municipally owned. Russian scholars are drawing on Soviet doctrine in order to understand the legal meaning of these legal constructs.

The new law on state and municipal enterprises adopted in 2002[21] shows that special property rights are needed in the legal regulation of entrepreneurship not only in the present time, but even in the future. Russian scholars are using also traditional classical jurisprudence for clarification of those legal institutions. Because the forms of quasi-ownership mentioned above continue to exist in the Russian economy, it is important to determine, for example, in joint investment projects, in which capacity Russian partners are participating, that is, the legal form of the property which they are contributing. Thus, the property problem connected with Soviet-era joint ventures persists to some extent even now. It is relevant in not only legal doctrine, but also legal practice.

A tendency can be seen in Russia whereby the state apparatus is playing a stronger role in the economy. The legal nature of the forms of quasi-ownership has been changed in the law on state enterprises (2002) as compared to the definition in the Civil Code. State and municipal organs have more possibilities to intervene in the activities of an enterprise when it has been created through public contributions. Here reference to the planned economy of the Soviet time is relevant.

19 Special rights to thing of persons who are not owners are: the right of inheritable possession for life of a land plot, the right of permanent (or perpetual) use of a land plot, the right of economic jurisdiction over property, and the right of operative management of property. "Grazhdanskii kodeks Rossiiskoi Federatsii", (30 November 1994) Law No.51-FZ, (hereinafter: the Civil Code of the Russian Federation), Art.216.

20 Anatolii Fedorovich Efimov and Nikolai Kirillovich Tolcheev, *Nastol'naia kniga sudì po zemel'nym sporam* (Prospekt, Moscow, 2008), 79.

21 Federal'nyi Zakon, "O gosudarstvennykh imunitsipal'nykh unitarnykh predpriiatiiakh", (14 November 2002) No.161-FZ (hereinafter: the Law on State and Municipal Unitary Enterprises).

A similar process can be observed in the case of joint stock companies in practice and in legislation. There are special regulations regarding state-owned joint stock companies, which are not covered by the ordinary law on joint stock companies.

Greater influence of the state can be observed in regulations concerning strategic fields of the economy in that the legislation minimizes the possibility of foreign participation. The question is the extent to which we should return to the law and jurisprudence of the Soviet era in understanding forthcoming legal solutions and structures in the Russian economy.

Freedom of Contract

A significant novelty in current Russian law is the principle of freedom of contract.[22] This principle is one of the fundamentals of the Russian Civil Code—along with private ownership and the equality of parties (§1). These innovations have become possible thanks to the democratic bases of society.[23] However, democracy is very weak in the Russian Federation, which may have serious effects on the development of the foundations of civil law.

In this context international relations are crucial, above all in the field of foreign economic co-operation. The unification of international trade law is having an important influence on the development of Russian civil law.[24]

Civil Procedure

A number of changes in the courts have been crucial for development of the new Russia. Creation of the civil society and a market economy based on the principle of the rule of law would not have been possible without fundamental changes in judicature. Even if the structure of the courts is very similar to that in the Soviet era,[25] there are totally different principles in civil procedure.

In some questions, Russian law makers cite principles that existed before the Revolution.[26] One of these is the active role of the judge in civil law proceedings.[27]

22 Oda, *op.cit.* note 1, 271-272.

23 O.A. Kuznetsova, *Normy-printsipy Rossiiskogo grazhdanskogo prava* (Statut, Moscow, 2006), 35-36.

24 Nina Grigorievna Vilkova, *Dogovornoe pravo v mezhdunarodnom oborote* (Statut, Moscow, 2002), 99-107.

25 Legeais, *op.cit.* note 1, 221.

26 Irina Valentinovna Reshetnikova, "Sudebnye reformy XIX i XXI vekov v oblasti grazhdanskogo sudoproizvodstva", in D.A. Medvedev (ed.), *Kodifikatsiia Rossiiskogo chastnogo prava* (Statut, Moscow, 2008), 308.

27 Vladimir Vladimirovich Iarkov, "Predlozheniia po kontseptsii, structure i soderzhaniiu Grazhdanskogo protsessual'nogo kodeksa Rossiiskoi Federatsii", in M.K. Treushnikov (ed.), *Put' k zakonu* (Gorodets, Moscow, 2004), 24.

The adversarial litigation in the new Russia has its roots in the imperial Russian legal reform of 1864.[28] The role of court decisions in Russian jurisprudence also reflects background influences from the Russian Empire and Soviet law.[29]

Another crucial influence on Russian legal principles is the country's membership in the Council of Europe and ratification of the European Convention for the Protection of Human Rights.[30]

One very difficult question for the Russian judiciary has been implementation of the principle of legal certainty. Russian legal doctrine before the October Revolution reflected an attitude similar to the one seen today in European legal practice. This attitude is in total contradiction to the practice and policy of Soviet courts.

It has been very difficult to change court practice and even the legislation, and even today there are many possibilities in Russian civil law proceedings to change the court's decision. This affects the finality of court awards, final legal judgments and the *res judicata*.[31]

However, it has been important in the field of civil procedure to honor old traditions, culture and habits, to engage not in revolution but evolution.[32]

From Russian Law towards CIS Law or Even Euro-Asian Law

One of the main questions with regard to the second side of the problem—the second phenomenon in the creation of Russian law today and the relevance of the Cold War for Russian jurisprudence—is the role of the Russian Federation in the development of law in the former Soviet countries and in other states.

28 Irina Valentinovna Reshetnikova, "The Role of Courts in Adversarial Litigation in Russia", 34(1) *Review of Central and East European Law* (2009), 1-2.

29 Vladimir Vladimirovich Iarkov, "Status sudebnoi praktiki v Rossii: nekotorye voprosy", *Vestnik Federal'nogo Arbitrazhnogo Suda Ural'skogo okruga* (2007) No.1, 95-108; and D.V. Litvinskii, *Priznanie inostrannykh sudebnykh reshenii po grazhdanskim delam* (Izdatel'skii Dom SPbGU, Sankt-Peterburg, 2005), 100-105.

30 Legeais, *op.cit.* note 1, 226.

31 William E. Pomeranz, "Supervisory Review and the Finality of Judgments under Russian Law", 34(1) *Review of Central and East European Law* (2009), 35; and M.A. Filatova, "Znachenie postanovleniia konstitutsionnogo suda Rossiiskoi Federatsii ot 5 fevralia 2007 g. No.2-P dlia reformirovaniia grazhdanskogo sudoproizvodstva", in E.A. Vinogradova and R.F. Kallistratova *et al.* (eds.), *Aktual'nye problemy razvitiia sudebnoi sistemy i sistemy dobrovol'nogo i prinuditel'nogo ispolneniia reshenii Konstitutsionnogo Suda RF, sudov obshchei iurisdiktsii, arbitrazhnykh, treteiskikh sudov i Evropeiskogo suda po pravam cheloveka: sbornik nauchnykh statei* ("Iuridicheskii Centr Press", Krasnodar, Saint Petersburg, 2008), 109-110.

32 Valerii Abramovich Musin, "Zakliuchenie kafedry Grazhdanskogo protsessa iuridicheskogo fakulteta Sankt-Peterburskogo Gosudarstvennogo Universiteta na proekt Grazhdanskogo protsessual`nogo kodeksa Rossiiskoi Federatsii", in Treushnikov, *op.cit.* note 27, 799.

After the collapse of the Soviet Union, there were joint activities between Russian and other Soviet-era lawyers and legal institutions, primarily within the CIS organization, to prepare similar legislation in new independent states. There are now several model laws and even recommendations by the inter-parliamentarian Assembly of the CIS countries, *e.g.*, the model civil code.[33] Several international conventions have been concluded by the CIS countries that play a very important role in unifying the legal bases for the different activities of people and states.

This kind of work continues, for example, within the inter-parliamentarian Assembly of the Euro-Asian Economic Union (*Mezhparlamentskoi Assamblei EvrAzES*).[34] It is clear that economic and other relations between former Soviet states are very close and active, and it is reasonable to harmonize the legal regulation governing collaboration in those regions.[35] In comparison, regional integration within the EU countries is far more highly regulated.

The policy of the Russian Federation does not clearly indicate whether the country prefers global economic and cultural co-operation with Western countries or whether closer co-operation and regional integration with Eastern European and Asian countries better serves its interests.

The state strategy of Russia will have a great relevance also for the legal co-operation and for the development of law in states more integrated with Russia. The EvrAzES has even prepared joint 'fundamentals of legislation' (*osnovy zakonodatel'stva*)[36] which are quite similar to the model of legislative drafting which was used in the Soviet Union. In this context, we should take into account not only the characteristics of law in the Soviet Union and the structure of the

33 Vilkova, *op.cit.* note 24, 83, 91. For a translation of, and unique commentary on, the most recent CIS model law in the private-law field, see 36(3/4)*Review of Central and East European Law* (2010), *The Harmonization of Corporate Law in the CIS. More Architecture of Choice*, William B. Simons (ed.), A *Review of Central and East European Law* Special Issue. Another issue of the *Review* contains discussions on—and, also, a translation of—CIS model legislation on bankruptcy. See 25(1/2)*Review of Central and East European Law* (1999), *The Legal Regulation of Bankruptcy: Russian Legislation and Models for the CIS*. Sarah Reynolds and William B. Simons (eds.), A *Review of Central and East European Law* Special Issue.

34 A.V. Toropygin and O.V. Mishal`tsenko, "Unifikatsiia i garmonizatsiia zakonodatel´stva v Evraziiskom Ekonomitseskom Soobshchestve", in D.V. Vinnitskii (ed.), *Rossiiskii ezhegodnik mezhdunarodnogo nalogovogo prava* (2009) No.1, 279-280.

35 D.V. Vinnitskii, "Evraziiskoe Ekonomicheskoe Soobshchestvo: pravovye instrumenty formirovaniia Tamozhennogo soiuza i Edinogo ekonomicheskogo prostranstva", in Vinnitskii, *op.cit.* note 34, 264-265.

36 *Ibid.*, 269-270.

state but, also, the fact that the law was created and had to operate under the pressure of ideology and politics.[37]

Observing the development of Russian jurisprudence in the framework of the global economy and legal world, the fundamental question is whether the Cold War was so long and the boundary between East and West so impenetrable as to isolate Russian law from the European legal civilization, from the previous bases of Russian Law. Even if there has been and still exists a strong policy aimed at integrating Russian law with the western European legal world, there are subjective forces and objective factors that focus more attention towards the eastern part of the world.

The focal historical question is whether we will see the creation and development of a new legal family, led by Russia that will replace the former socialist legal family.[38]

37 Legeais, *op.cit.* note 1, 109.

38 *Ibid.*, 200, 210, 230-231.

Russian International Law and Indeterminacy: Cold War and Post-Soviet Dynamics

Boris N. Mamlyuk[1]

In this chapter, I want to explore a paradox in the development of international legal theory at the height of the Cold War in the USSR and in its aftermath. Specifically, I want to analyze how—at the start of the Cold War (particularly the years 1953-1960)—leading Soviet international law theorists seemingly espoused a positivist framework for the preeminence of international law over international politics while simultaneously developing a set of indeterminate international legal theories and doctrines. Similarly, contemporary Russian approaches to international law and international institutions evoke 'exceptionalist' rhetoric;[2] yet, surprisingly, both theory and practice seem rooted in positivist conceptions. The main thesis here is that neither period represents a unique or paradoxical departure from mainstream international law. Rather, Soviet and contemporary Russian practice illustrate the indeterminate nature of international law at the high point of mid-twentieth century positivism, and that continuing legacy today.

This chapter explores this argument in three parts. The first section provides a very cursory overview of the indeterminacy critique of international law articulated by 'Newstream' international law scholars, led by David Kennedy and Martii Koskenniemi. The first section also invokes the typical characterization of Soviet approaches to international law as somehow trapped between strict positivism and *ad hoc* exceptionalism (*i.e.*, as indeterminate) rooted in the need for policy maneuverability. The second part analyzes the development—at the height

1 I owe a debt of gratitude to William Kratzke for re-familiarizing me with the work of Bernard Ramundo on peaceful coexistence; to Nikolay Mamluke for providing historical context; and to Tatiana Borisova and William Simons for their inexhaustible patience.

2 See R.B.J. Walker, "Lines of Insecurity: International, Imperial, Exceptional", 37(1) *Security Dialogue* (March 2006), 65, 69, (describing paradigmatic moments of transition and restoration (including Soviet & Russian) as inducing crises in the legitimacy of global order, leading to the characterization of the transgressing state as "international, imperial, exceptional"); Alexander I. Nikitin, "Russian Eurasianism and American Exceptionalism", in Michael D. Intriligator, A. I. Nikitin, Majid Tehranian (eds.), *Eurasia: A New Peace Agenda* (Elsevier, Amsterdam, 2005), 157, (comparing Russian and American national identities and drawing parallels between respective universalist ideologies and exceptionalist rhetoric); Aleksandr M. Tajmulin, "Globalization and Regionalization as Two Forms of World Order: Social-Philosophical Analysis", *Journal of Siberian Federal University: Humanities & Social Science* (2009), 379-383, available at <http://elib.sfu-kras.ru/bitstream/2311/1007/3/12_Tajmulin.pdf> (drawing on contemporary analyses of globalization and international law to argue that globalized processes are contrary to Russia's national interest); and Christopher J. Borgen, "The Language of Law and the Practice of Politics: Great Powers and the Rhetoric of Self-Determination in the Cases of Kosovo and South Ossetia", 10(1) *Chicago Journal of International Law* (2009).

Tatiana Borisova and William Simons, eds.
The Legal Dimension in Cold-War Interactions: Some Notes from the Field 81-104

of the Cold War—of the doctrine of peaceful coexistence and illustrates how Soviet theorists sought to formalize an indeterminate set of concepts concerning coexistence while preserving dueling and competing interpretations of coexistence for maximum policymaking advantage. The third section theorizes that the contemporary Russian fascination with natural law and positivist traditions in international law, in fact, is a retreat from allegations of Soviet-style duplicity in the use of international legal norms.

Indeterminacy, Generally, and Soviet Approaches to International Law

As suggested in the introduction, rather than prove exceptions, this chapter argues that both Soviet and contemporary Russian approaches to international law exemplify the indeterminacy and dynamics of contradiction in the structure of all international legal 'theories', positions, or arguments.[3] Whereas most Western scholars at the height of the Cold War saw Soviet attempts to balance competing contradictory positions of, on the one hand, an existing immutable global normative order, and on the other hand, a normative order based on the basis of evolving socialist state behavior as somehow disingenuous, a reexamination reveals that post-war Soviet international legal theory actually mirrored the patterns of legal indeterminacy which the Soviets saw in the 'bourgeois' West.

This is remarkable for two reasons. *First*, early Soviet international theorists such as Evgenii Pashukanis and Evgenii Korovin were among the first to articulate an indeterminacy critique of international law, and Interwar Soviet theory firmly rested on opposition to 'bourgeois' international law.[4] Therefore, it is important to understand the dynamics pursuant to which the Soviets interred their native critiques following the Second World War and appropriated dominant sets of international legal arguments.[5] *Second*, understanding the openness and mutability of Soviet international legal thought gives insights into contemporary Russian attempts both to constrain state behavior by international law while molding the content of such international rules, systems and processes. Before proceeding

3 See Martti Koskenniemi, *From Apology to Utopia: The Structure of International Legal Argument* (Finnish Lawyers' Publishing Company, Helsinki, 1989), 40-42; and Akbar Rasulov, "Writing about Empire: Remarks on the Logic of a Discourse", 23 *Leiden Journal of International Law* (2010), 449, 457.

4 See Boris N. Mamlyuk, *Perpetual Transition: Early Soviet and Post-Soviet International Legal Theory* (Martinus Nijhoff Publishers, Leiden, Boston, forthcoming); and Julius Stone, *Aggression and World Order: A Critique of United Nations Theories of Aggression* (Stevens & Sons, Ltd., London, 1958) 115 fn. 31 (discussing Pashukanis' later views that international law was merely an instrument of the struggle against the Western world).

5 This chapter is meant to suggest possible avenues for further research.

to the claims of Soviet indeterminacy, it is important to define the contours of the indeterminacy critique.

Generally, an indeterminacy critique of international law posits that in crucial doctrinal areas, international norms contain contradictory conceptions that allow state actors to make seemingly valid arguments by reference to either one of the competing interpretations of the doctrine, norm, rule, principle, etc.[6] Furthermore, the indeterminacy of particular norms of international law renders the entire international legal system unstable in that states can exploit contradictions in the rules to advance their political agendas. Simplified greatly, the indeterminacy critique thus attacks the very notion of objectivity in international law. It posits that in all doctrinal spheres, lawyers are left with seemingly valid arguments to challenge whatever position is opposed or to support whatever position is advanced.

As Koskenniemi points out, for an international legal rule to be objective—meaning that it is not rooted in ideological, political or personal subjectivity—a law must have concreteness and normativity.[7] By 'concreteness', Koskenniemi means that a law must be "verifiable, or justifiable, independently of what anyone might think the law should be".[8] 'Normativity', on the other hand, means that the law has to be "applicable even against a State (or other legal subject) which opposed its application to itself".[9] To render a rule objective, international actors (whether states or scholars) had to reconcile the contradictory demands for concreteness and normativity.[10] The process of reconciliation necessarily evokes 'descending' arguments for why a law is normative (and hence binding), countered by 'ascending' arguments for the law's concreteness.[11] As Koskenniemi writes:

> "The former [descending arguments] led beyond State will in a manner which seemed vulnerable because non-concrete (utopian); the latter [ascending arguments] led into particular State will because non-normative (apologist). [...] To make an ascending point you had to give a descending justification; and to [...] verify or justify your descending argument, you had to produce an ascending point."[12]

An easy example of an indeterminate character of an 'international law' is the contradictory definition of self-determination embodied in the 1970 UN Declaration of Principles of International Law. As one commentator has noted:

6 See, *e.g.*, David Kennedy, "A New Stream of International Law Scholarship", 7 *Wisconsin International Law Journal* (1988-1989); Martti Koskenniemi, "The Politics of International Law", 1 *European Journal of International Law* (1990), 4; and Nigel Purvis, "Critical Legal Studies in Public International Law", 32 *Harvard International Law Journal* (1991), 81.

7 Koskenniemi, *op.cit.* note 3, 458.

8 *Ibid.*

9 *Ibid.*

10 Koskenniemi, *op.cit.* note 3, 459.

11 *Ibid.*

12 *Ibid.*

> "On the one hand the Declaration proclaims that by virtue of the principle of self-determination 'all' peoples 'have the right freely to determine, without external interference, their political status' and that the modes of implementing this right are the 'establishment of a sovereign and independent state, the free association or integration with an independent state or the emergence into any other political status freely determined by a people'. On the other hand the declaration states that this shall not be construed 'as authorizing or encouraging any action which would dismember or impair, totally or in part, the territorial integrity or political unity of sovereign and independent states conducting themselves in compliance with the principle of equal rights and self-determination of peoples as described above and thus possessed of a government representing the whole people belonging to the territory without distinction as to race, creed or colour'. Thus there is no clear, coherent and determinate solution to the contradiction between the value of self-determination of peoples, on the one hand, and that of territorial integrity and political unity of states—on the other. This contradiction is merely restated."[13]

Charges of indeterminacy and nihilism were the essence of the Western critique of early Soviet international law. Post-WWII Soviet attempts to influence the development of international law (and, by extension, Soviet conduct in international relations) were also subject to the critique of indeterminacy.[14]

This is best illustrated by tracing the Soviet attempt to influence the development of the doctrine of non-aggression. On the one hand, the USSR was a champion of the codification of international law and a strident champion of efforts to develop an objective definition of 'aggression' in international law, primarily within the UN. At the same time, as shall be explored shortly, the Soviet Union's legal justifications for the 1956 suppression of uprisings in Hungary clearly fell both within and outside the Soviet definition, thereby rendering the Soviet definition indeterminate.

An early critic of this Soviet pattern of advocacy and avoidance was Julius Stone, who excoriated the Soviet stance on aggression because of its inconsistency, duplicity and ambiguity. Writing in 1958, Stone was keenly aware of the difficulty of defining aggression objectively although he believed in the theoretical possibility of a "determinate nucleus [of the law of aggression] within its otherwise indeterminate range and outline".[15] With respect to Soviet proposals, and Soviet policy justifications in support of such proposals, Stone remained skeptical.

Stone illustrated the indeterminacy of proposed definitions of 'aggression' by reference to the evolution of the definition proposed by the USSR to the International Law Commission in 1950 and the purported inconsistency of

13 Dencho Georgiev, "Politics or Rule of Law: Deconstruction and Legitimacy in International Law", 4(1) *European Journal of International Law* (1993).

14 See, generally, Zbigniew Brzezinski, *Ideology and Power in Soviet Politics* (Frederick A. Praeger, Publishers, New York, NY, 1967) (especially Chapter 5 discussing the role of ideology in shaping Soviet conceptions of international relations and Soviet desire to exploit ambiguities in ideology to select "various policy alternatives that may exist at any particular moment"); and *id.*, 136.

15 Stone, *op.cit.* note 4, 20.

Soviet action in Hungary in 1956 with its final proposed version.[16] To Stone, the fact that Soviets could simultaneously frame their arguments for the legality of the incursion into Hungary by distinguishing their actions from precisely that type of aggression they sought to define not only showed the indeterminate character of the proposed norm but, also, showed Soviet brazenness in deploying indeterminate legal arguments.

The Soviet proposal defined 'direct' or 'armed aggression' in the following way:

> "1. In an international conflict that State shall be declared the attacker which first commits one of the following acts:
>
> (a) Declaration of war against another state;
>
> (b) Invasion by its armed forces, even without a declaration of war, of the territory of another state;
>
> (c) Bombardment by its land, sea or air forces of the territory of another State or the carrying out of a deliberate attack on ships of another State or the carrying out of a deliberate attack on the ships or aircraft of the latter;
>
> (d) The landing or leading of its land, sea or air forces inside the boundaries of another State without the permission of the Government of the latter, or the violation of the conditions of such permission, particularly as regards the length of their stay or the extent of the area in which they may stay;
>
> (e) Naval blockade of the coasts or ports of another State;
>
> (f) Support of armed bands organized in its own territory which invade the territory of another State, or refusal, on being requested by the invaded state, to take in its own territory any action within its power to deny such bands any aid or protection."[17]

With respect to the proposed definition, the Soviet justification for the Hungarian incursion rested on 1(d) in that the Hungarian government requested aid from the USSR. Hence the 'leading in' of Soviet land and other forces was made with permission of Hungary.[18] According to Stone, this was incredible given that the Nagy government would not give permission for its own overthrow.[19] Consequently, the Soviet Union had to have an ancillary source of authority for permission to intervene. Indeed, the Soviets argued that Hungarian consent to intervene was part of the 'mutual defense' obligations of the Warsaw Pact of 14 May 1955.[20] To Stone, this also seemed disingenuous given that the mutual de-

16 *Ibid.*, 115. The 1950 proposal was based in substance on a 1933 proposal. The revised text was submitted to the International Law Commission in 1950, and a final proposal version appeared in 1953. *Ibid.*, 46, 115 fn. 32.

17 *Ibid.*

18 Stone, *op.cit.* note 4, 2, fn. 2.

19 *Ibid.*

20 *Ibid.*

fense obligations (Art.4 of the Warsaw Pact) envisioned defense against the armed attack of another state.[21] Because the factual context of the events in Hungary suggested an internal uprising, it was 'legally dubious' to invoke Article 4 mutual defense obligations.[22] Thus, the Soviets advanced a *further* legal rationale for the suppression of the internal uprising: that is, an interpretation of 'armed attack' as related to capitalist states *versus* relations among socialist states.[23] We shall revisit this Soviet distinction between capitalist-state relations and socialist-state relations, the so-called doctrine of 'socialist internationalism', in the following section. But, for present purposes, it is important to highlight Stone's criticism of Soviet attempts to advance a seemingly determinate definition of aggression while simultaneously exploiting ambiguities in the proposed norm to advance a diametrically different policy objective.

Returning to Koskenniemi's heuristic of ascending/descending arguments, we can conceive of the Soviet proposal as an attempt to establish the normativity of the prohibition of armed aggression. The descending argument for normativity was the prohibition of the threat or use of force found in Article 2(4) of the UN Charter, binding states by virtue of state consent (adoption of the Charter). The ascending argument for the concreteness of the prohibition of armed aggression was the supposedly categorical and determinate content of previous Soviet and non-Soviet proposals—the earliest Soviet ones being articulated as early as 1933.[24] Of course, the motivations for an objective definition of aggression were also dynamic and evolving. In the 1930s, the Soviet motivation was fear of interventionism and invasion, and the utopian hope that legal assurances (in the form of agreements of collective security, non-aggression, peaceful aid and cooperation), legal definitions (particularly of aggression), and legal institutions (Soviet accession to the League of Nations in 1934) would hold off attack.[25] To a lesser extent, Soviet advocacy for a determinate definition of aggression also served the propaganda purpose of showing the progressive nature of Soviet law *versus* reactionary 'bourgeois' practice, geared at dependent nations.

As explained below, the tactical necessity of defining 'aggression' in the early 1950s was similar although with additional nuances. Perhaps less concerned with its own strict territorial boundaries—due to the deterrent effect the Soviet nuclear arsenal had on any potential interlopers—the Soviet Union was extremely concerned with securing, by military and legal means, its exclusive right of maneuver in territories it controlled following WWII. As Stone pointed out, "the objective political meaning of a definition centered on armed invasion of territory

21 *Ibid.*

22 *Ibid.*

23 *Ibid.*

24 *Ibid.*, 115.

25 See *ibid.*, 115, fn. 31.

and declaration of war, is [intended] to give an extra stamp of legitimacy and collective guarantee to [post-WWII Soviet territorial] gains".[26] Together with the promulgation of the doctrine of peaceful coexistence, a definition of aggression would also have solidified the then-emerging Soviet sphere of influence, not only in its near abroad but, also, with respect to newly emerging states. This was particularly important following the Sino-Soviet split, resulting in part from Khruschev's announcement of peaceful coexistence in 1956. Lastly, defining aggression arguably lent support to (and helped to distinguish) related doctrines, such as the use of force to achieve self-determination—supported by the Soviet Union and emerging Third World states, but vehemently opposed by the West.[27]

Thus far, we have examined the general contours of the indeterminacy critique of international law and examined, at least, one line of Western criticism of the Soviet conceptualization of a particular international law doctrine (prohibition of armed aggression) as containing two competing and contradictory lines of authority: one categorically prohibiting aggression and labeling that state an 'attacker' which, for instance, issues a declaration of war or invades the territory of another state; another category that gives the right to land or lead in "land, sea or air forces inside the boundaries of another State [with] the permission of the Government of the latter".[28] We will return to Western critiques of the duplicitous use of international law by the USSR shortly; but, for the present, we shall turn to the development of a related doctrine, peaceful coexistence.

Study in Cold-War Soviet Indeterminacy: Peaceful Coexistence

It is commonly accepted that the origin of peaceful coexistence (*mirnoe sosushchestvovanie*) was Soviet Premier Nikita Khrushchev's address in 1956 at the Twentieth CPSU Congress signaling the ideological shift from continued and inevitable confrontation with the West to a policy of peaceful coexistence and cooperation in limited spheres.[29] The policy impetus for the recognition of the

26 *Ibid.*, 116.

27 Noah Weisbord, "Conceptualizing Aggression", 20 *Duke Journal of Comparative & International Law* (2009), 1, 25.

28 Comparing paragraph 1(b) and paragraph 1(d) of the 1953-1956 Soviet proposal, it is important to note how the language itself is suggestive of the contradiction and ambivalence of the norm—a state that 'invades' by way of, say, 'bombardment' is an 'attacker' committing armed aggression; a state that 'lands' its forces inside the permitting state has the right to 'stay', as long as the state 'leading in' or landing 'air forces', stays on the territory permitted by the host state, *i.e.*, so long as it does not overstay its welcome. See Koskenniemi, *op.cit.* note 3, xxi (discussing how legal argument proceeds by establishing a system of conceptual differentiations and using it to justify whatever doctrine, position or rule (*i.e.*, whatever argument) one needs to justify).

29 Grigorii I. Tunkin, *Theory of International Law* (1974), 36; and *id.*, "Coexistence and International Law", 95 *Recueil des cours* (1958).

doctrine was the realization—following the conclusion of the Korean War in 1953—that chemical, biological, and nuclear war between East and West would result in mutually assured destruction, and war and continued escalation of armed tensions between the Soviet Union and the US was not acceptable.[30] Although leading Soviet theorists like Tunkin sought to establish that principles of peaceful coexistence existed in early Soviet international legal theory,[31] coexistence as a strategic necessity and a doctrinal tenet of Soviet theory began to be fully articulated only after 1956.

From the Soviet perspective, peaceful coexistence implied the development of two competing international legal planes: (1) an international law governing relations among socialist states and capitalist states; and (2) a separate body of law governing relations among socialist states.[32] Given that post-WWII Soviet theorists continued earlier general critiques of 'Western' international law—particularly in the context of nonaligned countries and in the context of colonialism—peaceful coexistence also can be interpreted as embodying at least three additional legal planes: (3) relations among capitalist states (West-West relations); (4) relations among capitalist states and their colonies or protectorates; (5) relations among capitalist states and/or socialist states and nonaligned countries.[33]

On the most general plane, the international 'law of peaceful coexistence' was expressed as containing two discrete principles of general international law: peaceful coexistence (as a general principle recognized by all nations); 'socialist internationalism' (representing the highest level of cooperation and collaboration between members of the socialist bloc).[34] To attain recognition of the 'law of peaceful coexistence', Soviet theorists advanced four separate legal bases for the existence of the norm. *First*, peaceful coexistence was embodied in the UN Charter (just as with aggression) and, hence, binding as a principle of conventional law for UN members and also reflecting a generally accepted principle of international law. *Second*, for non-UN members, peaceful coexistence existed as a principle of customary international law.[35] *Third*, just as with the doctrine of aggression,

30 Bernard A. Ramundo, *Peaceful Coexistence: International Law in the Building of Communism* (Johns Hopkins Press, Baltimore, MD, 1967), 9; and Ivo Lapenna, "The Legal Aspects and Political Significance of the Soviet Conception of Co-existence", 12 *International and Comparative Law Quarterly* (1963), 737.

31 G.I. Tunkin, "Sorok let sosushchestvovaniia i mezhdunarodnoe pravo", *Sovetskii ezhegodnik mezdunarodnogo prava* (1958), 15. All translations from the Russian are by the author of this work unless otherwise noted.

32 Ramundo, *op.cit.* note 30, 10.

33 "Despite an early flirtation with the view that the principles of socialist internationalism govern relations between socialist and neutralist states, the Soviets now say that the applicable principles are those of peaceful coexistence." *Ibid.*, 11.

34 *Ibid.*

35 *Ibid.*, 13.

Soviets advocated for the codification of the principles of peaceful coexistence as a source of soft law, reflecting the opinions of the most highly qualified jurists.[36] *Lastly*, peaceful coexistence emanated as a *jus cogens* norm from the 'scientific international law' of Marxism-Leninism: "Peaceful coexistence is an historical fact, objective reality, the natural process of social development and the basic international legal norm."[37]

The emphasis on formality and the adoption of peaceful coexistence as an international norm had at least three purposes. *First*, as Koskenniemi writes, to seem legitimate, "a legal project for world order must appear formal".[38] By casting peaceful coexistence in formal terms, the Soviet conception of 'socialist internationalism'—distinguishing relations among socialist states *versus* capitalist-socialist or capitalist-capitalist relations—could gain legitimacy not just in the socialist bloc but, presumably, also in the West. As an alternative normative order, peaceful coexistence also would give legitimacy to the notion of perpetually contested international ideas—political ideologies, modes of economic development, human rights, and so forth—in different camps. *Second*, the emphasis on formality was necessary to reconcile Soviet theory with fundamental Marxist tenets of the withering away of the state during the higher phase of communism,[39] as well as to deal with the deeper dilemma that the need for coexistence did not stem from a conflict between the social productive forces and the relations of production, but from technological advances in weaponry.[40] *Third*, characterization of peaceful coexistence in formal terms was indispensable to maintain Soviet adherence to the very notion of a universal, consent-derived, general international law binding on all states.[41] Absent recognition or adoption of peaceful coexistence, international law would necessarily be fragmented into two systems—Western/capitalist international law and socialist international law—and the *de facto* and *de jure* schism would constrain Soviet foreign policy. Formal recognition of peaceful coexistence, on the other hand, would provide a legal basis for flexibility in the conduct of foreign relations, whether in the Soviet Eurasian sphere of influence, or with respect to military interventions in Africa

36 John N. Hazard, "Codifying Peaceful Co-Existence", 55 *American Journal of International Law* (1960), 109 (discussing early codification attempts by the International Law Association).

37 Ramundo, *op.cit.* note 30, 12, 16.

38 Koskenniemi, *op.cit.* note 3, 431.

39 A.K. Belykh, "On the Dialectic of the Withering Away of the State" (1963), in Zigurds L. Zile (ed.), *Ideas and Forces in Soviet Legal History: A Reader on the Soviet State and Law* (Oxford University Press, New York, NY, 1992), 404.

40 "Although the objective laws of social development are invoked, the heart of the matter is the impermissibility of nuclear warfare, producing the non-Marxist result that interdependence based upon technological advances in weaponry, rather than Marxism-Leninism, has dictated the policy and law of coexistence." Ramundo, *op.cit.* note 30, 16.

41 *Ibid.*, 18.

or (later) Afghanistan in support of proletarian revolutions, or softer forms of foreign assistance and intervention in neutralist states like Egypt.

This last point, the potential logical disconnect between universalism and peaceful coexistence of two diametrically different economic and social systems nicely illustrates the manipulability and reversibility of peaceful coexistence as a legal concept. As Koskenniemi argues, reversibility is the capacity of a given legal concept to be projected with a meaning which "links it both to the ascending and the descending conceptual scheme".[42] Whichever is chosen—whether descending (peaceful coexistence is a natural-law type doctrine that guaranteed largely peaceful relations between European states in the nineteenth century), or ascending (peaceful coexistence is a progressive principle sponsored by the Soviet state and other socialist states and recognized by other non-socialist states)—is not dependent on any natural essence but, rather, on the interpreter's position. From the standpoint of the Soviet Union, this broad and multi-pronged conception of the origins and scope of peaceful coexistence satisfied the need to provide Soviet policy makers with legal arguments that could support particular policy outcomes, even competing ones. In this way, we can imagine peaceful coexistence through a defensive *or* offensive lens, as a shield or a sword. Along with the proposed prohibition of armed aggression, peaceful coexistence could be deployed defensively in support of preserving the *status quo* standoff between East and West. Conversely, the legal doctrines could be deployed offensively to provide a limited (or expansive, depending on the context) right of engagement with nonaligned or neutral states. Moreover, because of its intentionally sweeping substantive scope, peaceful coexistence could be easily manipulated as a restatement of sovereignty principles or self-determination, further burnishing its rhetorical shine on the global political stage. Soviets could deploy this defensive interpretation to protect the right of socialist states to be left alone, and also to protect the rights of given non-aligned states to resist exploitative imperialists while awaiting their own revolutions.

From 1956, in an attempt to define peaceful coexistence in such a way as to reconcile socialist internationalism (the body of international law dealing with relations among socialist states) with universalism, Soviet theorists redefined and expanded traditional definitions of core international law concepts (including that of 'international law' itself) to place emphasis on the doctrine of peaceful coexistence.[43] The doctrine of coexistence was further fragmented so that coexistence principles on each plane of state relations could be connected to universal principles:

42 Koskenniemi, *op.cit.* note 3, 449.

43 Ramundo, *op.cit.* note 30, 24-25.

— Law of peaceful coexistence, operating on the plane of contemporary international law (universal, applying to all states);
— Principles of peaceful coexistence, operating on the plane of general international law (applying to nations in UN system);
— Socialist coexistence/principles of socialist internationalism, operating on the plane of relations among socialist states (applying to socialist states).[44]

More importantly, peaceful coexistence was defined by Tunkin as a programmatic concept, embodying future development:

> "Enriching the future development of international law, it [peaceful coexistence] at the same time contains the potential for a whole program of progressive development of international law, of many new principles and norms which are dictated by life and can be logically deduced from the principle of coexistence but which are still not generally recognized principles of international law."[45]

At the height of the Cold War, Bernard A. Ramundo—an American analyst and Russian-law scholar—readily identified the 'dualism' of the concept, "combining law in being and law in the making" and warned of the potential for abuse:

> "The law of peaceful coexistence must reflect, in Marxist terms of base and superstructure, the policy of peaceful coexistence dictated by the immutable, scientific laws of social development derivable from the basic tenets of Marxism-Leninism. Thus, either because the foreign policy of the Soviet Union presumptively is consistent with peaceful coexistence, or because the Community Party of the Soviet Union enjoys papal like authority in interpreting the basic laws of social development when formulating Soviet policy, *the basis is laid for an international legal order responsible to the policy needs of the Soviet Union.*"[46]

To Ramundo, the principle of peaceful coexistence seemed especially suspect since—combined with Soviet interpretations of self-determination and illegality of colonialism as *jus cogens* norms—peaceful coexistence gave additional legal justification for the Soviet anti-colonial policy of military support for national liberation movements.[47] Furthermore, since the USSR categorized neo-colonialism as functionally identical to nineteenth century armed colonialism, and placed in the former category indirect forms of colonialism—such as capitulations, vassal statehood, protectorates, mandates and trustee relationships,[48] direct economic and cultural aid, and the Peace Corps[49]—the law of peaceful coexistence did not preclude Soviet intervention against what *it* deemed as colonial practice or incur-

44 See *ibid.*

45 G.I. Tunkin, "Printsip mirnogo sosushchestvovaniia: general'naia liniia vneshnepoliticheskoi deiatel'nosti KPSS i sovetskoe gosudarstvo", 7 *Sovetskoe gosudarstvo i pravo* (1963), 26-27.

46 Ramundo, *op.cit.* note 30, 30 (emphasis added).

47 *Ibid.*, 147.

48 *Ibid.*, 143.

49 *Ibid.*, 148 (quoting Vladimir Kudryavtsev, "Asia and Africa: Solidarity v. Aggression", *Moscow News* (2 October 1965) No.40, 7).

sions. To emphasize this point further, because colonialism and neocolonialism were seen as Western institutions, Soviet forms of cultural, military and economic aid were consistent with coexistence; Western forms of aid were not.[50] In terms characteristic of more general Western critiques of the Soviet practice of advocating for general 'rules' of international law for the benefit of oppressed peoples and classes, Michael Akehurst, writing in 1970, commented that "it is the very vagueness of these rules which makes it possible for the Soviet Union to suggest them without running any risk of being regarded as guilty of violating them".[51]

At this point, we have examined the indeterminate nature of two separate international law doctrines from the standpoint of Cold-War Soviet theory: (1) aggression; and (2) peaceful coexistence (with its myriad constituent Medusa/*Matryoshka*-like doctrines). This section also endeavored to show how Soviet theory conflated peaceful coexistence principles with more established doctrines of self-determination and sovereignty. At this point, the question arises whether the indeterminate theories were actually put into practice or whether the aforementioned contradictory justifications for the invasion of Hungary, for instance, were anomalous, one-off, affairs. To put it more bluntly, was Soviet theory/practice essentially positivist with an indeterminate façade or was it indeterminate with a positivist façade?

In the period immediately after WWII, with the USSR's emergence as a true superpower on the world stage, many genuinely hoped that the Soviet Union's active stance at the UN reflected renewed potential for international law and global cooperation. Eminent Western scholars of Soviet law, such as Professor John N. Hazard, were cautiously optimistic that the realities of the Cold-War era would bring an end to the "spinning of fine theories",[52] and reorient Soviet-Western relations along more pragmatic lines. To non-area-specialists writing at the height of the Cold War, Soviet proposals for the recognition of the law of peaceful coexistence, general *jus cogens* norms of anti-colonialism, self-determination, efforts to define/codify aggression, were clearly aimed for the consumption by newly independent peoples in Afro-Asian countries—more propaganda than genuine attempts to redefine formal legal rules.[53] Western commentators were quick to point out that with respect to its relations with capitalist states, the Soviet Union maintained rigid adherence to positivist principles, developing state practice of punctilious treaty making and insisting on firm observation of United Nations procedural rules.[54]

50 *Ibid.*, 147 (describing Soviet categorization of its aid as "unselfish, fraternal assistance").

51 Michael Akehurst, *A Modern Introduction to International Law* (Atherton Press, New York, NY, 1970), 31.

52 John N. Hazard, "Pashukanis is No Traitor", 51 *American Journal of International Law* (1957), 385, 388.

53 Akehurst, *op.cit.* note 51, 31-32.

54 See Christopher Osakwe, *The Participation of the Soviet Union in Universal International Organizations: A Political and Legal Analysis of Soviet Strategies and Aspirations Inside ILO,*

But as argued above, a direct consequence of the adoption of the doctrine of peaceful coexistence was also its thinly veiled resurrection of traditional Westphalian notions of spheres of influence—best seen in Russia's justifications for armed suppression of anti-communist uprisings not just in Hungary but, also, in Czechoslovakia and elsewhere.[55] Returning to the Soviet justification for the invasion of Hungary, we can observe how the Soviet Union deployed different sets of arguments in support of its actions. As mentioned above, its original rationale was that Soviet armed action was necessary to provide 'mutual defense' of a signatory state in the Warsaw Pact, hence not 'aggression'. In November 1956, in response to growing pressure from the UN General Assembly,[56] which in resolutions asserted that the Soviet invasion violated Article 2(4) of the UN Charter, the Soviet Union changed its position. As noted by Stone, Soviet legal authorities claimed that the USSR "was acting in collective self-defense with Hungary under Article 51 of the Charter, and Article 5 of the Warsaw Pact, alleging 'indirect aggression' by other states against Hungary".[57] Whether or not this form of double entendre—the assertion of mutual-defense and non-aggression, followed by an assertion of self-defense in response to indirect aggression—was emblematic of the structure of general (not merely Soviet) international legal argument,[58] it carried life or death consequences insofar as it was invoked by Soviet authorities in support of particular decisions to intervene.

To what extent, however, was Soviet indeterminacy in the Cold-War period exceptional? Or, if not exceptional, were Soviet modes of argumentation in the contested domain of international law qualitatively different from Western ones? At this point, a set of general observations can suggest possible avenues for further research. *First*, I think it is vitally important to understand how the military stalemate between the Cold-War superpowers actually opened a creative

UNESCO and WHO (A.W. Sijthoff Publishers, Leiden, The Netherlands, 1972). See, generally, Jan F. Triska and Robert M. Slusser, *Theory, Law and Policy of Soviet Treaties* (Stanford University Press, Stanford-Palo Alto, CA, 1962).

55 Akehurst, *op.cit.* note 51, 12 (discussing Soviet Union's public justification for invasion of Czechoslovakia in 1968 as grounded in right to intervene in affairs of a state within a sphere of influence). Aside from Hungary and Czechoslovakia, the Soviet Union faced disaffection within the Warsaw Pact sphere in the form of, in chronological order: (1) Berlin uprising of 17 June 1953 (suppressed by Soviet troops); (2) the rise to power of Polish nationalist leader Gomulka in 1956; (3) the aforementioned Hungarian uprising in October-November 1956 (suppressed by Soviet troops); (4) the defection of Albania from the Warsaw Pact in 1960-1961; (5) Romania's assertions of national independence from 1962 onwards; (6) the aforementioned Czechoslovak 'spring' of 1968; and (7) the Polish 'workers' revolt' of December 1970. US Department of State, *Background Notes: USSR* (September 1975), 9.

56 The UNGA adopted resolutions calling for withdrawal of Soviet troops and admission of UN observers. UN A/RES/1127-1133(XI) (1956); and Stone, *op.cit.* note 4, 2 fn. 2.

57 Stone, *op.cit.* note 4, 2 fn. 2.

58 See, generally, David Kennedy, "Theses about International Law Discourse", 23 *German Yearbook of International Law* (1980), 353.

space for the re-imagination of international law along liberal, neo-progressive, or radical lines. If, as China Miéville argues, force typically resolves a contest between 'equal rights' (equally persuasive legal justifications on either side of an indeterminate international legal norm),[59] what alternative space was opened by the counterbalance of equal forces during the height of the Cold War? This is important, I think, to unlock our imaginings about alternative global structures or models of global governance that might have been—and may still be—possible. That is, even if political will and force ultimately drive policy, how will international law develop during the next phase of stalemate-configured force? *Second*, it is important to note that even though Soviet theory and practice clearly exploited dueling conceptions of international norms,[60] other international actors acted in functionally similar ways. In 1956 alone, concurrently with the drafting of the definition of aggression and the Soviet invasion of Hungary, Israel crossed its borders in Gaza and Sinai in an armed incursion to eliminate 'Fedayeen raiders', British and French troops carried out an invasion of the Suez Canal Zone, and instability prevailed in Indochina and Africa.[61] A *third* observation involves the effectiveness of international law as a rhetorical device to grant legitimacy to particular sets of doctrines rather than others. In the context of later periods in the Cold War, this can be studied by reference to, for instance, the failure of the US to label the Soviet war in Afghanistan as aggression,[62] and similar ambivalence on the part of the Soviet Union with respect to American incursions within the American sphere of influence of the time (*i.e.*, Grenada, Panama). Similarly, we can think of the impact of the Cold War on the foregrounding of certain qualitatively 'more-indeterminate' concepts such as self-determination and sovereignty over other 'less-indeterminate' concepts such as consensual jurisdiction to international tribunals or disarmament. *Lastly*, understanding these Cold-War dynamics also has the benefit of shedding light on the development of international law following the collapse of the Soviet Union, a topic that I would like to survey in the remaining pages of this chapter.

59 China Miéville, *Between Equal Rights: A Marxist Theory of International Law* (Haymarket Books, Chicago, IL, 2006).

60 Julius Stone, "Hopes and Loopholes in the 1974 Definition of Aggression", 71 *American Journal of International Law* (1977), 224, 234.

61 Stone, *op.cit.* note 4, 1.

62 Oscar Schachter, Deane R. Hinton, Rosalyn Higgins, Farooq Hassan, Stephen M. Schwebel and Benjamin B. Ferencz, "Legal Responses to the Afghan/Iranian Crises", 74 *Proceedings of the Annual Meeting (American Society of International Law)* (1980), 248-274.

Contemporary Russian International Law: Naturalism, Positivism and Indeterminacy

The usual starting points for a study of contemporary Russian international law are historical and conceptual. From the standpoint of international legal history, a typical comparative frame of reference is the late Soviet period (post-1970), followed by *perestroika* in the mid-1980s, followed by transformation and radical reform in the 1990s. Yet the post-Soviet period shares a number of deeply suggestive parallels with the early Cold-War period that are important to highlight. Both periods saw profound realignments: geo-politically (the rise of USSR as a superpower after WWII, the rise of the BRICs in the post-Soviet period); institutionally (the rise of the UN system in the post-WWII period, the coming of age of the WTO and the proliferation of regional trade bodies in the post-Soviet period); intellectually (liberal internationalism *versus* neo-liberalism), and so forth.

Conceptually, whether or not there is something akin to a unique Russian approach to international law emerging in the post-Soviet period is a subject outside of the scope of this chapter. Similarly, it is impossible to delve into the debates concerning Marxist influence on post-Soviet law. In fact, as has been suggested elsewhere, observance of Marxist principles in late Soviet international legal theory had long been illusory: in late Soviet theory and practice, Marxism was little more than a rhetorical tool used by Soviet theorists to conceal the problematic fact that there were only minor differences between Soviet conceptions of public international law and the then-dominant Western notions of the international legal order.[63]

Western scholarship presents divergent views on the question of development of a unique contemporary Russian international legal theory. For instance, in his 2003 introduction to the second edition of Professor Tunkin's *Theory of International Law*, the Soviet-Russian-law scholar Professor William E. Butler notes that "there is no 'substitute' or 'replacement' theory, as yet, to supersede the insights into international behavior identified [in the 1960-80s] by Academician G.I. Tunkin".[64] Others, such as Tarja Langstrom, suggest that Russia has indeed

63 G.I. Tunkin, "Mezhdunarodnoe pravo: nasledstvo XX veka", 7 *Rossiiskii Ezhegodnik Mezhdunarodnogo Prava* (1992), 16 fn.5 (this is a revised version of Ch. 3, § 3 of Tunkin's 1992 Hague *Cours*).

64 W.E. Butler, "Introduction", in G.I. Tunkin, *Theory of International Law* (Wildy Simmonds & Hill Publishing, Ltd., London, 2nd ed. W.E. Butler, transl. 2003), xiii. G.I. Tunkin (1906-1993) was the most prominent Soviet international lawyer of the post-WWII era. He served as the *doyen* of the international law profession in the Soviet Union, including as the president of the Soviet Association of International Law, as chief editor of the Soviet Yearbook of International Law, and as the leading publicist for over forty years from the early 1950s until his death in 1993. Tunkin read four lectures at The Hague Academy of International Law over the course of his career. These lectures were published in the following volumes: G.I. Tunkin, "Co-existence and International Law", 95 *Recueil des cours* (1958),

developed a replacement theory—idionsynchratic though it be—and that it is on its way to developing both a liberal international outlook and a system of domestic democratic governance.[65] Scholars such as Lauri Mälksoo and Tarja Langstrom have attempted to analyze the development of doctrinal pluralism in Russia by unpacking divergent theoretical streams in Russian international law hornbooks.[66]

Perhaps more important than Western views on the topic is the fact that leading contemporary Russian international lawyers have claimed that Russia has developed an alternative approach to international law, though in what respects and in what degrees remains to be seen.[67] Whether or not Russian approaches are markedly different from contemporary general international law doctrines, Russian theorists have clearly sought to project a new commitment to liberal internationalism—but with a somehow different Russian aspect. Typically, this takes the form of pronouncements regarding Russia's respect for the 'international rule of law' and the demise of ideology in Russian theory and practice. For instance, as early as 2001, writing in the introduction to the new Russian legal encyclopedia, Professor B.N. Topornin—then director of the Institute of State and Law of the Russian Academy of Sciences (*IGPAN*)—sought to signal a clear break with ostensibly exceptional earlier Soviet positions.[68] Topornin's editorial introduction is worth quoting at length:

> "Russia has a qualitatively new legal system. As a matter of fact, this does not mean mechanical replacement of Soviet legislation with new Russian codes. More substantively, the new Russian law derives from principles of private ownership and market economics, and the active and full participation of Russia in the system of international political, economic and cultural ties."[69]

1-81; *id.*, "The Legal Nature of the United Nations", 119 *Recueil des cours* (1966), 1-68; *id.*, "International Law in the International System", 147 *Recueil des cours* (1975), 1-218; and *id.*, "Politics, Law and Force in the Interstate System", 219 *Recueil des cours* (1992), 227-395. Volume 219 of the Cours was delivered in 1992 but published as the 1989 edition. G.I. Tunkin, *Theory of International Law* (1970); and Eric Myles, "Review: Tunkin, Theory of International Law", 41 *Canadian Yearbook of International Law* (2003), 619.

65 Tarja Langstrom, *Transformation in Russia and International Law* (Martinus Nijhoff Publishers, Leiden, Boston, 2003), 442.

66 Lauri Mälksoo, "International Law in Russian Textbooks: What's in the Doctrinal Pluralism?", 1 *Göttingen Journal of International Law* (2009), 279, 283; and Langstrom, *op.cit.* note 65.

67 Boris N. Mamlyuk, "International Law: A Russian Introduction (V.I. Kuznetsov, B.R. Tuzmukhamedov, eds.)", 35 *Review of Central and East European Law* (2010), 111 (review essay).

68 B.N. Topornin *et al.* (eds.), *Iuridicheskaia Entsiklopediia* (Jurist, Moscow, 2001).

69 *Ibid.*, vii.

The allusion to full integration in international affairs signaled Russia's commitment to international judicial tribunals, something Soviet practice discouraged.[70] Topornin continued:

> "The development of Russian law depends on the process of harmonization of different contemporary legal orders, first and foremost, continental and common law, but also the process of internationalization of legal institutions."[71]

More recently, in a 2009 article in the *Chinese Journal of International Law*, Professor Sergei Marochkin, an Honored Jurist of the Russian Federation,[72] sought to describe "the social nature of international law", in terms strikingly similar to classic Soviet themes of peaceful coexistence, observing that "[international law] has grown from the law of only the so-called 'civilized' nations into the law of communication among all States with different social systems and with different backgrounds, meaning developed States, developing States and emerging States".[73] Yet aside from prefatory remarks and general pronouncements, is there more substantial evidence of Russia's genuine shift towards liberal international models, or possibly other alternative outlooks on global governance?

In the remaining space of this chapter, I would like to discuss the theory of international law advanced by Stanislav Valentinovich Chernichenko (1935-) in his *Ocherki po filosofii i mezhdunarodnomu pravu* (*Essays on Philosophy and International Law*).[74] One of the leading contemporary Russian international legal theorists,[75] Chernichenko has been a longtime professor at the Ministry of Foreign Affairs' Moscow-based Diplomatic Academy (*MGIMO*) and has served in various leading diplomatic and academic roles in a long and distinguished career.[76] As a 1958 graduate of Moscow State University (*MGU*), Chernichenko presumably witnessed firsthand all five main periods in the development of Soviet/Russian international law: (1) pre-1956 'transition theory of international law' (Soviet accommodation to general international law in the period of the building of communism); (2) post-1956 emergence of the principle of peaceful coexistence; (3) liberalization from *perestroika* to the collapse of Soviet Union;

70 Triska *et al.*, *op.cit.* note 54, 384.

71 *Ibid.*, vii.

72 Sergei Yu. Marochkin, "On the Recent Development of International Law: Some Russian Perspectives", 8 *Chinese Journal of International Law* (2009), 695.

73 *Ibid.*, 3.

74 S.V. Chernichenko, *Ocherki po filosofii i mezhdunarodnomu pravu* (Nauchnaia Kniga, Moscow, 2009).

75 S.V. Chernichenko, *Teoriia mezhdunarodnogo prava* (NIMP, Moscow, 1999); and *id.*, *Mezhdunarodnoe pravo: sovremennye teoreticheskie problemy* (Mezhdunarodnye Otnosheniia, Moscow, 1993).

76 "Stanislav Valentinovich Chernichenko", *Bol'shaia biograficheskaia entsiklopediia* (2009), available at <http://dic.academic.ru/dic.nsf/enc_biography/16288/Черниченко>.

(4) transition to monism[77] in the immediate wake of the collapse of the USSR; and (5) theoretical reformulation following Russia's reemergence as a regional hegemon.

More importantly, in the deeply fragmented Russian academic sphere, where rigid disciplinary divides usually discourage sweeping interdisciplinary studies of international law, philosophy, sociology and international relations, a work by a leading theorist encompassing precisely this scope is, frankly, rare. That Chernichenko's *Essays* represent one of the first major attempts by a post-Soviet theorist to present a systematic overview of the nature, function, and limits of international law makes the work clearly deserving of much greater study than can be attempted here. Nevertheless, a more limited examination is certainly warranted and possible. Specifically, my goal is to interrogate whether Chernichenko's philosophy presents a novel approach regarding the nature of international law from the perspective of the post-Soviet state, or whether Chernichenko's philosophy retraces the familiar naturalistic or positivistic tropes that dominated Western international legal theory in the nineteenth and twentieth centuries and, hence, subject to the same indeterminacy critique advanced above with respect to general international law (section 1) and classic Soviet international law (section 2).

The starting point for Chernichenko is a disclaimer of previous Marxist conceptions of international law—a common technique adopted in post-Soviet international law literature.[78] In the preface, epilogue[79] and elsewhere in the text, Chernichenko makes clear that his attempt to build an epistemology of international law is premised on a depoliticized, de-ideologized, objective view of international law and international relations.[80] Although such a claim is *a priori* suspect to one versed in critical approaches to international law, the claim of objectivity is worth exploring for it is, ironically, rooted in Hegelian and Marxist logic.[81] In other words, while dismissing Soviet Marxist ideology, Chernichenko is firmly committed to Soviet Marxist 'scientific' method. Therefore, Chernichenko

77 Monism, or the primacy of international law over domestic law, was enshrined in Art.15(4) of the 1993 Russian Constitution.

78 See George Ginsburgs, *From Soviet to Russian International Law: Studies in Continuity and Change*, in William B. Simons (ed.), *Law in Eastern Europe*, No.48 (Martinus Nijhoff Publishers, Leiden, Boston, 1998).

79 Chernichenko, *op.cit.* note 74, 761.

80 "At one point, humanity believed in the illusion that the teachings of Marx and Engels would unlock the secrets of social development [...] but life has shown this to not be true." *Ibid.*, 19. "In my previous days, I used to advance novel conceptions of how international law as superstructure 'develops' from the interrelationship of various bases. It is not worth mentioning that in domestic Soviet legal scholarship, such debates carried ideological stamps. Returning to these positions now is senseless." *Ibid.*, 675.

81 *Ibid.*, 728.

studies international law as a material reality, amenable to scientific inquiry.[82] While it is influenced by sociological, political, moral and other influences, law does have an immutable essence, an objective kernel that can be identified, found and studied. This naturalistic view forms the *first* level of international law for Chernichenko.[83] However, natural law cannot regulate social life; it merely informs our understanding of international law—what Chernichenko calls our 'international legal consciousness' (*mezhdunarodno-pravovoe soznanie*).[84] "International law does regulate social relations, not directly, but through positive law."[85] Therefore, Chernichenko invokes positive state-made law as the *second* level of law on the international plane. Positive law is created as a result of state-to-state relations, whether in the context of treaty-making or as a result of state practice and the development of firm customs.[86] From there, states form what Chernichenko labels subjective international law, that is, particular states' interpretation/implementation of treaties or customary norms.[87] *Next*, Chernichenko identifies international legal consciousness as the subjective interpretation of agents of state actors, whether commentators, diplomats, or other leading political figures.[88] International legal consciousness is informed by natural law or positivistic principles, but it is inherently subjective, being the product of competing state interests, actors and the actors' agents (scholars, judges, policymakers, etc.).[89] *Lastly*, Chernichenko invokes a vaguely defined category of 'anti-law' ('*anti-pravo*'), diametrically opposed to forms of objective or subjective law, and presumably representing policy preferences that cannot be supported by even subjective international law.

To summarize, Chernichenko's stratification of international law may be presented as follows, roughly corresponding to similar domestic lines:

Natural law (objective moral imperatives);

(1) Positive law (state-made law, derived from consent of states as actors);

(2) Subjective international law (subjective rights and duties carried by states as a result of interpretation of positive law);

(3) International legal consciousness (subjective understanding of international obligations carried by state agents); and

82 *Ibid.*, 14.

83 *Ibid.*, 22.

84 *Ibid.*, 722.

85 *Ibid.*, 721.

86 *Ibid.*, 22.

87 *Ibid.*, 720-722.

88 *Ibid.*

89 *Ibid.*, 721.

(4) International anti-law (policy directives of particular states unsupported by any of the above sources of law).

With respect to the history of international law, Chernichenko follows the general liberal narrative of the progressive, though tentative, development of international law from early European origins to the present.[90] Here, perhaps, one gets the best appreciation for the way in which Chernichenko conceives of the dynamics of international law and its guiding forces:

> "Throughout history, the development of the norms of international law and individual international law principles (and their precursors) [...], international actors behave selfishly, constrained only by their relative abilities (taking into account their own power and the power of their partners [and counterparts]). But international law develops (positive international law, and subjective international law), as a result of coordination, assimilation, combination of given elements of international legal consciousness, as a result of conflicts and competition."[91]

This constant tension among states poses fundamental challenges to the universality of natural and positive international law, given that states will maneuver for maximum advantage given their subjective motivations. Chernichenko seems aware of this fluctuating and unstable field of actors, and their consequent inability to formulate a unifying global order; but he intentionally avoids reconciling his theory of a universal natural law with conflicting subjective international legal interpretations. In fact, at moments Chernichenko flatly contradicts himself. For instance, while Chernichenko offers numerous examples of natural law precepts in international law—*i.e.*, justice,[92] good faith,[93] *pacta sunt servanda*—he is simultaneously uncomfortable with categorizing logical corollaries of 'justice-based' international law concepts as somehow springing from eternal values and natural law. For instance, Chernichenko is keenly aware of the internal contradictions and mutability of core doctrines, such as the notion of 'just war'.[94] At other times, it is not clear whether certain international legal doctrines are of positive or natural character. For example, he argues that sovereignty and subjecthood are absolute, almost natural, rights under international law:[95]

90 *Ibid.*, 727 (discussing progressive development of the norm of prohibition of force or threat of use of force); *id.*, 728; and Kennedy, *op.cit.* note 6, 15-23 (describing the liberal enlightenment struggle for an "international order of respected will").

91 Chernichenko, *op.cit.* note 74, 723.

92 *Ibid.*, 704.

93 *Ibid.*, 709-710 (discussing notions of justice and good faith as natural law concepts).

94 *Ibid.*, 728.

95 S.V. Chernichenko, "Gosudarstvo kak lichnost', sub"ekt mezhdunarodnogo prava, i nositel' suvereniteta", *Rossiiskii ezhegodnik mezhdunarodnogo prava* (1993-1994), 13-14 (also as "State as a Personality, Subject of International Law and Bearer of Sovereignty", *Russian Yearbook of International Law 1993-1994* (Rossiia-Neva, St. Petersburg, 1995)] (hereafter, Chernichenko, *State as Personality*).

"One cannot be so-so [slightly] a subject of international law; international legal personality, like domestic legal personality, is a quality. One cannot be more or less a legal subject."[96]

Characterizing Chernichenko's theory by reference to canonical Western figures is difficult. At certain points, particularly his invocation of the moral imperatives grounding natural law, Chernichenko is a Kantian. He believes in a universal international law that can be rationally studied by reference to universal reason, similar to Tunkin's neo-Kantian turn in the dying days of the Soviet Union.[97] At other moments, Chernichenko is a Kelsian formalist, struggling like Kelsen to reconcile the relationship between the domestic and international legal orders through simultaneous reference to state consent and descending normativity as justifications for the binding nature of international law.[98] Just as Kelsen was a strict monist in the years preceding WWII, followed by Kelsen's adoption of a modified, optional monist view in the years after the war, Chernichenko's transformation from a strict dualist to a modified monist is reflective of political considerations (for instance, Russia's adoption of strict monism in the 1993 Constitution). At still other moments, Chernichenko exhibits characteristics of a Hobbesian realist:

"For the philosophy of international law, it seems to me, it is important to point out that human society on the whole is incapable of eliminating armed conflicts, just as it is incapable of eliminating any other social ills."[99]

Chernichenko's polemical style makes it difficult to relate these admittedly essentialist badges to his outlooks on particular doctrinal areas. This task is further complicated by Chernichenko's insistence that his philosophy of international law is apolitical and his disciplined unwillingness in the *Essays* to consider the policy dimensions or implications of his work. Nonetheless, just as with the Cold-War period, we can draw several tentative observations about the development of Chernichenko's outlook as a leading contemporary Russian theorist, especially by contextualizing his work in the larger constellation of political forces at play in the late 1990s and early 2000s.

First, and at the most general level, we can attempt to theorize the impetus behind the emergence of a neo-naturalist turn within the Russian legal academy. Just as the devastation of WWI caused the revival of metaphysical natural law concepts in 1920s European international legal discourse,[100] the reasons for

96 Chernichenko, *op.cit.* note 74, 652.

97 G.I. Tunkin, "Politics, Law and Force in the Interstate System", 219 *Recueil des cours* (1989), 227, 292.

98 See, generally, Martti Koskenniemi, *The Gentle Civilizer of Nations: The Rise and Fall of International Law: 1870-1960* (Cambridge University Press, Cambridge, 2002).

99 *Ibid.*, 726.

100 Jochen von Bernstorff and Thomas Dunlap, *The Public International Law Theory of Hans Kelsen: Believing in Universal Law* (Cambridge University Press, Cambridge, 2010), 48 fn. 24.

Chernichenko's naturalist turn are manifold. As a legacy of Cold-War postures of intellectual competition, contemporary Russian theorists are extremely mindful of Western critiques of Russian law. While Western scholars were cautiously optimistic regarding post-Soviet reforms, especially in the turbulent 1990s, the charge that Soviet domestic and international legal theory carried Soviet-style indeterminacy over to Russian international law continues.[101] Resort to natural law principles, Kantian moral imperatives, and *grundnorms* can be seen as absolving contemporary Russian theorists of the sins of Marxist moral agnosticism.

Second, Chernichenko's theory of the coordination of domestic and international legal orders (both reflecting the same fundamental natural law truths) has the practical effect of supporting his modified monist conception. This, of course, has tremendous practical consequences, particularly in the context of the debates over the primacy of international law and domestic transformation/implementation of international human rights norms following Russia's ratification of the European Convention on Human Rights in 1998. In other words, if domestic law reflects the same naturalist Ultimate Truth as international law, then resort to international law for domestic subjects is unnecessary. Chernichenko's strict opposition to the 'illusion' of individuals' recourse to international mechanisms evidences this. To Chernichenko, the ECHR did not grant individuals the right to petition the courts but, rather, compelled member-states of the Convention to provide such a right, and he took great umbrage at the suggestions of judges of the ECtHR, who—speaking at the Institute of State and Law in Moscow—argued that "it is necessary to be pragmatic and to acknowledge that the European Convention on Human Rights gives individuals the right to resort to the ECtHR".[102] If domestic implementation reflected the same fundamental values as the treaty, individuals could obtain identical Ultimate Justice in domestic tribunals as they would at the ECtHR in Strasbourg.

Third, in a much more skeptical vein, we can imagine the contemporary Russian naturalist turn as simply the latest incarnation of a utopian trope to consciously or subconsciously conceal the indeterminate and political nature of law.[103] Just as with early Cold-War Soviet attempts to reconcile universalism

101 Nigel J. Jamieson and Alexander Trapeznik, "A Legislative Logico-Linguistic) Analysis of the Common Law Components of the Russian Constitution", 16 *Transnational Law & Contemporary Problems* (2007), 431 (describing the expression of *vlast'* in the Russian Constitution as suffering from 'majestic indeterminacy' along with other constitutional provisions).

102 Chernichenko, *State as Personality*, *op.cit.* note 95, 13-14.

103 Borgen, *op.cit.* note 2, 26 (quoting Russian Foreign Minister Sergei Lavrov: "International law [...] is the embodiment of the moral principle in relations among states. Indeed, international law is our ideology in international affairs. To use Fyodor Tyutchev's phrase, we want 'once and for all to establish the triumph of law, of historical legality over the revolutionary mode of action'.").

with socialist internationalism in such a way as to give the Soviet state maximum policy maneuverability, Chernichenko's dualist comparison of international *versus* domestic law reflects the process of reconciliation between concrete and normative orders, so well-articulated by Koskenniemi.[104] For instance, with respect to human rights, Chernichenko's insistence that international human rights law is undeveloped and cannot be applied to a state which opposed its application (ascending argument designed to show the concreteness of sovereignty) is directly countered by the example of military intervention for *gross* violations of human rights in limited circumstances (descending argument designed to ensure international law's normativity).[105] In other words, the flexibility of 'objective' natural law or positive law is ensured by the competing political preferences of given state actors and by the competing interpretive frames of state agents. It is for this reason, perhaps, that the same Chernichenko can be, and is, cited by Russian policymakers and commentators in opposition to Kosovar independence and self-determination and in support of, for instance, Abkhazian independence and self-determination.[106]

Conclusions

This chapter has tried to suggest a number of avenues for further research on the nature and function of Soviet and post-Soviet approaches to international law. The importance of re-examining Soviet theory during the Cold-War period cannot be overstated, as the readings in this volume attest. *First*, an appreciation of the intellectual foundations of Soviet international law and contemporary Russian law is fruitful in its own right. *Second*, recent political developments (Russia's so-called illiberal slide back to 'state capitalism' and reemergence as a regional hegemon under Vladimir Putin) suggest the importance of reviving serious study of Russian approaches to international law, international trade, and regional/global governance. In short, while the Soviet and contemporary Russian 'theories' of international law offer historical tropes of development that are different from the histories of 'Western' international law and, therefore, are

104 "The existence of general principles of law common to international law and to domestic law depends on the point of view [of one advancing the position]. This can be argued in the affirmative or negative." Chernichenko, *op.cit.* note 74, 707.

105 Compare *ibid.*, 754-755 (discussing inadvisability of humanitarian intervention to prevent gross human rights violations); with *id.*, 733 (discussing permissibility of intervention in support of a domestic violent armed conflict); with *id.*, 726 (discussing need to constrain the expansion in the definition of armed conflict to prevent expansion of legal grounds for intervention). See, also, Koskenniemi, *op.cit.* note 3, 458-459.

106 See Borgen, *op.cit.* note 2, 21-24; and T.M. Shamba and A.Iu. Neproshin, *Abkhaziia: Pravovye osnovy gosudarstvenosti i suvereniteta* (2003), available at <http://abkhazia.narod.ru/SH/list.html>.

amenable to comparative study,[107] it is important to debunk the myth of Soviet and now Russian exceptionalism—lest we return to precisely those adversarial Cold-War postures which we believed we all defeated, not only with respect to Russia but, so too, with respect to competing 'other' approaches to international law and global governance.

107 Martti Koskenniemi, "FYBIL 20 Years On: The Case for Comparative International Law", 20 *Finnish Yearbook of International Law* (2009); and Boris N. Mamlyuk and Ugo Mattei, "Comparative International Law", 36 *Brooklyn Journal of International Law* (2011), 385.

Separation of Powers without Checks and Balances: The Failure of Semi-Presidentialism and the Making of the Russian Constitutional System, 1991-1993

William Partlett

In 2007, soon-to-be Russian President, Dmitrii Medvedev, dropped a constitutional bombshell. Responding to a journalist's question, he stated that he thought that the Russian President should be a member of a political party. He argued that Russia was changing: "Today our country is more ready for a partisan president, than 10 to 12 years ago, when a president who was a member of a political party would have destroyed our country."[1]

Medvedev's opinion was controversial. According to a poll taken a year earlier, 62% of Russian voters believed that the Russian President should not be the member of a political party.[2] Moreover, Vladimir Putin also disagreed: "As I have repeatedly said, and my opinion on this matter remains the same today, I would consider it inappropriate if the head of state [the Russian President], no matter his political sympathies, were to head one of the parties."[3]

Two years later, after he had been elected President with backing from a broad coalition of political parties, Medvedev once again stated that he thought that the Russian President should be a member of a political party. He acknowledged, however, that the "unique Russian tradition" of the President as the "guarantor of the Constitution" and "the symbol of the unity of the nation" made this development difficult.[4] Sergei Mironov, the then-head of the upper house of the Russian Parliament (the Federation Council), defended the idea of a nonpartisan president: "The President of the country should be above all parties and should not take party positions. [...] This comes from our principled belief in the nonpartisan position of president."[5] Other major political figures agreed with Mironov. Leonid Belov, a representative in the upper house of the Russian Parliament, said that "it might be possible to conceive of a partisan president

1 Informatsionnoe agentsvo "Khakasiia", "Dmitrii Medvedev schitaet chto v Rossii mozhet byt' partiinyi prezident", *RIA Novosti* (1 October 2007), available at <http://www.19rus.info/news/20592.html>.

2 "Bol'shinstvo Rossiian khotiat, chtoby prezident ostavalsia bespartiinym", *Newsru.com* (25 July 2006), available at <http://www.newsru.com/russia/25jul2006/party.html>.

3 "Vladimir Putin: Partiinyi prezident – eto netselesoobrazno", *Komsomol'skaia Pravda* (15 April 2008), available at <http://spb.kp.ru/online/news/78377>.

4 Irina Gusakova, "Dmitrii Medvedev nameknul, kto stanet sleduiushchim prezidentom", *News-info.ru* (15 September 2009), available at <http://www.newsinfo.ru/articles/2009-09-15/valdaj/722137>.

5 "Ne dolzhno byt' partiinogo prezidenta", *Gazeta.ru* (10 April 2009), available at <http://www.gazeta.ru/interview/nm/s2969481.shtml>.

Tatiana Borisova and William Simons, eds.
The Legal Dimension in Cold-War Interactions: Some Notes from the Field 105-140

sometime in the future, when our political system is better developed. [...] but now at such an early stage, it is necessary for the president to remain neutral and non-partisan".[6] Nikolai Bezborodov, a member of the Fair Russia party (*Spravedlivaia Rossiia*), stated "in today's conditions we need a nonpartisan leader. This type of leader will better be able to associate with all party interests and will have greater authority than a partisan president".[7] Finally, Nikolai Mitrofanov, a member of the Liberal Democratic Party (*Liberal'no-Demokraticheskaia Partiia Rossii*), said that a partisan president would lead to unseemly partisan battles for the position of the president.[8]

Russia's Rejection of Western-Style Constitutional Design

This controversy highlights a critical aspect of Russian constitutional design: standing above the system of separated powers and wielding a 'fourth' kind of power in Russia's constitutional system, the President is a *de facto* elected monarch. As the only state institution that is elected by all the people, the Russian President embodies the unity of the Russian state and, therefore, is constitutionally required to ensure that the political parties and interests that operate in the separated branches of government coordinate in the interests of the entire nation.

Russian Constitutional Design

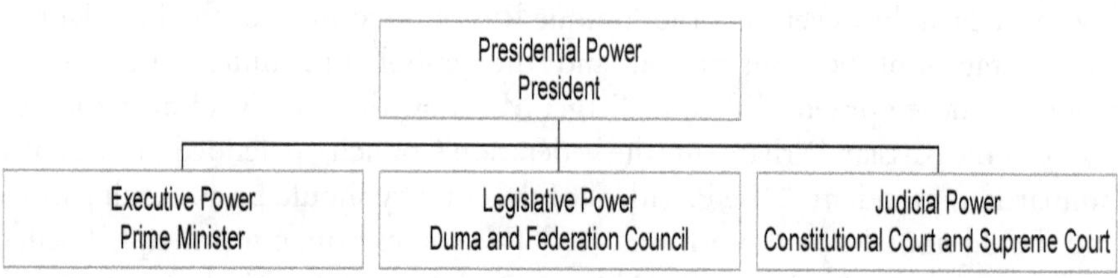

Any presidential party affiliation would undermine the President's constitutional role as guarantor of both the Constitution and the unity of the Russian state. Marat Baglai, a former Chief Justice of the Russian Constitutional Court, explained the President's unique role in Russia's constitutional system:

> "[T]he Russian President stands outside the interests of specific political parties or societal groups, as a unique rights-protector and 'lobby' for all the people. The President's interaction with the parliament, which is founded on party representation, should protect the unity of the general government and regional interests. This service of the general will [*obshchenarodnoe sluzhenie*] is found in the president's oath, in which he swears to 'faithfully serve the people'."[9]

6 "Partiinyi prezident – khorosho, bespartiinyi – luchshe", *Regions.ru* (18 February 2007), available at <http://www.regions.ru/news/2058174>.

7 *Ibid.*

8 *Ibid.*

9 Marat Baglai, *Presidenty Rossiiskoi Federatsii i Soedinnennykh Shtatov Ameriki: rol', poriadok vyborov, polnomochiia* (Norma, Moscow, 2008), 20-21.

This constitutionally privileged position of the President reflects a deliberate intent to avoid meaningful legislative or judicial checks on presidential power. Russia's 1993 Constitution, therefore, rejected a western-inspired constitutional design that would place any serious structural limitations on the power of the president.

Western Constitutional Design, Separation of Powers, and Constitutionally Limited Government

A normative theory of constitutional design—describing the 'correct' institutional architecture that should be outlined in a constitution—has long been at the center of the western political thought. Well before political thinkers were discussing the importance of constitutional rights, they were debating the best constitutional design for ensuring both individual liberty and just government. The most dominant theory—most famously spelled out by Charles de Montesquieu in the *Spirit of Laws*—counsels that the best constitutional design for limiting the arbitrary abuse of governmental power is a system divided into executive, legislative, and judicial branches.[10] As Montesqueiu wrote:

> "When the legislative and executive powers are united in the same person, or in the same body of magistrates, there can be no liberty. [...] Again, there is no liberty, if the judiciary power be not separated from the legislative and executive. Were it joined with the legislative, the life and liberty of the subject would be exposed to arbitrary control; for the judge would then be the legislator. Were it joined to the executive power, the judge might behave with violence and oppression. There would be an end to everything, were the same man, or the same body, whether of the nobles or of the people, to exercise those three powers, that of enacting laws, that of executing the public resolutions, and of trying the causes of individuals."[11]

The simple tripartite separation of powers, however, is incomplete: this constitutional design only places constraints on the power of government and protects individual liberty when it is combined with the theory of checks and balances.[12] Placed together, the branches of government are separated to the extent that they can check any encroachment by the other.[13] This system of separated *and* balanced

10 Charles de Secondat Montesquieu, *The Spirit of Laws*, Vol. 1 (Printed for G. and A. Ewing and G. Faulkner, 1751).

11 *Ibid.*, 185.

12 M.J.C. Vile writes:

> "The doctrine of the separation of powers, standing alone as a theory of government, has, as will be demonstrated later, uniformly failed to provide an adequate basis for an effective, stable political system. It has therefore been combined with other political ideas, the theory of mixed government, the idea of balance, the concept of checks and balances, to form the complex constitutional theories that provided the basis of modern Western political systems."

Constitutionalism and the Separation of Powers (Liberty Fund, Indianapolis, IN, 1998), 2.

13 "The traditional theory of the separation of powers sought to divide the functions of government between three branches of government and to keep the personnel of the three

government harnesses inter-branch political competition for public support into a self-enforcing, structural limitation on the reach of government.[14]

This theory of constitutional design was at the very forefront of the debate during the drafting of the United States Constitution. For many of the drafters, constitutional structure—not constitutional rights—was the primary safeguard of individual liberty. In the debate over the correct constitutional structure, the drafters sought to balance effective government with structurally limited one. With memories of the ineffectiveness of the legislatively dominated Articles of Confederation fresh in their memories, the drafters justified the creation of an independent executive—a president—by appealing to the separation of powers and its ability to provide "energy" in government. Hamilton wrote:

> "Energy in the executive is a leading character in the definition of good government. [...] There can be no need, however, to multiply arguments or examples on this head. A feeble Executive implies a feeble execution of the government. A feeble execution is but another phrase for a bad execution; and a government ill executed, whatever it may be in theory, must be, in practice, a bad government."[15]

The drafters were, however, wary of too much energy in their government:

> "On comparing these valuable ingredients [energy and stability] with the vital principles of liberty, we must perceive at once the difficulty of mingling them together in their due proportions."[16]

The drafters, therefore, rejected a pure separation of powers system and blended powers to ensure that each branch was co-equal and could balance against the other. As James Madison wrote:

> "[T]he great security against a gradual concentration of the several powers in the same department, consists in giving to those who administer each department the necessary constitutional means and personal motives to resist encroachment of the others."[17]

Placing Russian Constitutional Design in the Western Tradition of Constitutionally-Limited Government: The Transition Paradigm

Commentators and scholars describing Russia's post-Soviet constitutional development mistakenly believed that Russia was attempting to import this western tradition of separated and balanced constitutional design. This belief stemmed

branches separate. The evident inability of this arrangement to control abuses by government led to the modification of the theory by grafting on to it checks and balances derived from the mixed constitution of eighteenth-century Britain." *Ibid.*, 405.

14 For more on how this system works in practice, particularly given the rise of partisan politics in democracies, see Darryl Levinson, "On Parchment and Politics: The Positive Puzzle of Constitutional Commitment", 124 *Harvard Law Review* (2011), 657.

15 Alexander Hamilton, *No. 37*, in *The Federalist Papers* (1788, reprinted: Arlington House, New Rochelle, NY, 1966), 423.

16 James Madison, *No.37*, in *The Federalist Papers* (1788, reprinted: Arlington House, New Rochelle, NY, 1966), 227.

17 James Madison, *No.51*, in *The Federalist Papers* (1788, reprinted: Arlington House, New Rochelle, NY, Robert Scigliano, ed. 2001), 321-322.

from a powerful assumption that the fall of communism was the 'end of history'[18] and the culmination of a massive 'third wave'[19] of worldwide democratic revolution in a world where there was no longer any alternative to western-style, free markets and liberal democracy. This powerful ideological movement spawned both a massive cottage industry of democracy promotion organizations as well as the emergent academic field of 'transitology'.[20]

This ideological trend also helped create an analytical framework for understanding post-communist political change: the 'transition paradigm'.[21] The central assumption in this paradigm was that a movement away from previous forms of dictatorship automatically signaled a desire to move toward democratic government. In Russia, commentators perceived Boris El'tsin's relentless push to destroy the Soviet form of government as proof that he was leading Russia towards a wholesale reorientation of its "entire political, economic, and legal system toward capitalism and democracy".[22]

This paradigm played a powerful role in shaping western scholars understanding of Russian legal development, "predispos[ing] scholars to assign certain meanings to Russian law, ask particular questions of its development, and look for specific conclusions in their final analysis".[23] Those following Russia's constitutional development therefore proclaimed Russia's 1993 Constitution to be the product of "one of the most extensive transfers of legal ideas in the modern history of law".[24] As a result, the dominant interpretation of Russia's constitutional system is that Russia's 1993 Constitution was an attempt—albeit

18 Francis Fukuyama, *The End of History and the Last Man* (Avon Books, Inc., New York, NY, 1992).

19 Samuel Huntington, *The Third Wave: Democratization in the Late Twentieth Century* (University of Oklahoma Press, Norman, OK, 1991).

20 'Transitology' can best be traced to the seminal work of Guillermo O'Donnell and Phillipe Schmitter. See *Transitions from Authoritarian Rule: Tentative Conclusions about Uncertain Democracies* (Johns Hopkins University Press, Baltimore, MD, 1986).

21 Thomas Carothers, "The End of the Transition Paradigm", 13(1) *Journal of Democracy* (2002), 5.

22 William Partlett, "Reclassifying Russian Law: Mechanisms, Outcomes, and Solutions for an Overly Politicized Field", 2(1) *Columbia Journal of East European Law* (2008), 42.

23 *Ibid.*, 8.

24 Robert Sharlet, "Legal Transplants and Political Mutations: The Reception of Constitutional Law in Russia and the Newly Independent States", 7 *East European Constitutional Review* (1998), 59. Many saw this transfer as facilitated by a massive influx of scholars and consultants.

> "The opening of new areas (both geographic and substantive) to American influence, the removal of the principal rivals to U.S. power and American-supported ideologies, and the seemingly sweeping embrace of principles that official and unofficial U.S. actors have seen as congenial (or even as proprietarily American) thus have provided the setting for countless U.S. legal export-promotion and advice-offering activities that have sought to respond to the demands and opportunities of the era."

Jacques deLisle, "Lex American? United States Legal Assistance, American Legal Models, and Legal Change in the Post-Communist World and Beyond", 20 *University of Pennsylvania Journal of International Economic Law* (1999), 181.

an ultimately failed one—to transplant western, constitutional design. Indeed, scholars perceived President El'tsin's frequent appeals to the separation of powers and the eventual adoption of separated powers in Russia's 1993 Constitution as a reflection of his intention to found a western-style, constitutional design.[25] In so doing, they mistakenly assumed that the separation of powers alone limits the power of government. Furthermore, they ignored the fact that—taken alone—the separation of powers is a theory of government that has been used to enable governmental power.

As soon as the Russian Constitution was ratified in 1993, scholars immediately hailed it Russia's first post-Soviet constitution as a symbolic marker of a "new beginning"[26] for Russian democracy and "a crucial component in the establishment of a constitutional society in Russia".[27] Richard Sakwa argued that Russia's adoption of a constitution in 1993 put an end to a period of "phoney democracy"[28] and was a critical first step away from its authoritarian and communist past: "The final vestiges of the communist legacy were swept away as the new document promised economic liberalism and the democratic separation of powers."[29] This understanding of the Russian founding period has remained dominant until today. A 2008 report from the Woodrow Wilson Institute states:

> "The present Russian Constitution represents a clear break with its most direct predecessor, the 1977 Brezhnev Constitution. Gone are the references to the supremacy of the Communist Party and the requirement that the citizens comply with standards of socialist conduct. Instead, the Constitution contains specific sections devoted to civil rights, the division of powers. [...]"[30]

Seeing the 1993 Russian Constitution as a western transplant, commentators have labored to place the Russian constitutional system within the framework of Western constitutional design. Most saw Russia's system of government as a mixture of the American and French constitutional traditions. Robert Sharlet wrote that "[t]he Russian Federation Constitution of 1993 can be seen as the

25 See Art.3, Russian Constitution, originally published in *Rossiiskaia Gazeta* (25 December 1993).

26 Bruce Ackerman, "The Rise of World Constitutionalism", 83 *Virginia Law Review* (1997), 786.

27 Dana Atchison, "Notes on Constitutionalism for a 21st-Century Russian President", 6 *Cardozo Journal of International and Comparative Law* (1998), 351.

28 Richard Sakwa, *Russian Politics and Society* (Routledge, New York, NY, 4th ed. 2008), 40.

29 Richard Sakwa, "The Struggle for the Constitution in Russia and the Triumph of Ethical Individualism", 48 *Studies in East European Thought* (1996), 131.

30 F. Joseph Dresen and William E. Pomeranz (eds.), "The Russian Constitution at Fifteen: Assessments and Current Challenges to Russia's Legal Development", conference proceedings at the Woodrow Wilson International Center for Scholars, Washington, DC (19 March 2009), 3, available at <http://www.wilsoncenter.org/topics/pubs/KI_090623_Occ%20Paper%20304.pdf>. It is worth noting that the most direct predecessor to Russia's current Constitution was not the 1977 Brezhnev Constitution but the 1978 RSFSR Constitution.

constitutional equivalent of Europe's Airbus, assembled from parts manufactured in a number of countries. [...] French and US influences are apparent in the presidency chapter of the Russian Constitution".[31] Rett Ludwikowski made a similar observation:

> "The Constitution of the Russian Federation of December 12, 1993 was also a product of the constitutional melting pot. The drafters attempted to duplicate the American system of checks and balances but ended up with a model which combined both French and American features."[32]

The comparisons to the French constitutional system have led many scholars to classify Russia's constitutional system as 'semi-presidential', a form of government characterized by the combination of a "popularly elected [president] with a head of government who is responsible to a popularly elected legislature".[33] The defining characteristic of this type of constitutional government is the possibility of a split executive—called 'cohabitation'—when an elected president must share executive power with an opposition prime minister who has support in the parliament.

Others saw Russia's constitutional system as a 'super-presidential' version of the American constitutional system, providing "an unequally balanced three-way separation of powers" that afforded too much executive power to the President.[34] One scholar summarized this approach: "The 1993 Russian Constitution prescribes a governmental system roughly similar to the United States model. Its executive powers, however, echo those of a presidential dictatorship."[35] These imbalances were seen as dangerous to Russia's assumed goal of creating a checks-and-balances system: "[The Russian Constitution] is plagued by contradictions that undermine the separation of powers in the new Russian government."[36]

31 Robert Sharlet, "Legal Transplants and Political Mutations: The Reception of Constitutional Law in Russia and the Newly Independent States", 7 *Eastern European Constitutional Review* (1998), 64.

32 Rett Ludwikowski, "Mixed Constitutions: Product of an East-Central European Constitutional Melting Pot", 16 *Boston University International Law Journal* (1998), 41.

33 Cindy Skach, "The Newest Separation of Powers: Semipresidentialism", 5 *International Journal of Constitutional Law* (2007), 93. See, also, Tiffany Troxel, *Parliamentary Power in Russia, 1994-2001: President vs. Parliament* (Palgrave MacMillan, Houndmills, UK, 2003), 33.

34 Robert Sharlet, "Reinventing the Russian State: Problems of Constitutional Interpretation", 28 *John Marshall Law Review* (1995), 777. Stephen Holmes was perhaps the first to describe the Russian constitution this way, arguing that "[t]he system established by Yeltsin's constitution, in fact, can most succinctly be described as superpresidentialism". Stephen Holmes, "Superpresidentialism and Its Problems", 2(4) *Eastern European Constitutional Review* (1993), 123.

35 Joshua Briones, "Religious Minorities in Russia", 8 *University of California Davis Journal of International Law and Policy* (2004), 338.

36 Jeffrey Waggoner, "Discretion and Valor at the Russian Constitutional Court: Adjudicating the

The 'Failure' of the Russian Constitution?

As it has become increasingly clear that the Russian Constitution was not fostering limited government, western scholars have faced a problem: Why did Russia's supposed western constitutional design fail to limit government power?[37] Some have explained this dilemma as a simple reflection that the Russian Constitution cannot overcome Russia's long history of autocratic government.[38] For instance, they argue that Russia's ingrained culture of leader worship has overcome the power of the constitutional rules:

> "[T]he Russian Constitution of 1993 is flawed not because of its imperfect separation of powers but because its effectiveness ultimately relies upon the individuals occupying the various offices of state power and much less upon the ideals on which the Constitution is based."[39]

Others have argued that Russia's semi-presidential system of checks and balances has broken down. In particular, they argue that this system of government is particularly prone to autocratic backsliding. Cindy Skach, for instance, has argued that Russia's adoption of a semi-presidential form of constitutional government in 1993 undermined its pursuit of limited government by creating incentives for "legislative immobilism, presidential-legislative deadlock or impasse, and the resulting use of presidential decrees to counteract immobilism".[40]

Russian Constitutions in the Civil-Law Tradition", 8 *Indiana International and Comparative Law Review* (1997), 191.

37 For a detailed description of post-Soviet mechanisms for faking democracy, see Andrew Wilson, *Virtual Politics: Faking Democracy in the Post-Soviet World* (Yale University Press, New Haven, CT, 2005). Furthermore, Freedom House has labeled the majority of post-Soviet republics, including Russia, as 'not free'. Robert W. Ortung, *Nations in Transit: Russia* (Freedom House, New York, NY, 2008), available at <http://www.freedomhouse.hu/images/fdh_galleries/NIT2008/NT-Russia-final.pdf>.

38 Kim Lane Scheppelle, "We Forgot About the Ditches: Russian Constitutional Impatience and the Challenge of Terrorism", 53 *Drake Law Review* (2005), 963-1027.

39 Ian Brown, "Clinging to Democracy: Assessing the Russian Legislative-Executive Relationship under Boris Yeltsin's Constitution", 33 *Vanderbilt Journal of Transnational Law* (2000), 663. The underlying approach was that the Russian president had excessive executive power: "Yeltsin's exercise of super-presidential power threatened the precarious separation of powers contained in the 1993 Constitution." William Hayden, "Seeds of Unrest: The Political Genesis of the Conflict in Chechnya", 24 *Fletcher Forum of World Affairs* (2000), 69. "The principal drawback of the Constitution is its tendency to centralize power in the executive branch to an extent that will render meaningless any constitutional limitations in the presence of an executive who chooses to disregard them." Molly Lien, "Red Star Trek: Seeking a Role for Constitutional Law in Soviet Disunion" 30 *Stanford Journal of International Law* (1994), 110.

40 Skach, *op.cit.* note 33, 108. Her analysis, based on a history of both France and Weimar Germany, suggests that this system of government can quickly lead to constitutional breakdown.

An Authoritarian Version of Separated Powers

This chapter provides a much simpler answer: the drafters of the 1993 Constitution never intended to place any structural constraints on the power of the Russian President. For them, a legitimate democratic constitution was one that concentrated power in a stable and energetic president. They rejected a structural system of checks and balances as a dangerous system of 'dual power' that would endanger Russia's territorial integrity and slow down radical economic reforms. Thus, many western commentators have gotten it backward: the 1993 Constitution rejected rather than embraced the western constitutional tradition of balanced and self-limiting government.

This chapter will describe how El'tsin and his supporters advanced separated powers as a 'democratic' solution to the problems of constitutionally-limited, semi-presidential government. This story begins prior to the collapse of the Soviet Union, when the Russian parliament amended the communist-era constitution to include a popularly-elected president and a constitutional court. These changes created a semi-presidential system of structural checks and balances, which was enforced by an assertive constitutional court. President El'tsin and his supporters, however, did not accept the limitations that this system placed on presidential power and ruthlessly attacked its legitimacy. Facing resistance from both parliament and the constitutional court, El'tsin finally suspended the constitution, dissolved parliament, and called for a referendum to ratify a new constitution. This new constitution formalized a presidentially-dominated vision of constitutional government which elevated the elected president above the system of separated executive, legislative, and judicial powers. The Russian President had replaced the 'guiding role' of the Communist Party of the Soviet Union (Party).

To tell this story, this chapter will draw on two main sources. *First*, it will draw on newspaper reports from this period. These newspaper reports provide an unfiltered view of the constitutional debate during this turbulent period of constitutional crisis. *Second*, it will reference the debates from the Constitutional Convention that helped to draft the Russian Constitution. The twenty volumes of the Constitutional Convention are an invaluable and surprisingly neglected source for understanding the way that the Russian Constitution was understood by President El'tsin and his supporters, the public officials that continue to lead Russia today.[41]

41 Vladimir Putin's chief patron, the late Anatolii Sobchak, was a key El'tsin supporter and organizer of the Constitutional Convention.

The Failure of Semi-Presidentialism in Russia

Soviet Constitutional History: Unwritten and Written Constitutions

In the Soviet Union, there were two sets of overlapping institutions: the Party apparatus and the state system.[42] The Soviet Union's real constitution—which was unwritten—placed supreme power in the Party and made state institutions into mere transmission belts of Party policy. The formal written Soviet Constitution was simply a blueprint for structuring the state system and therefore did nothing to limit Party power.[43]

The Soviet Union adopted a new formal written Constitution in 1977 and Russia did the same in 1978.[44] These new Constitutions created a formal governmental system of legislative supremacy with an all-powerful parliamentary assembly that elected and oversaw the Council of Ministers (which acted as the formal executive branch of the government).[45] These Constitutions also took a small step toward reflecting the real unwritten constitutional structure by proclaiming the Party to be "the leading and guiding force of Soviet society, the nucleus of its political system and of all state and public organizations".[46]

As Gorbachev and his allies sought to reform the Soviet Union in the mid 1980s, they faced strong Party resistance. Gorbachev used constitutional change—or, as he called it, *perestroika*—to reshuffle institutions and transfer his power base away from the Party to the state system. First, he amended the 1977 Soviet Constitution to create a new two-tiered legislative body, consisting of the Congress of People's Deputies and a smaller Supreme Soviet—a working parliament that was elected by the Congress. He also ended the Party's monopoly over the state system by instituting semi-competitive elections to this new parliament for the first time.

42 For more on the institutional tension between the Party and the state in the Soviet constitutional system, see Stephen Kotkin, *Magnetic Mountain: Stalinism as a Civilization* (University of California Press, Berkeley, CA, 1995).

43 In fact, each of the Soviet Union's constitutions created a system of state power that was loosely modeled on a western European constitutional model of parliamentary sovereignty within a federal system.

44 See Robert Sharlet, *Soviet Constitutional Crisis: From De-Stalinization to Disintegration* (M.E. Sharpe, Inc., Armonk, NY, 1992).

45 For more on the constitutional structure of the 1977 Soviet Constitution, see Christopher Osakwe, "The Theories and Realities of Modern Soviet Constitutional Law: An Analysis of the 1977 USSR Constitution", 127 *University Pennsylvania Law Review* (1979), 1350.

46 For instance, see Art.6, *Konstitutsiia RSFSR* (1978), originally published in *Vedomosti VS RSFSR* (1978) No.15 item 407. It is also important to note that both the 1977 Soviet and 1978 Russian Constitutions guaranteed the role of the *All-Union* Soviet Communist Party. No Russian-level Communist Party existed during the Soviet period.

Although these elections still gave a competitive edge to the Party, they helped undermine Party legitimacy: the new parliament's reflection of the will of the people far outweighed the Party's claim to the 'virtual' representation of the popular will.[47] This was by design. Appeals to popular sovereignty would become a key tactic for Gorbachev in his attempt to reform the Soviet Union: "the later phase of *perestroika* was an attempt to establish a political system based not on one party, claiming to represent the people, but on the people in fact".[48]

Although weakening Party power, this new legislative body proved a slow and unwieldy base for Gorbachev's ambitious reform agenda.[49] To ensure more effective reform, Gorbachev hastily pushed through another amendment to create another state institution: a presidency.[50] In order to ensure his own transition to the presidency, the first President of the Soviet Union was to be elected by the Congress. Gorbachev became the first Soviet President soon after.[51]

With these changes, Gorbachev seemed to be creating a semi-presidential system in which a President stood next to a Council of Ministers and two-tiered parliament.[52]

47 "Constitutional amendments introduced at that time led to the country's first competitive elections in March 1989 and the transformation of the moribund Soviet parliament into a lively, two-tiered legislature." Eugene Huskey, *Presidential Power in Russia* (M.E. Sharpe, Inc., Armonk, NY, 1999), 14.

48 Hans Oversloot, "Uncivic Culture and Presidential Power in Contemporary Russia", 26(2) *Review of Central and East European Law* (2000), 164. Gorbachev also often resorted to such popular appeals when facing opposition. For instance, in trying to hold the USSR together, Gorbachev argued that a referendum would not encroach on the sovereignty of the union republics like Russia "because the decision is taken by the people, and the expression of the people's will is the source of all that happens on earth, including the people's opinion on the fundamental issues of the country". *Izvestiia* (25 December 1990), quote from *ibid.*, 165.

49 Gorbachev's decision to use state institutions as his power base and ignore the Party was evidenced by the fact that he began to spend more time in the Kremlin (parliamentary and government headquarters) than on Old Square (Party headquarters). Huskey, *op.cit.* note 47, 14.

50 Gorbachev saw this new institution as critical in ensuring 'acceleration'. *Ibid.*, 15.

51 *Ibid.*, 19.

52 As in all semi-presidential systems, the critical question was whether the president or the parliament would control the power ministries in the Council of Ministers. As noted earlier, in a typical semi-presidential design, the head of the government (prime minister and his subordinate power ministries) was ultimately responsible to the parliament, creating a situation where a popularly elected president is forced to share executive power over the power ministries with a prime minister.

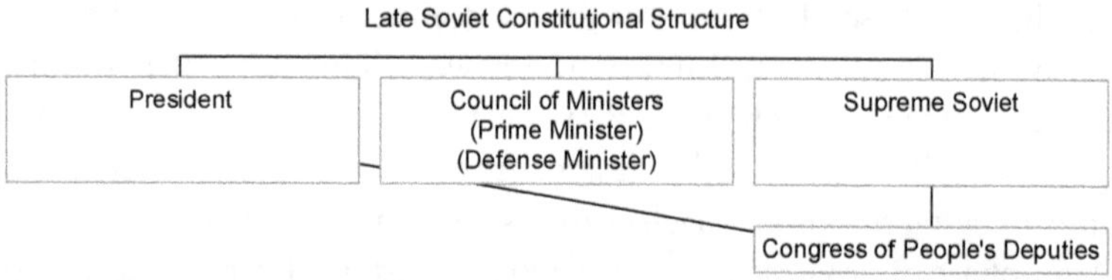

Gorbachev, however, had different ideas. He saw the president acting "above the unpleasant business of managing a vast and inefficient bureaucracy, which was left to the prime minister. [...] Removed from daily politics, the president could aspire to the majesty of an 'enlightened monarch.'"[53] Essentially, he perceived the Soviet president replacing the Party's role as the guiding force in Russian politics.

> "[He] saw the president operating above the fray of daily politics and administration in a realm that transcended the traditional branches of government. He remarked to deputies in the weeks before becoming president that he would be a mediator between the executive [Council of Ministers] and the legislature."[54]

This belief was further underlined by Gorbachev's move to extend his own presidential apparatus to "gradually take over the Central Committee (of the Communist Party) apparatus"[55] before the dissolution of the Soviet Union on Christmas Day 1991. Thus, Gorbachev's institutional restructuring was not an attempt to eliminate the concept of a guiding institution in the unwritten Soviet constitution; it was instead an attempt to replace the 'guiding' Party with a 'guiding' President.

The Construction of a Semi-presidential System in Russia: October 1989-December 1991

As Gorbachev was transforming the Soviet institutional structure, Boris El'tsin and the leadership of the Russian Republic moved aggressively to assert Russian sovereignty from the Soviet center. Constitutional change was at the center of Russian-level strategy: El'tsin and his team sought to make deeper democratic institutional reforms to increase the power and legitimacy of the Russian state *vis-à-vis* the federal Soviet state.

In October 1989, the Russian Parliament amended the 1978 Russian Constitution to adopt a two-tiered legislature, with a structure that paralleled the Soviet parliament.[56] At its base was the Congress of People's Deputies (Congress), a body that was comprised of 1,098 members and met two to three times per

53 Huskey, *op.cit.* note 47, 16.

54 *Ibid.*, 18.

55 *Ibid.*, 16.

56 Thomas F. Remington, *Russian Parliament: Institutional Evolution in a Transitional Regime 1989-1999* (Yale University Press, New Haven, CT, 2001), 85.

year. The Congress had the power to amend the constitution, pass laws, elect a chairman, and approve the head of government as well as other state officials.[57] "The Congress functioned in some respects like a constituent assembly, which assumes control of the state temporarily in a time of crisis in order to lay the constitutional foundations of a new political order."[58]

To govern between meetings, the Congress elected a permanent standing body, the Supreme Soviet. This 252-member body had its own executive committee—called the Presidium—which acted as a kind of collective chief executive. The head of the presidium had "wide powers to coordinate and manage the legislative process and set the agenda for both congress and Supreme Soviet sessions"[59] and was functionally similar to the western Prime Minister, enjoying the support of the Parliament and directing the development of legal policy through parliamentary committees. The presidium also assumed many executive functions, including the power to issue decrees (*postanovleniia*) with normative force. The head of the presidium also enjoyed many powerful mechanisms to ensure parliamentary support:

> "[He] managed the extensive physical resources of the Supreme Soviet (which included, besides the White House itself, apartment buildings and dachas, a large car park, and such administrative support services as the parliamentary library and the computer center); and issued orders and policy decisions in its own name."[60]

In drawing up the electoral law for the new Russian Congress, the Russian leadership rejected the semi-competitive electoral rules used at the Soviet level; instead, it drafted a law allowing for completely open elections to each of the seats in the Congress. The elections in March 1991 for the Russian Congress were the first open, democratic elections to any Russian-level institution and were highly competitive: on average, 6.3 candidates competed for each seat.[61] In the end, "[a]bout 40 percent of the deputies voted rather cohesively in support of the democratic reform positions, and about 40 percent of the deputies opposed them; the remainder formed a wavering center".[62] When the First Congress convened on 16 May 1990, El'tsin was elected chairman, drawing his support from a coalition of democratic activists and conservative nationalists who supported El'tsin's pro-Russia stance.

As Russia fell deeper into economic troubles and sought to assert its independence from the Soviet Union, El'tsin followed Gorbachev's example and proposed the creation of a Russian President. Supporters of a Russian President

57 *Ibid.*

58 Huskey, *op.cit.* note 47, 17.

59 Remington, *op.cit.* note 56, 85.

60 *Ibid.*, 128.

61 *Ibid.*, 91.

62 *Ibid.*, 9.

argued that it would help serve as a juggernaut for democratic reform and help finish the destruction of the Soviet Union and its organizational backbone, the Party.[63]

In May 1991, the Congress enacted legislation creating the first Russian Presidency. The new law placed the President at the head of the executive branch, stating that "[t]he Council of Ministers is responsible to the President".[64] The law also afforded the President the authority to veto laws, the power to name the head of the government with the agreement of the Supreme Soviet, and the ability to issue edicts. The President did not, however, have the power to dissolve the parliament.[65] Finally, the drafters sought to maximize Russia's democratic legitimacy and specified that the President was to be directly elected. This would prove to be an important choice as it grafted an elected presidency onto Russia's existing system of parliamentary sovereignty.

The leadership in the Congress also pushed aggressively for the creation of a Constitutional Court. In July 1991, the Congress passed a law giving the Russian Constitutional Court broad powers to review and strike down parliamentary laws, presidential edicts, and government acts. This broad drafting sprung from a strong constituency in favor of the Court, including many parliamentarians who supported the Court as "another propaganda tool for the Russian executive to gain political capital relative to the Soviet executive".[66]

The majority of the judges chosen for this new Court were "favored law professors and those who worked closely with the Supreme Soviet and Constitutional Commission".[67] None of them were former judges from the Soviet period, meaning that they had not been socialized into a system of deference to the other branches. The Chairman (*predsedatel'*) of the Court and the top vote getter in the Parliament was Valerii Zor'kin. A highly acclaimed academic, Zor'kin was an expert on the history of western constitutional ideas in Russia and had written a biography of Boris Chicherin, one of the leading liberal constitutional thinkers in the Tsarist period.[68] Zor'kin's jurisprudence and stewardship of the Court would reflect this background, as he would emerge as a major proponent for transplanting a western-style system of checks and balances.

63 Huskey, *op.cit.* note 47, 28.

64 Art.123, RSFSR Constitution.

65 See Art.121(5), part 11, RSFSR Constitution.

66 Carla Thornson, "Why Politicians Want Constitutional Courts: The Russian Case", 37 *Communist and Post-Communist Studies* (2004), 195-96.

67 Alexei Trochev, *Judging Russia: Constitutional Court in Russian Politics* (Cambridge University Press, Cambidge, 2008), 71.

68 Valerii D. Zor'kin, *Chicherin* (Iuridicheskaia literatura, Moscow, 1984).

Building a Presidential Vertical of Power: August-December 1991

Boris El'tsin won the first ever Russian presidential election in June 1991 with sixty percent of the vote. The formal constitutional position of the newly elected Russian President was clear: the amended 1978 Constitution created a form of semi-presidentialism where a system of legislative supremacy coexisted alongside an elected president. Informally, however, many viewed the newly created President much as Gorbachev did: as an elected replacement to the Party and the new guiding force in Russian politics. This informal view of presidential power was amplified by the fact that the President was elected by the entire Russian people. At El'tsin's inauguration, the head of the Russian Orthodox Church stressed this point: "[E]lection by the people and the will of God have entrusted supreme political power in [President El'tsin]."[69] In his initial speech, El'tsin also described the President's expansive powers stemming from the will of the people: "For centuries in our country, power and the people were at opposite poles. [...] That time when the people kept silent is receding into the past, never to return. [...] There is no higher position to which citizens of a state can elect someone."[70]

Soon after taking office, El'tsin began to build an apparatus that would help him realize this view of presidential power, constructing a "hierarchical structure of executive authority that would extend from himself, the President, to leaders at the provincial and local level".[71] To do this, El'tsin made two major administrative moves. *First*, he established a system of presidential representatives, the "chief purpose of these officials was to monitor implementation of presidential edicts and instructions".[72] *Second*, he created a new institution in the region—the head of administration (*glava administratsii*)—each of which would operate like a 'little president' in each respective region. This was a massive transformation in the organization of power in Russia:

> "[T]he executive and administrative functions of state government in territories, provinces and autonomous provinces and regions are henceforth to be exercised by heads of administration appointed by the RSFSR President and accountable only to him. The head selects a 'team' at his own discretion, and he has broad powers—for example, he can veto the decisions of local soviets."[73]

This process of institutional change was catalyzed by the failed Party coup in August 1991. As Tim McDaniels writes, "[El'tsin was] the hero of the August

69 "We Can be Fully Confident that Russia Will Revive", *Izvestiia* (10 July 1991), 1, 3, in 43(28) *Current Digest of the Post Soviet Press* (hereinafter *CDPSP*) (14 August 1991), 1-3.

70 *Ibid.*

71 Darrell Slider, "Federalism, Discord, and Accommodation", in Theodore H. Friedgut and Jeffrey W. Hahn (eds.), *Local Power and Post-Soviet Politics* (M.E. Sharpe, Inc., Armonk, NY, 1994), 251.

72 *Ibid.*

73 Aleksandr Dergachov, "The First Days of the Russian President's Local Representatives", *Izvestiia* (28 August 1991), 2, in 43(35) *CDPSP* (2 October 1991), 21-22.

events, showing undeniable courage in defying putschists and rallying the opposition around himself [...] his mandate to lead was based on the perception that he could perform miracles".[74] With broad new powers freshly delegated from the Russian Parliament, El'tsin moved to accelerate the liquidation of the Party, decreeing that "political parties could not maintain primary organizations within state enterprises or organizations".[75] El'tsin's new system of 'administrative heads' and representatives now began to operate in the Party's place. These administrative heads would remain accountable to El'tsin: claiming that elections were "too risky", he persuaded the Congress to allow him to appoint these regional heads until 1995.[76]

This top-down presidential apparatus so closely co-opted the Party that even El'stin supporters complained that "unfortunately, there are familiar faces among the representatives of the President of Russia—the same party functionaries who compromised themselves long ago in the eyes of the local residents".[77] As El'tsin built his presidential apparatus of power, "[t]his [was] a fundamental change in the institutional balance that existed previously because it removed the selection of leaders of the executive branch of the government from the control of the legislature".[78] The top-down Party-controlled apparatus was now being replaced with a top-down Presidential apparatus. The unwritten, Soviet constitution lived on.

Semi-Presidentialism in Action: January 1992-November 1992

The Soviet Union ceased to exist in December 1991 and Russia emerged as an independent country in January 1992. Formally and constitutionally, it remained a western-style, semi-presidential republic. Informally, however, the broad delegation of appointment and edict power that El'tsin enjoyed allowed him to continue to construct a presidential apparatus that was increasingly filling the Party's unwritten constitutional position. In this process, El'tsin relied heavily on "the Russian tradition of executive law-making prerogatives".[79] The real question for Russia now would be whether this emerging form of presidential

74 Tim McDaniel, *The Agony of the Russian Ideal* (Princeton University Press, Princeton, NJ, 1996), 174.

75 Remington, *op.cit.* note 56, 101.

76 John F. Young, "Institutions, Elites, and Local Politics: The Case of Omsk", in Jeffrey W. Hahn (ed.), *Regional Russia in Transition: Studies in Yaroslavl'* (Woodrow Wilson Press, Washington, DC, 2001), 138-61, at 142.

77 *Izvestiia* (7 October 1991), 2.

78 Jeffrey Hahn, "The Political Transformation of Yaroslavl': Transition to Democracy", in Hahn, *op.cit.* note 76, 51-52.

79 Eugene Huskey, "Executive-Legislative Relations", in Eugene Huskey (ed.), *Executive Power and Soviet Politics: The Rise and Decline of the Soviet State* (M.E. Sharpe, Armonk, NY, 1992), 90-91.

power would overwhelm the formal semi-presidential constitutional system. As Robert Sharlet described it:

> "Political power no longer lurked behind the 'magic wall' of party secrecy; it has metamorphosed into a form of constitutionalism. The question for the future became, could the new constitutional forms impose reasonable limits and encourage the exercise of restraint, or would these arrangements eventually become merely a more routinized and efficient means of societal domination?"[80]

As Russia's economy continued to collapse and El'tsin's popularity waned, El'tsin "relinquished much of his will and his ability to maintain majority support within parliament".[81] Meanwhile, El'tsin's successor as head of the Supreme Soviet—Ruslan Khasbulatov—increasingly asserted the formal constitutional rules in the amended constitution, which explicitly afforded the Congress the power to both amend the constitution and revoke delegated powers to the President.[82]

Zor'kin and the Constitutional Court played a key role in mediating this emerging institutional rivalry. In its first case, the Zor'kin Court signaled its clear intention to interpret the semi-presidential system in Russia's 1978 constitution as one which placed limits on both presidential and parliamentary power. In striking down a El'tsin edict seeking to merge the Internal Police and the *KGB*, the Court opened its decision with a broad statement that "[o]ne of the fundamental principles of a constitutional system is that each government institution may only make decisions and carry out actions that are within its competency, determined in the Constitution".[83] It went on to explain that "[t]he President is not able to contradict the Constitution and the laws of the Russian Federation or *the elements of a system of checks and balances*, underpinned by the principle of separation of powers based in Article 3 of the Russian declaration of sovereignty".[84]

El'tsin and his supporters—opponents of strong judicial checks on presidential power—fought the implementation of the judgment. Under pressure from the El'tsin administration, the newspaper charged with printing Constitutional Court decisions (*Rossiiskaia Gazeta*) failed to mention that El'tsin's edict had been struck down as unconstitutional. Instead, it printed remarks from El'tsin advisor Sergei Shakhrai attacking the decision for being too political. El'tsin eventually accepted the ruling but only after some 'coaxing' by Zor'kin.[85]

80 Robert Sharlet, *op.cit.* note 44, 98.

81 Remington, *op.cit.* note 56, 86.

82 Khasbulatov used a number of mechanisms to fight back against El'tsin's growing informal power, including control over the Central Bank and the Procuracy. Huskey, *op.cit.* note 47, 33.

83 *Vestnik Konstitutsionnogo Suda Rossiiskoi Federatsii* (1993) No.1, 11-19.

84 *Ibid.*

85 Robert Ahdieh, *Russia's Constitutional Revolution: Legal Consciousness and the Transition to Democracy* (Penn State University Press, University Park, PA, 1997), 80.

As Zor'kin sought to enforce the formal constitutional rules as limitations on political power, he would have little choice but to thrust himself into the political world. This task would prove difficult, as both the presidential and parliamentary political elite were unaccustomed to constitutional limitations on the practice of political power. As Zor'kin explained in a speech to the Congress in spring 1992:

> "One of the reasons for the rivalry between the executive and legislative branches is the disregard for the constitutional principle of separation of powers. This principle in sum is not conceived on the basis of the practice where each branch is completely independent in the boundaries of its own power, but is based on the relationship between powers in which there is cooperation, mutual control and equilibration over the responsibilities for their decisions and actions."[86]

Semi-Presidentialism in Crisis: November 1992-March 1993

In November 1992, El'tsin's broad delegated powers lapsed. When it became clear that the Congress had no plans to renew these powers, rumors of a presidential *coup d'état* spread through Russia. Even leaders of Russia's democratic movement—including Democratic Reform Movement leader Gavril Popov—called for a temporary presidential dictatorship.[87]

In his struggle with parliament, one of El'tsin's chief strategies was to attack the amended 1978 Constitution's parliamentary sovereignty for violating the separation of powers. In his 2 December 1992 speech to the Congress, El'tsin outlined his vision for the 'correct' separation-of-powers system for Russia. This constitutional framework—which owed much to the Soviet-era unwritten constitution—was centered around the necessity of a strong and independent president in Russia in keeping the country together and carrying out the necessary economic reforms. Presidential—not Parliamentary—power, he argued, was critical for Russia's next top-down political and economic experiment: free market capitalism.

In making this argument, El'tsin drew heavily on the theory of a pure separation of powers:

> "The root of many problems lies in the fact that there are still normative provisions, both in the Constitution and the laws that are at variance with the principle of separation of powers. [...] .[T]he executive branch does not possess the necessary powers and independence, and therefore it cannot bear full responsibility for the state of day-to-day administrative affairs."[88]

El'tsin returned to this theme in his December 10 speech to the Congress, where he stated that "[t]he constitution, or what has become of it, is turning the Su-

86 *Vestnik Konstitutsionnogo Suda Rossiiskoi Federatsii* (1993) No.1, 3.

87 "The Russian Democratic Reform Movement is for Presidential Rule", *Nezavisimaia Gazeta* (5 November 1992), 2, in 44(45) *CDPSP* (9 December 1992), 1.

88 "The Seventh Congress of People's Deputies", speech by B.N. El'tsin, *Rossiiskaia Gazeta* (2 December 1992), 3-4, in 44(48) *CDPSP* (30 December 1992), 2-4.

preme Soviet, its leadership and its Chairman into the absolute rulers of Russia [...] accustomed to giving orders without being accountable".[89]

El'tsin realized that the parliament would not readily yield to this vision; thus, he appealed to the people directly as the only legitimate source of power. He therefore called for a referendum to decide the correct nature of Russia's constitutional system:

> "[I]n this situation, I consider it necessary to appeal directly to the citizens of Russia, to all the voters. To those who voted for me in the election and thanks to whom I became President of Russia. [...] My proposal is based on the constitutional principle of people's rule, on the President's constitutional right to appeal to the people, and on the President's constitutional right of legislative initiative. [....] The Congress and the President have but one judge—the people."[90]

This rivalry between the parliament and president was seemingly bringing Russia to the brink of outright civil war. Zor'kin helped broker a compromise: Speaker Khasbulatov agreed to a referendum in April 1993 in return for El'tsin naming a Prime Minister from the three candidates having the broadest support in the Congress.[91]

This compromise, however, would not last long. In January 1993, Khasbulatov sought to back away from a referendum. He argued that he had only agreed to a referendum because "considerations of sociopolitical advisability outweighed considerations of consonance with constitutional law".[92] He attacked a referendum for offering Russian voters a false choice:

> "I expect that, during the process of agreeing on the final wording, it is likely that the terms 'presidential republic' and 'parliamentary republic' may be proposed [but...] they are too insubstantial and abstract. [...] These terms are being imposed for only one purpose: to distract public opinion from the truth, to separate people into the 'just' (supporters of the strengthening of presidential power) and the 'unjust' (the anti-reformers' and all those reactionary deputies) and to establish some type of dictatorial regime (a regime of mob rule)."[93]

In response, El'tsin and his advisers increased their attacks on the legitimacy of the existing Constitution, accusing it of being 'unconstitutional' and ill-suited to the needs of present-day Russia. Underlying this argument was the contention that the existing constitution conflicted with the 'higher' constitutional principle of separation of powers (as well as the unwritten constitutional conception of the necessity of a guiding force in politics). A Constitutional Court judge later

89 "The President of Russia Sees Holding a Nationwide Referendum as the Only Way Out of the Crisis", *Izvestiia* (10 December 1992), 1, in 44(50) *CDPSP* (13 January 1993), 1.

90 *Ibid.*

91 Huskey, *op.cit.* note 47, 31.

92 Ruslan Khasbulatov, "The Congress of People's Deputies and Constitutional Reform", *Rossiiskaia Gazeta* (9 January 1993), 2, in 45(2) *CDPSP* (10 February 1993), 7.

93 Ruslan Khasbulatov, "The Congress of People's Deputies and Constitutional Reform", *Rossiiskaia Gazeta* (10 January 1993), 2, in 45 (2) *CDPSP* (10 February 1993), 8.

remarked that "[a]t that time, some great minds started to develop the idea of the 'non-constitutional nature of the Constitution'".[94]

One of El'tsin's close constitutional advisors and a leading academic, Professor Sergei Alekseev, began this line of attack by challenging the constitutionality of parliamentary sovereignty in the constitution:

> "What can one say when, with respect to Congress, Article 104 of the Constitution currently in effect says in plain language that the Congress is 'the supreme body of state power' (not of representative or legislative power, but of state power as a whole) and that it is authorized to deal with any—!!—question coming within the jurisdiction of the Russian Federation? This situation has become—paradoxical as it might seem—unconstitutional."[95]

For Alekseev, separation of powers meant a president that was a Party-like, guiding force in Russian politics: "The point is that the institution of the presidency, as it is understood today, is an institution of a head of state who is called upon—along with performing other functions—to ensure the optimal and balanced functioning of the legislative, executive, and judicial branches."[96] Anatolii Vengerov, another of El'tsin's supporters, also argued that the only legitimate constitutional system included a strong and independent president:

> "Russia has always needed strong executive authority at major turning points in its history. [I]f we want Russia to be preserved and not to break up into appanage principalities, it needs that kind of authority—both because of its geopolitical position and large dimensions and because of its ethnic makeup, which has always been a special problem for us."[97]

El'tsin also reiterated this position, arguing that any parliamentary reforms that weakened his powers "not only upset the balance among the government's branches but also change the constitution fundamentally. I did not swear to uphold that kind of constitution".[98] He also sent a draft letter to Zor'kin questioning the constitutionality of the current system, asking him to pay special attention to the crisis and "to the relationship between Article 3 [establishing separation of powers], on the one hand, Articles 104 and 107 [stating that the Parliament was the highest organ of state power], on the other".[99]

94 Leonid Nikitsky, "Interview with Boris Ebzeev, Justice of the Constitutional Court of the Russian Federation", 6 *Eastern European Constitutional Review* (1997), 86.

95 S. Alekseev, "Absolute Power for the Soviets is Incompatible with True Democracy", *Izvestiia* (4 February 1993), 5, in 45(6) *CDPSP* (10 March 1993), 8. Alekseev also had been the first Chief Justice of the USSR Committee of Constitutional Supervision, the forerunner of the RF Constitutional Court.

96 *Ibid.*

97 Interview by Aleksandr Sidiachko, *Megapolis-Express* (19 May 1993), 23, in 45(19) *CDPSP* (9 June 1993), 4.

98 Nikolai Troitskii, "What does Yeltsin Want?" *Megapolis-Express* (3 March 1993), 3, in 45(9) *CDPSP* (31 March 1993), 1.

99 "The President's Appeal to the Constitutional Court and Supreme Soviet" *Izvestiia* (2 March 1993), 1, in 45(9) *CDPSP* (31 March 1993), 4.

As the constitutional debate raged on, the Congress met again in March 1993. In Khasbulatov's speech to the Congress, he proclaimed that El'tsin's "attempts to devalue the existing Constitution, destabilize the political situation [...] have a certain logic, which consists, apparently, in implying that the potential for carrying out ultra-radical reforms by constitutional, democratic methods have been exhausted".[100] The next day, El'tsin appealed to the assembled deputies not to weaken the presidency, describing the necessity of a strong presidency in Russia's constitutional system: "I am a strong proponent of presidential power. But not because I am President, but because without the presidency Russia would not survive [...] because the President is elected by the entire people, he *embodies* the integrity and unity of Russia."[101] The Congress, however, did not listen and stripped the President of his extraordinary powers "to issue edicts with the same force as parliamentary laws, to appoint presidential envoys or heads of administration, [and] to appoint government ministers without the approval of parliament". The President was now limited to its more limited role as head of the executive branch in a formal semi-presidential, separation-of-powers system.

El'tsin would not accept this arrangement. On March 20, he gave a televised speech and called for "special administrative rule, a condition in which the Supreme Soviet and the Congress of People's Deputies would be subordinated to the President and would not have the right to cancel his edicts or to pass laws contradicting them".[102] In support of this extraordinary measure, he tied the Congress to the old Soviet system of government and argued that the Congress was undermining the people's ability to exercise their power through the President:

> "The eighth Congress was, in point of fact, a dress rehearsal for revenge by members of former Party *nomenklatura*. They simply want to deceive the people. We hear them lie in the oaths of loyalty to the Constitution that they continually take; from Congress to Congress, that document is bent and reshaped in their own interests, and blow after blow is dealt to the very foundation of the constitutional system of people's rule."[103]

El'tsin also reiterated his belief that the Congress's actions were violating the separation of powers: "The separation of powers as a principle of Constitution is being eliminated, to all intents and purposes."[104]

Reaction was swift. Vice President Rutskoi spoke out against the speech in a hastily convened session of the Presiding Committee of the Supreme Soviet

100 "Speech by R. Khasbulatov, Chairman of the Supreme Soviet", *Rossisskaia Gazeta* (11March 1993), 1, in 45(10) *CDPSP* (7 April 1993), 1.

101 "If you Destroy the Presidency, you Destroy Russia", *Izvestiia* (12 March 1993), 1.

102 Roy Medvedev, *Post-Soviet Russia: A Journey through the Yeltsin Era* (Columbia University Press, New York, NY, 2000), 96.

103 "Boris Yeltsin Offers the Country a Peaceful Way Out of the Crisis", *Rossiiskie Vesti* (23 March 1993), 1-2, in 45(12) *CDPSP* (12 April 1993), 1.

104 *Ibid.*

that Saturday night.[105] The Constitutional Court convened a special session on Sunday, 21 March and declared El'tsin's speech unconstitutional on Monday morning. The Congress met on 21 March and called an emergency session for 26 March. El'tsin had no choice but to back down: the published edict from his speech on 24 March deleted any mention of 'special administrative rule'.[106]

The Congress convened a special session on 28 March to consider El'tsin's impeachment and the referendum. Outside in Red Square, El'tsin gave a speech to a throng of supporters claiming that the impeachment vote did not matter because he would only submit to the 'verdict of the people'.[107] Sixty-six percent of the deputies called for his impeachment, perilously close to the seventy-five percent needed. They also voted to hold a referendum on 25 April 1993.

The April Referendum and the Construction of a New Constitutional System: April 1993-December 1993

The Congress approved four questions for the April 25 referendum:

1. Do you have confidence in Boris El'tsin, the President of Russia?
2. Do you approve the social and economic policy of the President of Russia and Russia's government since 1992?
3. Do you consider early presidential elections necessary?
4. Do you consider early elections for the full Parliament to be necessary?

The legal meaning of the upcoming referendum results ended up in the Constitutional Court. In a carefully reasoned decision, the Constitutional Court held that the first two questions did not have 'legal significance' and, therefore, would not result in any legal changes to the constitution. Thus, for these questions to be deemed 'passed' they would not require more than fifty percent of the entire Russian electorate, but just fifty percent of those voting in the election.[108]

For El'tsin and his team, however, a victory in the referendum would be a vindication of their vision of a presidentially-dominated system of constitutional government with no structural limitations on presidential power. One constitutional advisor stated:

105 Medvedev, *op.cit.* note 102, 96. According to Medvedev, El'tsin had taped the speech on the morning of 20 March and had distributed tapes to the foreign embassies before consulting his advisors. The Chair of El'tsin's Security Council, Iurii Skokov, refused to endorse the new edict and tried to persuade El'tsin not to take this step.

106 *Ibid.*, 97.

107 *Ibid.*, 97.

108 Andrew Felkay, *Yeltsin's Russia and the West* (Praeger Publishers, Westport, CT, 2002), 74.

"If the President receives a vote of confidence on the first referendum question while on the fourth question the electorate votes for early elections for the People's Deputies, he will fully implement the provisions in his March 20 televised address to the people."[109]

In the campaign prior to the April referendum, El'tsin and his newly built presidential apparatus worked hard to ensure a large vote in support of El'tsin. These El'tsin-appointed administrators worked against regional legislatures in the high-stakes referendum over the future direction of the Russian political system.[110] El'tsin's main strategy was to appeal to the Russian people by arguing that a vote of no confidence in him would be a vote to return to the communist past. For instance, pro-El'tsin newspapers framed the choice as one of moving forward or backward:

"Peasants—you who feed Russia—Do you want to go back to the state farms, without the slightest hope that, if not you, at least your grandchildren will own land? [...] Intelligentsia [...] What will your life be like under a regime of information blockades and ideological clichés, the regime that the Soviets have already begun to explore?"[111]

In the end, 58.05% of participants voted that they had confidence in Boris El'tsin.[112] El'tsin's team immediately saw these results as a popular ratification of presidentially dominated government. El'tsin proclaimed that "[t]he Russian Soviet Federation Socialist Republic has been peacefully replaced by the Russian Federation. The state has changed its legal identity."[113] Shakhrai held a press conference and stated that the Congress could no longer legally remove the President from his post, force the government to resign, or adopt a new constitution.[114] Asked what would happen if the Congress failed to comply, he said: "The president and the government received a vote of confidence in the referendum. They will conduct the economic reform on the basis of their own decisions."[115]

109 Viktor Kozhemiako, "Threat of a State of Emergency", *Pravda*, 1, in 45(16) *CDPSP* (19 May 1993), 9.

110 Sergei Chugaev, "The Russian Federation Supreme Soviet is Conducting a Political Campaign using the Taxpayers' Money", *Izvestiia* (21 April 1993), 1-2, in 45(16) *CDPSP* (19 May 1993), 7.

111 Editorial, "Think Again", *Rossiiskie Vesti* (24 April 1993), 1, in 45(16) *CDPSP* (19 May 1993), 11.

112 Georgii Ivanov-Smolenskii, "According to the Latest Data from the Central Election Commission, 58.05% of Russian Citizens Participating in the Referendum Cast their Votes for Boris Yeltsin", *Izvestiia* (28 April 28 1993), 2, in 45(17) *CDPSP* (26 May 1993), 1.

113 Vasilii Kononenko, "President of Russia begins Promised Changes by Presenting Draft of New Constitution", *Izvestiia* (30 April 1993), 1-2, in 45(17) *CDPSP* (26 May 1993), 7.

114 Sergei Shakhrai, "The Deputies Must Repeal their Most Recent Decisions", *Rossiiskie Vesti* (28 April 1993), 1, in 45(17) *CDPSP* (26 May 1993), 3-4.

115 *Ibid.*

Not long after, El'tsin issued an edict calling for a Constitutional Convention.[116] El'tsin chose the delegates himself and speculated that the Convention could emerge as a kind of proto-government: "It seems to me that the Constitutional Convention can be transferred into a Federation Council and will be one of the houses of parliament."[117] El'tsin drew the authority to create a new parallel representative body alongside Parliament from his popular mandate in the April referendum: Shakhrai stated that El'tsin's referendum result "mean[s] that the President [...] possesses the constitutive power to form other state institutions".[118]

El'tsin produced a draft constitution for consideration at the Convention on 29 April 1993.[119] This document formalized the 'unwritten Soviet-era constitution' that El'tsin and his team had been pressing for the last year. It outlined the El'tsin administration's view of the correct separation-of-powers system: one that placed the president in the old position of the Party and above the tripartite system of separated power. As the embodiment of the people and the head of the unitary state, the President was the guarantor of the constitution and ensured the harmonious interaction of the branches.[120]

This draft was immediately controversial, particularly for its broad view of presidential powers. In an interview discussing this draft constitution, Alekseev stated boldly: "We are not yet ready for a parliamentary form. That requires a developed political system—one that has parties, a special level of sophistication, and firmly stated rules of play. [...]" When asked whether the Presidential draft would create a constitutional monarchy, he said:

> "The position is not Tsar but President. Although I will say candidly that some Russian traditions have been incorporated, because Russia is a country that has an authoritarian state as one of its foundations. It used to be a monarch, now it's a President. Generally speaking,

116 Perhaps the best example of this was when the Soviet coup plotters in August 1991 sought to ensure that the Soviet Union would not break up into independent republics, relied on constitutional procedure. "While any Latin American *junta* would unhesitatingly have cut off communications and arrested political challengers, the Soviet conspirators were concerned to cite Article 127, Section 7 of the USSR Constitution on the transfer of power from the president to the vice president." Sharlet, *op.cit.* note 44, 113.

117 "Vlasti posle referenduma: Prezident naznachaet datu konstitutsionnogo soveshchaniia", *Kommersant, Vlast'* (12 May 1993).

118 Sergei Chugaev, "S. Shakhrai on the New Constitution", *Izvestiia* (30 April 1993), 2, in 45(18) *CDPSP* (2 June 1993), 6.

119 Levent Gönenc, *Prospects for Constitutionalism in Post-Communist Countries*, in William B. Simons (ed.), *Law in Eastern Europe*, No.50 (Martinus Nijhoff Publishers, Leiden, Boston, MA, 2002), 161.

120 Chugayev, *op.cit.* note 118, 6.

> since 1918 we have been moving—not in words but in deeds—toward a constitutional monarchy."[121]

Once underway, El'tsin did not intend any serious compromises with parliamentary delegates at the Convention. Speaker Khasbulatov was shouted down when he attempted to speak at the Convention and walked out with seventy representatives from local parliaments, calling the conference a sham. Another parliamentarian was ejected for 'disorderly conduct' after he attempted to introduce a new draft for discussion.[122] The sessions were closed, and proposed changes had to be approved by the working commission—a smaller body that was comprised solely of El'tsin's closest advisors and appointed executive representatives from the regions.

In his speech to the Convention, El'tsin outlined the key goals of the Convention. El'tsin's speech began with an outright attack on parliamentary government: "In opposition are not two branches of government, but instead two independent political systems." He tied parliamentary government with the Soviet Union, discussing how the assembly-based power (*sovetskaia vlast'*) was unable to achieve reform, leading him to the remarkable conclusion that "assemblies [*sovety*] and democracy are not compatible". He also drew directly from the pure version of separation of powers in saying that the "system of parliamentary sovereignty, given to Russia by Soviet power, cannot achieve the necessary agreement" and is "dangerous [and] chaotic".[123]

El'tsin went on to argue that Russia's new constitution should adopt a 'new approach' to the organization of power.[124] Clearly referencing the constitutional deadlock that had plagued the country over the previous year, he described the new constitution as creating an effective form of presidential power that could effectively transform the country in its time of need: "[...] to ensure effective power, which will protect the rights and freedoms of the individual, and will become the pivot for the legal system for the economic well-being of the country."[125] Thus, the key goals of the constitution were to be: "The protection of the unity of the Russian government and overcoming the weakness of government power."[126] Reflecting his intention that this president should not face any structural checks or balances, El'tsin proclaimed: "We should depart from copying the American,

121 "No, not a Tsar but a President", interview with S. Alekseev by Elena Dikun, *Megapolis-Express* (5 May 1993), 26, in 45(18) *CDPSP* (2 June 1993), 7.

122 Ahdieh, *op.cit.* note 85, 59.

123 *Konstitutsionnoe soveshchanie. Informatsionnyi biulleten'* (Iuridicheskaia literatura, Moscow, 1993), 14.

124 *Ibid.*

125 *Ibid.*, 14.

126 *Ibid.*, 17.

French, or other models, and return to Russian roots in order to honor our very own democratic experience."[127]

Professor Alekseev, the chief architect of the constitutional draft, was the next to speak to the Convention and further described the vast powers of the Russian president. "[The president was the] head of state. [...] His responsibility is the structural integrity of the government. He takes measures, so that the entire government apparatus will work, averts different types of crises, and directly runs the Government."[128] He went on to explain that the constitutional role of the President was different from western constitutional systems. The Russian President is not the same as:

> "[...] imagined in textbooks or in its classical form. The fundamental concept of the presidency is as the superior power. The presidency ensures the idea of an independent and responsible Government, formed in order to decide questions of governmental operation. And the presidency ensures that the Government works with the regional legislatures in the creation of a single governmental vertical."[129]

This "stable, strong, and capable organization of power" was democratic, Alekseev argued, because it is rooted in a "democratic basis: sovereignty [*narodovlastie*]. [...] The people decide the matter".[130]

As the conference went forward, delegates questioned why the president was not in the executive branch and why the Constitution simultaneously called for a separation of powers and governmental unity. In response to one of those questions, a close El'tsin advisor, Anatolii Sobchak, effectively summed up the system: "The separation is not into separate trees of power, but into separate branches, which come from the same core, the same trunk."[131] The president would be the trunk of state power from which the separated branches would emanate.

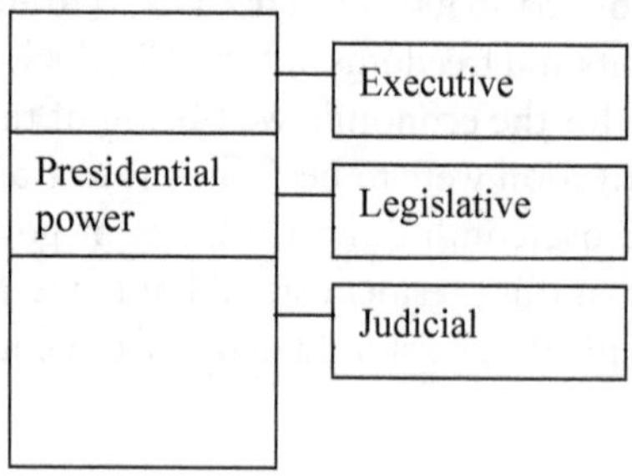

127 *Ibid.*

128 *Konstitutsionnoe soveshchanie: Stenogrammy. Materialy. Dokumenty. 20 aprelia-10 noiabria 1993 g. v 20 tomakh*, Vol.1 (Iuridicheskaia literatura, Moscow, 1995), 7.

129 *Ibid.*

130 *Ibid.*

131 *Ibid.*, Vol.2, 382. Sobchak previously had been on the Law Faculty of Leningrad State University and thereafter had become the first elected, post-Soviet mayor of St. Petersburg in mid-1991.

Sergei Shakhrai, another member of the constitutional drafting team, explained that placing the president outside the executive branch was a way to strengthen the president: "The President is weaker if he is the head of the executive branch." Shakhrai stated that this extra power would be safeguarded by the fact that the president is "elected by all the people".[132] One participant mentioned that in France, in 1958, they were considering two models of government (presidential and parliamentary) and had created a new one (semi-presidential). He stated that the Russians were now creating a fourth model of government to deal with its own unique political situation.[133]

In the wake of the constitutional convention, El'tsin's draft remained largely unchanged in its most important provisions. El'tsin now searched for a way to ratify this draft. Opposition in the regional assemblies meant that El'tsin had to abandon his initial plan to present the draft to each subject of the federation for ratification.[134]

El'tsin decided to take matters into his own hands. On 21 September 1993, he issued Edict Number 1400, disbanding the Russian Parliament (and the regional legislatures) and ordering the Constitutional Court to refrain from meeting. The edict nullified all parts of the 1978 Constitution that contradicted its terms. In its opening paragraph, the edict based its legitimacy on: "[the parliament's] direct opposition to the will of the people, reflected in the referendum of 25 April 1993. This referendum had the highest possible legal force across the entire Russian nation."[135]

The Constitutional Court declared this edict unconstitutional and authorized the legislature to impeach El'tsin. Under Article 121 (6) of the Russian Constitution, the President's powers were immediately suspended if the President attempted to disperse a legally elected representative body. At a meeting of the Congress in the Russian White House, Aleksandr Rutskoi became President and began issuing edicts.[136] The Supreme Soviet and Rutskoi called for a mass strike to resist El'tsin's unconstitutional actions. A tense standoff ensued. El'tsin refused to compromise and called on the Army to disperse the 'illegal' Parliament. El'tsin, in his own memoir, recalled how close he was to losing control of the country at this point.[137]

In the crucial moments—as the army wavered—control of public opinion became critical. Fighting broke out between pro-parliamentary troops and pro-El'tsin troops over control of the Moscow television and radio tower, Ostankino.

132 *Ibid.*, Vol.12, 284.

133 *Ibid.*, Vol.6, 48.

134 Ahdieh, *op.cit.* note 85, 63.

135 Edict No.1400, *Rossiiskaia Gazeta* (14 January 1994 and 19 January 1994).

136 Medvedev, *op.cit.* note 102, 107.

137 Boris El'tsin, *Zapiski Prezidenta* (Ogonek, Moscow, 1994), 381.

Despite the fact that a majority of the officer corps did not want to intervene in the political situation, Defense Minister Pavel Grachev reluctantly agreed to intervene to put down the disturbances and forcibly disbanded the Parliament, shelling the Russian Parliament.[138] No one took to the streets to protest the gross violation of the amended, communist-era Constitution; El'tsin's campaign to undermine its legitimacy had succeeded. Russia's short-lived experiment with constitutionally limited government was over.

El'tsin's team worked quickly to establish the legitimacy of his actions. In speaking to an American audience, a prominent political thinker in the *perestroika* and post-*perestroika* periods explained:

> "The Congress of People's Deputies simply was unable to comprehend any rule of law higher than constitutional law, and that the Congress is unable to distinguish constitutional law from constitutional principles. The principles expressed in the current Constitution have never achieved the level of being 'constitutional'. Instead, the constitution of the Russian Federation itself might be unconstitutional. This idea is based upon the simple notion that the current Constitution expresses principles that are in direct conflict with the will of the Russian people."[139]

The Ministry of Justice also issued a statement, asserting that:

> "[although the President] acted beyond the formal legal framework, he acted in accordance with the constitutional principles of government by the people, insurance of the country's security and protection of the rights and lawful interests of citizens [...] although, as a formal matter, he exceeded his powers, he used this violation, not to usurp power but to protect the will of the people."[140]

In October and November, El'tsin reconvened a rump constitutional convention that further entrenched the power of the Presidency. A key figure in El'tsin's administration, Sergei Filatov, stressed that Russia was not ready for the destabilizing effects of a structurally balanced constitutional system:

> "I said this at the first meeting and I want to repeat my opinion that references to international practice are often inappropriate for Russia. We are special. And when we talk about the separation of powers—the full isolation of one branch of government from another, then we can see the history, which has just happened—it is history, but it is still fresh in our minds—this shows us that we have chosen the path away from partnomenklatury [...] and away from the path to war."[141]

138 James H. Brusstar and Ellen Jones, *The Russian Military's Role in Politics* (National Defense University Institute, Washington, DC, 1995), 24.

139 Alexander Iaklovev, "Russia: The Struggle for a Constitution", 7 *Emory International Law Review* (1993), 291.

140 Statement of the Ministry of Justice at the Constitutional Meeting. See *Informatsionnyi Biulleten'* (1993) No.2, 26.

141 *Konstitutisonnoe soveshchanie, op.cit.* note 128, Vol.18, 96.

As they were finalizing the draft, El'tsin issued an edict stating that the Constitutional Conference's draft would be placed before the Russian people in a nation-wide referendum on 12 December 1993.[142] He based this decision on:

> "The unshakable nature of the people's rule as the foundation of the Russian Federation's constitutional system, cognizant of the fact that the repository and sole source of power in the Russian Federation is its multinational people, and with a view to implementing the people's right to directly resolve the most important questions of the life of state."[143]

The official draft constitution was published on 9 November 1993.[144] The President remained above the tripartite system of separated power and exercised significant presidential power over each branch of government. *First*, the President had a virtual monopoly over executive power. Article 111 (4) of the Constitution provided that if the lower house of the Parliament (the *Duma*) rejected the President's choice as head of the government (Prime Minister), the President must then appoint a Prime Minister and dissolve the *Duma*. Furthermore, the President had the power to annul any executive branch edicts. As one newspaper columnist stated:

> "The draft virtually precludes the possibility of forming a coalition government [...] emphasis is placed not on having various political parties represented in the Cabinet [...] but on having a unified, functional body that acts in accordance with the President's political will."[145]

Second, the President exercised significant constitutional power to control the legislative branch of the government, particularly over the upper house of the Russian Parliament: the Federation Council. Article 95 (2) stated that the Federation Council was comprised of "two representatives from each of Russia's subjects: one from the executive branch and one from the legislative branch". Furthermore, according to Article 77 (2), the bodies of executive power in the federal center and in the regions formed a "unified system of executive power". Because of the President's monopoly of executive power, one-half of the 'senators' in the Federation Council were therefore subordinated to the President. This was by design: El'tsin had originally seen the Federation Council as a consultative body that would help the Russian President exercise power in the regions.[146]

142 "Decree of the President of the Russian Federation", *Rossiiskie Vesti* (19 October 1993), 1, in 45(42) *CDPSP* (17 November 1993), 7.

143 *Ibid.*

144 Dmitry Volkov and Aleksei Zubro, "Boris Yeltsin's Basic Law", *Segodnia* (11 November 1993), 1, in 45(45) *CDPSP* (8 December 1993), 1-2.

145 *Ibid.*

146 El'tsin's Edict No.1400 (*op.cit.* note 135) disbanding the Parliament initially stated that the upper house would be automatically made up of the heads of the executive and representative branches of government in the regions. Most of these executive representatives were El'tsin appointees. However, because of the widespread opposition to his disbanding of the legislative assemblies in the regions, he temporarily decided that elections would yield a more pliant group of legislative representatives in the Federation Council. See Aleksei Zuichenko and Lev Bruni, "The Council of Federation Will be Formed by the Voters", *Segodnia* (12 October 1993), 1, in 45(41) *CDPSP* (10 November 1993), 16.

In order to ensure that this body would remain in this role, El'tsin personally intervened in the final days before releasing the draft and insisted that the Federation Council be 'formed' rather than 'elected' as originally envisioned by the Constitutional Convention.[147] In making this change, El'tsin hoped to ensure that this powerful body—which had the power to veto bills passed by the lower house and confirm judicial appointments—would stay out of party politics and remain subordinated to the presidential apparatus.[148] As the Chairman of the Federation Council said in 1999:

> "The upper house of the Federal Assembly is an element of stability; in a period of abrupt change it protects the country from social upheaval. For the first time in the history of Russia, a non-political organ has emerged which influences state policy and stands by the people."[149]

Third, the President had full control over the judicial branch of government. The President appointed all of the judges to both the Supreme Court and the Constitutional Court with the consent of the Federation Council.[150] Because the Federation Council was a rubber-stamp body largely under Presidential control, the President had no real check on his or her appointment power.

Campaign and Ratification

During the campaign to ratify this constitution and the elections to the new bicameral legislature, El'tsin refused to join a political party. He also forbade any candidates in the Parliamentary elections—which were taking place simultaneously with the referendum—to campaign against the Draft Constitution.

El'tsin himself made a series of speeches seeking to persuade the Russian people to ratify the Constitution. He began by explaining that the system of power outlined in the Constitution was the only way to ensure the expression of the unified will of the people and avoid civil war:

> "Only by relying on the will of the people, can we strengthen Russian statehood and overcome the legacy of the Communist and Soviet past and the consequences of *dual power.* […] The constitution raises a firm barrier to confrontation among the branches of power."[151]

147 See Paul Chaisty, *Legislative Politics and Economic Power in Russia* (Palgrave Macmillan, New York, NY, 2006), 104.

148 Furthermore, the President would exercise significant informal control over this body through the president's role in choosing the Chairman of this part-time, non-partisan chamber. The presidentially-appointed "Commission on the Legislative Proposals under the Administration of the President of Russia" specified that: "The Federation Council would not be party run or party oriented. Instead, it would be overseen by a chairman and deputy chairmen." Remington, *op.cit.* note 51, 180.

149 Quoted from Chaisty, *op.cit.* note 147, 105.

150 Art.83, Russian Constitution.

151 "Boris Yeltsin: The New Constitution Will Protect Democracy in Russia", *Izvestiia* (10 November 1993), 1, in (45)45 *CDPSP* (8 December 1993), 1-2.

In a later interview, El'tsin explained the importance of a president serving as a guiding force in Russian politics:

> "In a country that it used to tsars or great leaders, in a country where clear-cut interest groups have not been defined and normal parties are just beginning to emerge, in a country where executive discipline is extraordinarily weak and where legal nihilism is enjoying an unrestrained spree—in such a country, should we place our stakes only or mainly on parliament? In six months, if not before, people would be demanding a dictator. Such a dictator would quickly be found, let me assure you."[152]

El'tsin went on to explain that the draft constitution placed limits on this newly envisioned presidential power:

> "The President's power is limited by the fact that he implements basic policy guidelines within the framework and on the basis of the Constitution, which has rather stringent norms. [...] Moreover, the President did not arrogate this role to himself, he did not inherit it—he received it from the people in the form of a clear political mandate."[153]

In addressing the Russian people before the referendum on the Russian Constitution, El'tsin once again returned to the unwritten constitutional principle that Russia needs a strong guiding force to avoid fragmentation and civil war:

> "Russia is an enormous country, which occupies a significant part of two continents—Europe and Asia. The president, who is elected by the entire population, by all the people who are citizens in all the regions, or, as they say in Rus', by the earth, is called to embody all of Russia. The president, therefore, is the chief garantor of Russia's unity and carries the serious responsibility for the country. For these reasons, the president should have powers equal to these responsibilities."[154]

Another of El'tsin's supporters sought to place this referendum in the western tradition: "After Dec. 12, either we follow the path of Gen. de Gaulle proposed for France at the time of the Fifth Republic, when a presidential constitution adopted by referendum brought the county out of an impasse, or we repeat our own history at the beginning of the century."[155]

The Constitution received a bare majority in the national referendum. In the aftermath of the ratification of the Constitution, El'tsin stated:

> "A popular mandate to strengthen the system of government has been received. [...] No matter whom the voters cast their votes for, they were agreed on one point: Russia needs strong rule, Russia needs order, people are irritated by the amorphous nature of power, they are tired of inconsistent and halfhearted decisions, and they are exasperated by the rise in crime."[156]

152 "As President I Have a Greater Stake than Others Do in Social Stability", interview with Boris El'tsin, *Izvestiia* (16 November 1993), 1, 4, in 45(46) *CDPSP* (15 December 1993), 9.

153 *Ibid.*

154 "To Adopt the New Constitution Means Saving Russia from a Repeat of the October Events", *Izvestiia* (10 December 1993), 1, in 45(49) *CDPSP* (5 January 1994), 1-2.

155 Vladimir Lysenko, "At a Fork in the Road", *Nezavisimaia Gazeta* (11November 1993), 1, in 45(45) *CDPSP* (8 December 1993), 3.

156 Vera Kuznetsova, "Will a Fundamentally Reformed Government be Able to Conduct Fundamental Reform?", *Nezavisimaia Gazeta* (23 December 1993), 1, in 45(51) *CDPSP* (19 January 1994), 1.

El'tsin's aides were not shy about the nature of the constitutional system that they had created. The reporter, David Remnick, reported that: "[El'tsin's aides] admitted that the illusion of a smooth and swift transfer from a dictatorship to a free-market democracy is gone. [...] Now the talk is of a transitional regime of 'enlightened authoritarianism' or 'guided democracy' or some such hybrid that makes no secret of the need for a prolonged concentration of power in the presidency."[157]

Enforcing the Constitutional System: 1994-Present

Now that El'tsin's team had formalized a system of government in which the President took on the unwritten functions that the Communist Party performed during the Soviet period, they sought to promote its authority. El'tsin and his team saw the formal legal power of the 1993 Constitution as another key tool in rebuilding the Russian state and reforming the country.

This desire to build the legitimacy of the Constitution meant that the Constitutional Court was preserved.[158] In fact, members of the Constitutional Court, including the acting Chief Justice, Nikolai Vitruk, and the other sitting justices, played an important role in drafting the enabling legislation for the Constitutional Court law, finally approved on 12 July 1994. Furthermore, Zor'kin was never removed from the Court and became its Chief Justice again in 2003 under Vladimir Putin.[159] At the same time, however, in order to ensure that the Court would not revert to its old ways and attempt to limit presidential power, El'tsin added six new judges to the Constitutional Court, which "would provide a minimal pro-El'tsin majority on the bench".[160]

When the Court finally returned to making decisions in 1995, the Court worked to slowly rebuild its power in the Russian constitutional system. Despite repeated appeals by members of the *Duma* against what were perceived to be unconstitutional presidential actions, the new Court consistently interpreted the language of the Constitution in line with the drafter's broad view of presidential power.

Two decisions are particularly characteristic. In 1996, members of the *Duma* claimed that a El'tsin edict reorganizing the institutions of executive power was unconstitutional because this reorganization should be based on federal law and not a presidential edict.[161] The court disagreed and upheld the edict, arguing that textual requirement that the President "protect the harmonious interaction

157 Huskey, *op.cit.* note 47, 32.

158 For more on the continued power of the Constitutional Court in Russia, see Trochev, *op.cit.* note 67.

159 Walter Moss, *A History of Russia: Since 1855* (Anthem, London, 2000), 557.

160 Trochev, *op.cit.* note 67, 76.

161 *Postanovlenie* (30 April 1996), *Vestnik Konstitutsionnogo Suda Rossiiskoi Federatsii* (1996).

of the organs of state power" justified edict-based legislation as long as it did not contradict federal law or the constitution. In a scathing dissent, Luchin attacked this broad and potentially limitless vision of presidential power:

> "In Russia we are seeing the de facto return of edict-based legislation [*ukaznoe pravotvorchestvo*], which we used to see during the Soviet period when the Presidium of the USSR Supreme Soviet would issue normative acts. [...] The President gives himself not just the right to appoint the heads of the regions, but also the right to suspend or forbid elections to the head of the administration. [...] This 'self-regulation' does not have any limits, is dangerous, and does not accord with the separation of powers."[162]

In 1998, the Constitutional Court interpreted the provision of the constitution affording the President the power to appoint the Prime Minister (the head of the executive branch).[163] In relevant part, this provision stated:

> "After the State *Duma* thrice rejects candidates for Chairman of the Government of the Russian Federation nominated by the President of the Russian Federation, the President of the Russian Federation shall appoint a Chairman of the Government of the Russian Federation, dissolve the State *Duma*, and call a new election."

Representatives of the *Duma* argued that this provision did not allow the President to propose the same candidate each time and then dissolve the parliament after the third rejection.

The Constitutional Court disagreed with the *Duma*. After noting that the text did not compel a result, the Court reasoned that it would have to interpret the provision in light of the goals of the constitutional system. It began its analysis arguing that: "the legal logic of Article 111 is that [...] the only source from which these [separated] powers come is the Russian multinational people [...]". From there, the Court reasoned that there must be methods for the President in ensuring the coordination of the branches of government. As the 'head of government' and coordinator of these branches of government, the Court argued that the constitution does not limit the power of the President to appoint the same candidate each time.

Thus, the text of the constitution and the context of its creation have proved important in Russia's post-1993 constitutional law. Despite some vigorous dissents, the majority of the Court has found very few limitations on presidential power in the 1993 Constitution. Thus, El'tsin had proven successful in resisting the real constitutional revolution—the western-style structural limitations in the amended 1978 constitution—while converting the unwritten constitution into a formal, textually based 'presidential' one.

Conclusions

The end of the Cold War has had a lasting effect on Western understandings of the 1993 Russian Constitution. In their belief that Russia was 'in transition'

162 *Ibid.*

163 *Postanovlenie* (11 December 1998), *Vestnik Konstitutsionnogo Suda Rossiiskoi Federatsii* (1998).

to democracy, western commentators mistakenly saw El'tsin's attacks on the Soviet-era state system to be proof of a desire to move toward constitutional democracy. Furthermore, they misunderstood El'tsin's appeals to the separation of powers as proof of his desire to establish structurally limited government. This misunderstanding of the intent of Russia's first post-Soviet constitutional system has plagued subsequent commentary and scholarship.

Cleared of these flawed assumptions, it is clear that Russia's 1993 constitutional system and its central institution, the presidency, was the culmination of an attempt to build a system of government that would avoid the inefficiencies of constitutionally-limited government. Divorcing separation of powers from the theory of checks and balances and appealing to the will of the people, El'tsin's team were able to undermine the legitimacy of the 1978 Constitution and introduce a constitutional system that reintroduced the unwritten constitutional concept of the need for a 'guiding force' in Russian politics. 1993 therefore represented a counter-revolution against the true western constitutional transplant: the amended 1978 Constitution. Ironically, the brief tenure of Russia's amended Communist-era Constitution is the closest Russia ever moved toward western-style, constitutionally limited governmental design.

These conclusions help us understand the rightful role of western ideas of constitutional design in Russia's post-Communist period. *First*, these findings explain why constitutionally-limited government did not spread to Russia. Since 1993, Russia has operated under a formal constitutional system of government that was not intended to place structural limitations on political power: the President has taken the position (and actual office space) that the Party used to occupy. Putin, therefore, is unfairly charged with Russia's autocratic backsliding; instead, his ability to build consensus across the subordinate branches of government—particularly in reaction to threats from terror and financial crisis—have helped him push the powers of the presidency to their constitutional limit. In this way, he has been able to accomplish what El'tsin's erratic and personalized leadership style was unable to do: realize the textual powers of the President as the guiding force in Russian politics.

Second, the constitutionalization of presidential power also reflects the surprising importance of formal constitutional rules in the exercise of political power in Russia. The amended 1978 Constitution's hastily-constructed semi-presidential system of balanced government proved difficult for El'tsin to overcome. Furthermore, even though El'tsin's team rejected check and balances in the constitution, they also valued constitutional rules, explicitly outlining the contours of presidential power in the 1993 Constitution (rather than simply mentioning the President as the 'leading force' in society). Although few constitutional limits are placed on the President, those that do limit presidential power have proved important: for instance, Putin's decision to step down from the Presidency in 2008—despite large scale attempts in Russian society to either amend the Constitution or declare Putin the father and leader of the nation through extra-constitutional means—suggests that the current political elite also see the text of the constitution as placing limits on presidential power.

Third, in vesting such strong constitutional powers in the President, the Russian Constitution has set the example for other countries that used referendums and appeals to separation of powers to pass new constitutions that elevate the President above the system of separated powers. For instance, since El'tsin's actions in 1993, Belarus, Kazakhstan, and Armenia have transformed their communist-era constitutional systems of parliamentary sovereignty into presidential republics, declaring the President to be head of state, guarantor of the constitution, and coordinator of state bodies of power.

Fourth, this chapter reveals Russia's surprisingly strong domestic tradition of respect for constitutionally-limited government. The Zor'kin Court's attempts to enforce checks and balances have been echoed in the post-1993 period by scathing dissents attacking the new constitutional system for its failure to limit presidential power. Furthermore, a growing number of influential Russians are beginning to argue that conditions have changed and Russia is now ready for more limitations on presidential power. In a recent conference, Russian President Dmitrii Medvedev admitted that the Russian constitution was not 'ideal' but that it was still needed during Russia's ongoing transition to democracy.[164] He did, however, leave open the possibility that constitutional changes might be made in the future. Those interested in promoting constitutionally-limited government in Russia would be well-served in nurturing this tradition.

Finally, this chapter suggests broader lessons for post-authoritarian constitutional transformation. The preceding analysis suggests that constitutional structure is critical in securing individual liberty in post-authoritarian nations with ineffective judiciaries. The structural competition for power amongst different branches helped limit the power of the Russian government between 1992 and 1993 far more than the extensive rights provisions in the El'tsin Constitution have since 1993. Furthermore, this chapter reveals the dynamics of constitution-making in a common post-authoritarian setting: a situation where countries inherit both a purely symbolic, liberal constitution and a real, illiberal unwritten one.[165] The Russian example suggests that one of the primary dangers for this kind of post-authoritarian constitutional change is that the unwritten, illiberal constitution will re-emerge. Assumptions that popular uprisings against authoritarian regimes are enough to signal an abandonment of this unwritten constitution are fallacious. On the contrary, because post-authoritarian popular uprisings frequently bring about crisis, there is often pressure to reassert unlimited power to reduce chaos.

164 "A Conversation with Dmitry Medvedev", *Council on Foreign Relations*, (15 November 2008), available at <http://www.cfr.org/publication/17775/conversation_with_dmitry_medvedev.html>.

165 This constitutional duality is present in many authoritarian countries today, including China.

Post-authoritarian constitutional construction therefore is often best served by amending the formal, authoritarian constitution and making it 'matter', rather than by formulating a brand new one.

The Impact of the Cold War on Soviet and US Law: Reconsidering the Legacy

Paul B. Stephan

Introduction

Twenty years out, the impact of the Cold War on US and Soviet, then Russian, law deserves a reappraisal. How much did the Cold War affect developments in each legal system and was the impact symmetrical? This chapter takes a broad-brush view, emphasizing highlights rather than carefully analyzing systematic changes. It argues that the effect of the Cold War on both country's laws and legal institutions was not all that great but that the impact was greater on the United States.

During the course of the Cold War, one can detect some significant developments in US law that reflected at least indirectly that country's perception of the pressures of the superpower competition. Symmetrically, the unwinding of that conflict had a notable impact on the United States, both in its participation in international institutions and its approaches to international law as well as in its domestic legal reforms. The Soviet Union and Russia were different. Although consciousness of the superpower rivalry was broad and acute in the Soviet Union, important developments in law can mostly be laid at the feet of domestic forces. Symmetrically, although the collapse of the Soviet system had an overwhelming and largely disorienting impact on Russia, the legal changes there responded largely to domestic imperatives rather than foreign pressure (the presence of foreign technical advisors notwithstanding).

What explains this difference? For the United States, the challenges that coalesced into what became the Cold War coincided with a striking new stage in its history. Internationally isolated for most of its history, that country suddenly found itself saddled with broad geopolitical responsibilities and concerns. Peacetime international engagement in the role of a superpower was an entirely new task for the United States and required investment in new institutions and legal strategies. The Soviet Union, in contrast, experienced its struggle with the United States more as a continuation of the existential crisis that the Soviet state had faced since its inception.

Sometime between May 1945 and December 1946, the US people recognized—for what amounts to the first time in its history—that their country could emerge from open, unlimited warfare and still find itself engaged in an international struggle that challenged its identity as a nation and threatened its

Tatiana Borisova and William Simons, eds.
The Legal Dimension in Cold-War Interactions: Some Notes from the Field 141-158

continued existence.[1] The Soviet Union, by contrast, had known only fundamental threats and (both real and imagined) baleful foreign influence since its inception.

During the Cold War, the United States responded to its new place in the world by reexamining and, in some cases transforming, its fundamental institutions. Although the ensuing story was complicated and US actions varied, the country never lost its sense of the importance and difficulty of its competition with the Soviet Union and its allies. When that competition ended, the United States believed that the world had changed and that it had triumphed, with predictable if regrettable consequences. During the same period, the Soviet Union underwent several profound institutional transformations, but none had a direct link to what was officially depicted as the capitalist menace. When the Soviet regime collapsed, many inside—as well as outside—the country perceived the outcome as the result of internal forces rather than foreign pressure. The legal changes that followed reflected an internal struggle for power and control over the nation's wealth, rather than a response to what the United States believed it was holding out as new models for Russian society and politics.

This chapter begins by sketching the main developments in US and Soviet law through the Cold-War period and showing the ways that they were and were not tied to the superpower competition. In each country, it divides this time into periods corresponding to the tenure of particular leaders. One might argue that this focus on the political leadership misses too much to be helpful. But in the case of Russia, for much of the twentieth century Moscow dominated the country—much as Paris still monopolizes the French sense of self. Prime Minister Putin's rather risible effort to shift institutions and resources to St. Petersburg exposes exactly how important Moscow remains. Within Moscow, a company town not unlike Washington, DC, the moods and decisions of the top reverberate throughout society. And for most of the Soviet period, the top meant one prominent leader and a small clique of associates. This was especially true for law, which—at least in the formal sense—responded largely to top-down direction, with only interstitial reactions to local or sectoral influences. In the case of the United States, Washington's influence on the country as a whole may have been less significant. But the national elections that produced particular Presidents bore at least some relation to broader changes in the culture that in turn influenced legal change.

After reviewing the impact of the Cold War proper on the two countries' legal systems, the chapter looks at how both the United States and Russia responded once peace broke out. Put broadly, the United States reveled in what it believed

1 The impact of the immediate postwar period on the broader US legal culture, as well as on the Supreme Court in particular, is discussed in Paul B. Stephan, "Treaties and the Court, 1946-2000", in William S. Dodge, Michael D. Ramsey and David Sloss (eds.), *International Law in the US Supreme Court: Continuity and Change* (Cambridge University Press, New York, NY, 2011).

to be a great victory—only to come back to earth a decade later. Russia struggled through a period that Muscovites compared to the 'time of troubles' that scarred the country so badly in the early seventeenth century. The chapter concludes with a review of Russian arguments that the Cold War has not yet ended and nostalgia among a handful of Western legal scholars for the Soviet system.

Reaction under Stalin and Truman's Internationalism (1945-1953)

For the United States, the Cold War represented a sharp break with the past. The United States never before had maintained a large military establishment—much less a worldwide network of foreign military bases—during peacetime.[2] The specter of subversion by undisclosed agents of a foreign power was not quite so unique, but the extent of the reaction to the perceived threat was. The Korean War underlined both of these trends, even as it suggested limits to both US international power and the feared domestic threat. The dominant trend in the legal culture was one of consolidation of Executive power, with only minimal pushback from the judiciary.[3]

The flip side of this anxiety about foreign threats was the undertaking of great international projects, principally the United Nations and the Marshall Plan. In these early years, the United Nations had not yet become the place where dreams of international cooperation went to die. Most significantly, because of the Soviet decision to withdraw from Security Council activity just as the crisis on the Korean peninsula got under way, the United States was able to obtain the United Nations' blessing for its expeditionary force to repel the North's invasion. President Truman in turn used the UN endorsement as a ground for not seeking a declaration of war from Congress.[4] The Marshall Plan at one point consumed one-tenth of the national budget. The seeds of the global institutionalism that seemed so promising during the 1990s were sown during this period.

As for the Soviet Union, it faced the consequences of its terrible triumph in what it called the Great Patriotic War. On the one hand, through conquest and

2 American imperialism, at least in the formal sense of direct management of foreign states, emerged as the aftermath of the Spanish-American War. But the occupation of the Philippines and the sporadic takeover of Cuba and Haiti in the years before World War II paled in comparison to the military as well as diplomatic presence that arose after 1945.

3 See Stephan, *op.cit.* note 1, 321-326; *Chicago & Southern Air Lines v. Waterman SS Corp.*, 333 US 103 (1948) (recognizing unreviewable presidential discretion in international negotiations); *Dennis v. United States*, 341 US 494 (1951) (upholding convictions of accused Soviet-influenced subversives); *Youngstown Sheet & Tube Co. v. Sawyer*, 343 US 579 (1952) (requiring legislative authorization of seizure of steel production assets); and *United States v. Reynolds*, 345 US 1 (1953) (recognition of official secrets privilege).

4 See UN Security Council Resolution 82, S/RES/82 (1950); UN Security Council Resolution 83, S/RES/83 (1950); UN Security Council Resolution 84, S/RES/84 (1950); and UN Security Council Resolution 85, S/RES/85 (1950).

a series of concessions at international conferences, it had acquired suzerainty, if not sovereignty, over a wide strategic corridor in Central and Eastern Europe, in addition to a significant adjustment of its borders at the expense of Poland and Romania. On the other hand, the nation had absorbed great casualties, certainly many more than the twenty million officially claimed as war dead. Moreover, its subjects, as soldiers in the Red Army, had wandered well outside the borders of the Soviet Union and in many cases had fraternized with members of the Allied armies. Each of these circumstances produced a reaction, which in the loosest sense one might call a component of the Cold War. But the reaction seemed much more about general Soviet fear and anxiety than about any specific threat from the West.

First, the Soviet Union had to devise a legal structure to manage its relations with the territory of Europe that had come within its control, but not within its boundaries. What the Soviet leadership, first and foremost Stalin, saw as pressing security concerns greatly limited the range of options, but the exact form of domination and control was not foreordained. There is a basis for the argument that active involvement of Soviet security organs in the domestic affairs of the subject countries and the liquidation of non-Communist elements in the coalition governments that initially governed Bulgaria, Czechoslovakia and other conquered nations was as inevitable as was, twenty-some years earlier, the rise of the *Cheka* and the expulsion of the left Social Revolutionaries from Lenin's ruling coalition. The actual architecture of the postwar control system, specifically the creation of the Warsaw Pact (1955) and the Council for Mutual Economic Assistance (1949), doubtlessly owed something to an inclination to mirror the institutions created in the West, namely NATO (1949) and the European Coal and Steel Community (1952). But the firmness of the Soviet guiding hand, orchestrating murderous show trials and vicious repressions as well as rigid barriers against Western contamination, was remarkable and disproportionate to Western actions.

Indeed, the extension of Soviet power outside of Soviet borders, in particular through the establishment of the Eastern Bloc and the provision of military assistance to North Korea in its conflict with South Korea and the United Nations (1950-1953), did not lead to any significant conceptual breakthroughs in Soviet theories of international law. Rather, the late Stalin regime pragmatically addressed what it regarded as its fundamental security interests. The more important changes in the legal environment involved the domestic consequences of the late war. These fell into two categories: retribution and decontamination.

Because the Germans had occupied a large part of the western Soviet Union and in some instances had enjoyed initial popular support as liberators from the Stalin regime, there existed a host of candidates for punishment as collaborators, traitors and war criminals. Some had thrown in their lot with the Nazis to the point of participating in the administration of the terror and genocide that became Nazi occupation policy. Others had simply struggled to survive.

The Soviet regime dealt with this task in various ways. Especially prominent individuals met justice through war crime trials, an institution that continued up to the 1980s. The regime famously participated in the Nuremberg tribunals, now hailed as the birth of international criminal justice and a worthy blow against the culture of impunity. National tribunals, however, both in the Soviet Union and the subject states, absorbed a far greater burden, and produced a much larger number of trials. Soldiers who had become German prisoners of war either were shot or went to the camps, normally for a ten-year sentence. Officers and soldiers who had fraternized with British or US troops fell under a cloud, and often ended up in the camps as well. One can see weak parallels with the fate of the officers of the Russian army that had invaded France in 1815. The distinctive contribution of the later Stalin regime to the law of postwar retribution, however, was the identification of entire nationalities as traitors subject to group punishment. People classified as Crimean Tatars, Chechen, Ingush, Volga Germans, Meskhetian Turks and other ethnic groups in the North Caucasus and Crimea were deported *en masse* from their native lands to Central Asia and other points east. The transport killed hundreds of thousands, with the harsh conditions that greeted the survivors killing more. Some won the right to end their exile under Khrushchev, while others regained their civil rights only during the Gorbachev period.

The link between retribution, decontamination, and nationalist consciousness was both explicit and deeply disturbing in the case of the Jews. On the one hand, during the immediate postwar period the Soviet Union presented itself to the outside world as the state that had done more than any other to protect European Jewry from the Nazis, an image burnished by its being the first country to recognize Israel.[5] On the other hand, the leadership perceived Jews as having links to a wider community outside the enlarged boundaries of the Soviet empire. The 'fatherland' (*otechestvo*) for which the Great Patriotic (*Otechestvennaia*) War was fought seemed, after the fact, to require blood identity that excluded outsiders—especially those who seemed more European than Russian. A vicious and deadly campaign against Jews ensued. Signs of a new program of official anti-Semitism—including the arrest of high-level party cadres with Jewish backgrounds—appeared in 1946, but a fully fledged campaign against 'rootless cosmopolitans' did not get under way fully until 1948. Show trials of prominent academics, including leading members of Moscow State University's law faculty, followed, culminating in the notorious 'doctors' plot' of 1952.

Masha Gesson, in her remarkable essay about her two grandmothers, conveys something of the strangeness of this period. One grandmother, the daughter of Zionists, had good Hebrew and, after the War, needed to support an infant and an invalid husband. One day in 1948 she showed up for a job interview with the

5 *Cf.* Ben-Cion Pinchuk, "Was There a Soviet Policy for Evacuating the Jews? The Case of the Annexed Territories", 39 *Slavic Review* (1980), 44.

Jewish Anti-Fascist Committee, only to discover that over the previous weekend the state security forces (at that time the *MGB*, the immediate predecessor of the *KGB* and the descendent of the *Cheka* and the *OGPU*) had arrested everyone associated with that organization. She went home, resigned to the inevitable, and when the phone call came dutifully reported to the designated entrance of the *MGB* headquarters, carrying winter clothing and stale toast to survive the train ride east. The guard at the entrance laughed at her: she had been summoned to the entrance for prospective employees, not the one for persons subject to repression. It turned out that the *MGB* indeed had uncovered her job application in the course of its crackdown on the Committee, but decided that it needed to hire a Hebrew linguist in support of espionage and covert action responsibilities generated by the Soviet Union's relationship with the new State of Israel.[6]

The arrests and trials, centered in Moscow, had implications for the several million Jews who lived in the Soviet Union after the War. During this period, the authorities gave renewed attention to the Jewish Autonomous Region in the distant and inhospitable borderland with China. The Soviet Union had created this entity before the War as a potential buffer against the notoriously anti-Semitic White Guards and Cossacks who had settled in Manchuria in the wake of the Revolution. After the War, newspapers carried stories explaining that Soviet Jews wanted to settle in the Autonomous Region to ensure their protection from unspecified forces that threatened them. As Gesson's memoir indicates, many Jews of the time believed that the authorities' real intentions were to use the Autonomous Region as a platform for liquidating the Soviet Union's Jewish population. According to these accounts, Stalin's death cut short an extermination campaign that would have rivaled the Holocaust.

It is tempting to personalize and displace these grotesque events as simply a manifestation of Stalin's increasing dementia, brought on perhaps by atherosclerosis and presenting itself as acute paranoia. For the purpose of this chapter, what matters is that the traumatic efforts to punish groups seen as insufficiently loyal and to cauterize the 'wound' of foreign contamination, themselves a reflection of the terrible dislocations and suffering of the War, created an environment that made both constructive engagement with the West and legal innovation at home extremely difficult. An event that epitomizes Soviet behavior under these constraints is its aforementioned boycott of Security Council meetings during the summer of 1950—as the legalities of the conflict in Korea were being sorted out. Rather than wielding a veto that would impede the formation of a Western alliance in aid of the South, the Soviet delegation simply refused to engage.

Some argue, I think implausibly, that the Cold War brought about Stalin's reactionary policies by creating a sense of danger.[7] Rather, an ongoing foreign

6 Masha Gessen, "My Grandmother, the Censor", *Granta* (1998) No.64, 165, 176-179.

7 *E.g.*, Eric Hobsbawm, *The Age of Extremes: A History of the World, 1914-1989* (Pantheon Books, New York, NY, 1994), 230-233.

threat provided justification, not inspiration, for these policies. The leaden atmosphere and general anxiety that the repressions produced in turn contributed to a downward spiral in relations between the Soviet camp and the United States, if only by shaping US apprehensions, both reasonable and irrational, of its adversary. This trend made cooperation through international institutions, first and foremost the United Nations, virtually impossible, thus stunting the development of any kind of a common international law.

The First Reforms (1953-1964): De-Stalinization and Desegregation

In the United States, the period from Eisenhower's inauguration to Johnson's election was one of profound social reform, especially with respect to race. The Supreme Court brought down *Brown v. Board of Education* in 1954.[8] Over the next decade the Warren Court issued a number of far reaching decisions in criminal law, free expression, and election law, with restructuring of racial relations a common thread. The rest of the country gradually got behind the project, if never completely or wholeheartedly.[9]

The connection between the civil rights struggle in the United States and the Cold War is a matter of controversy. One scholar has made her reputation by characterizing the domestic reforms as primarily the product of the international context, describing desegregation as a 'Cold War imperative'.[10] A less monolithic view might concede that the Justices of the Supreme Court themselves were conscious of the international costs of the existing system of racial apartheid in the South, but that in the broader polity arguments about international pressure impeded rather than advanced efforts to dismantle segregation.[11] More generally, one can trace the influence of the superpower competition in these fundamental developments in US law without asserting strict causality between the one and the other.

The question of reform in the Soviet Union was of a different order of magnitude due to the extreme social and political deformities of the Stalinist legacy. The Soviet people greeted Stalin's death in March 1953 largely with grief

8 *Brown v. Board of Education*, 347 US 483 (1954).

9 See *Mapp v. Ohio*, 367 US 643 (1961) (establishment of exclusionary rule in state criminal cases); *Baker v. Carr*, 369 US 186 (1962) (creating principle of proportionality in election districts); *New York Times Co. v. Sullivan*, 376 US 254 (1964) (First Amendment limits on civil suits for libel of public officials); and *Miranda v. Arizona*, 384 US 436 (1966) (mandated warnings to criminal suspects).

10 Mary L. Dudziak, *Cold War Civil Rights: Race and the Image of American Democracy* (Princeton University Press, Princeton, NJ, 2000).

11 See Michael J. Klarman, *From Jim Crow to Civil Rights: The Supreme Court and the Struggle for Racial Equality* (Oxford University Press, New York, NY, 2004), 182-184, 375-376.

and anxiety: they had learned to fear change. Within a few months, however, some of the political figures jockeying to take over the leadership signaled an intention for others to see them as reformers willing to break with the Stalinist system. Ironically, the first to do so was Lavrentii Beriia, who as head of the security organs had more blood on his hands than did any of his competitors for power. Khrushchev—after putting Beriia and his closest associates to death—eventually adopted reform and dismantling of the most extreme aspects of Stalinism as the platform for his claim to the status of supreme party leader. This struggle came to its climax with the suppression of the 'Anti-Party Group' (*i.e.*, Stalin's most loyal lieutenants) in 1957, a year after the CPSU Twentieth Party Congress had introduced the theme of de-Stalinization (cryptically called the Struggle against the Cult of Personality). In the course of reconsidering the historic destiny of the Soviet Union, the leadership gave new attention to legal architecture.

One instance where the reformist spirit extended into legal practice involved the doctrine of international law that Soviet scholars packaged as the Theory of Peaceful Coexistence.[12] Leon Lipson wrote (and spoke) brilliantly about this development.[13] He saw PCX—as he called it (so as to avoid confusion with peace or coexistence)—as a second-order theory of international law. PCX opened the door to binding customary norms, a concept that prior Soviet approaches had ruled out, but maintained that no norm could arise unless it represented the coordinated wills of the two opposing camps in the international struggle. PCX, in other words, gave the socialist bloc a veto over all international law norm formation while admitting the existence of a process that could proceed alongside positive treaty law.

Compared to the bizarre combination of isolationism and belligerence that preceded it, PCX represented a more rational form of reengagement with the non-socialist world. Indeed, Lipson and others feared that people in the West might make too much of this change in direction, and in particular might misjudge the extent to which the Soviet leadership still saw its interest as adverse to that of the United States and its allies. Lipson also questioned the strength of the intellectual foundations for this supposed break with the past, which replaced one form of conceptual unilateralism (no international obligations without the express consent of the Soviet state) with another (no international norms that conflicted with PCX, which required the approval of the socialist camp).

On the domestic front, law reform reflected and drew spirit from the cultural ferment associated with the 'thaw'. A program to rewrite the 1936 Stalin Constitution got under way, although it failed to make much headway. A kind

12 G.I. Tunkin, "Coexistence and International Law", 95 *Recueil des Cours* (1958), 1; and N.S. Khrushchev, "On Peaceful Coexistence", 38 *Foreign Affairs* (1959), 3.

13 Leon Lipson, "Peaceful Coexistence", 29 *Law and Contemporary Problems* (1964), 871; and *id.*, "The Rise and Fall of 'Peaceful Coexistence' in International Law", *Papers on Soviet Law* (1977), 6.

of formalistic federalism appeared as part of a broader law revision project. The Soviet legislature would enact 'fundamentals' (*osnovy*) in fields such as civil law, criminal law, criminal procedure, and the like, leaving it to the fifteen Republics to enact law codes that filled in the gaps. This approach marked a slight loosening of the bonds of centralization that had prevailed under Stalin. Finally, a number of discrete law reform projects came to fruition, including the re-legalization of abortion (then the principal family planning device) and the renunciation of administrative imposition of criminal punishment.

Under Khrushchev, the authorities also undertook various administrative changes—largely to address internal agendas. The Crimea, previously a part of the Russian Soviet Federated Socialist Republic, became the possession of the Ukrainian Republic. A Russian bureau appeared within the CPSU structure, and the position of regional party leader became bifurcated into a first secretary for industry and another for agriculture. Khrushchev changed his job title from General Secretary to that of First Secretary to create semantic space between himself and Stalin. None of these reforms directly affected the legal system, but each hinted at an underlying administrative instability that—as it progressed over three decades—eventually brought down the Soviet Union.

One might interpret the thaw and the associated legal reforms as an effort to compete more effectively with the West along the ideological dimension of the Cold War. Khrushchev, so the argument would go, sought to create a kinder, gentler Soviet state so as to present a more appealing face both to the Soviet people and to the non-aligned world. But to reach this conclusion, a defender of the foreign-competition thesis must pull off three improbable moves: (a) posit some sort of mechanism through which the Soviet people held their leaders accountable for their shortcomings in comparison with the West; (b) assign to Soviet law a significant role in ideological competition outside the Soviet Union; and (c) disregard the various domestic factors that explained these reforms. While the ultimate judgment of history remains unformed, the most plausible conclusion is that Khrushchev sought to make a break with the more arbitrary and violent aspects of the Stalinist system principally because the political élite wanted more security—not to gain any advantage over the West. Compare this with desegregation in the United States, where Cold-War concerns helped shape elite support for reform, even if they did not have much effect on the broader public.

Retrenchment under Brezhnev and a Crisis of Confidence in the United States (1964-1982)

In the United States, the period from Johnson's election through Reagan's first term saw waves of first cultural, then economic and political ferment and disorder, marked by a shattering of confidence in the capacity of traditional élites to manage government generally and foreign policy in particular. One dimension of this conflict was a debate over the validity of the Cold War. Much of the drama and deepening sense of dismay stemmed from growing disgust with the Vietnam War—perhaps the nastiest and most disillusioning of the country's sallies into superpower competition. Opposition to that intervention led to many voices arguing either that the Soviet Union never had presented a serious threat to the United States or that it had ceased to do so. Skepticism about national security claims grew in the wake of the Vietnam disaster. Both the legislature and the judiciary asserted wider control over national policy, including foreign relations, as confidence in the Executive's capacity to manage US national interests collapsed.[14]

This crisis of confidence in the United States may have contributed to the retrenchment in the Soviet Union that later became known as the 'period of stagnation', but domestic factors seemed far more important. Khrushchev's efforts to push the Soviet system in various directions, subsequently known as his 'hare-brained schemes', ended up alienating almost every interest group with a say in Soviet politics—but none more so than the leading cadres of the CPSU. His reforms, although not as dangerous to them as was Stalin's terror, undermined their authority and the stable if informal patronage relationships that they had built up. Accordingly, he became in 1964 the only Soviet leader ever to be overthrown by the Party organization.

The new leadership brought about changes in legal policy both internationally and at home. As Lipson noted, the Brezhnev period witnessed the decline—although never the denunciation—of the theory of peaceful coexistence. PCX never had addressed relations among socialist states, but until 1968 one might have hoped that socialist internationalism, the doctrine that explained intra-camp affairs, might accommodate a modicum of sovereign independence on the part of socialist states. True, the invasion of Hungary in 1956 had coincided with Khrushchev's critique of Stalinism at the Twentieth Party Congress, but one might have cabined that episode both as premature and as extreme (towards the end the Hungarian leader Nagy had tried to throw in his lot with the West). The 1968 invasion of Czechoslovakia—and the subsequent enunciation of the Brezhnev doctrine to justify it—put an end to any hope of reconciling socialist internationalism with national independence. From then on, the rules of the game seemed clear: any state that sought to deviate too greatly from a line set in Moscow could expect armed intervention if other corrective efforts failed. Henceforth, from the socialist end of the international spectrum, PCX seemed dubious if only because it promised the capitalist world so much more than the Brezhnev doctrine permitted.

And for the West, something new was on offer. The concept of *detente*, first worked out with the Germans and French and then extended to the United States, implied both a more cooperative relationship than mere coexistence

14 See, generally, Paul B. Stephan, "Courts, the Constitution, and Customary International Law: The Intellectual Origins of the Restatement (Third) of the Foreign Relations Law of the United States", 44 *Virginia Journal of International Law* (2003), 33.

and the transition to yet another, presumably higher state of cooperation and interdependence. This policy had its apotheosis in the 1975 Helsinki Conference, which ratified the post-War *status quo* in Central and Eastern Europe at the price of a more explicit international commitment to human rights. The leading legal science research center—the Institute of State and Law of the USSR Academy of Sciences—dutifully created a new human rights section to buttress the Soviet side in a new realm of ideological combat. These scholars and other official intellectuals attacked the lack of positive rights in capitalist countries while loudly insisting on the principle of noninterference in domestic affairs to insulate from international scrutiny their practice with respect to negative rights.

In retrospect, the bargain struck by the Soviet leadership at Helsinki may have given it cause for regret. Ratification of the post-war *status quo*—and in particular of the incorporation of the Baltic states into the Soviet Union—was not meant to and did not produce any legal consequences. When independence movements began to stir in Central and Eastern Europe during the late 1980s, the United States felt no obligation to withhold its support. But by arguing that the 'Basket III' human rights component of the Helsinki Accords interpreted and developed preexisting legal instruments, in particular the UN Charter and the Universal Declaration on Human Rights, the West managed to suggest that the Soviet side had conceded something significant and potentially transformative.[15] Many thinkers and activists within the Eastern bloc began to use Basket III as a rallying point for their efforts to challenge the system, and Western governments relied on the same provisions to justify their involvement in these domestic struggles.

Outside the sphere of international law, the retrenchment period witnessed several important developments. The Brezhnev regime undertook a certain degree of cultural repression, including the use of show trials to excoriate prominent dissident thinkers. This tendency culminated in acts of parliament expelling from the country Aleksandr Solzhenitsyn, an especially dangerous personality because of his Russian nationalism, and exiling to a remote backwater Andrei Sakharov, a critic whose ideas resonated more with the West than with Soviets. An especially cruel innovation was the use of forced psychiatric hospitalization to discredit opponents of the regime, including General Grigorenko, a war hero who had taken up the cause of the Crimean Tatars. But unlike the Stalin period, people did not automatically pay for dissent with their lives, and the repressions were more targeted than massive.

Ironically, the Brezhnev era also saw a major increase in the resources devoted to lawyers and legal institutions. Most of the growth occurred in the ranks of

15 The Helsinki Accords, more formally known as the Final Act of the Conference on Security and Cooperation in Europe, contained three 'baskets' of consensus: a statement on European borders and noninterference in internal affairs, a statement on economic, scientific and environmental cooperation, and one on humanitarian cooperation, including respect for human rights. The last was the third basket that took on a life of its own.

iuriskonsults, legally trained specialists assigned to state-owned enterprises with the task of reining in the more freewheeling managers who used creative accounting and informal patronage ties to evade the rigors of state planning. But legal education and the prestige of law professors also rose as the political authorities sought to impart a sense of stability and formal coherence to a system that had lost whatever inspirational force it once enjoyed. A milestone in this kind of legalization of Soviet society occurred in 1977 when the Supreme Soviet adopted a new constitution for the Soviet state. The Brezhnev Constitution produced no significant institutional changes or legal breakthroughs, and critics noted that it used a sloppy and ungrammatical Russian that was far inferior to that of the 1936 instrument, but the new law did signify the desire of the leadership to present the regime as formalized, law-based, and stable.[16]

The other important story of the Brezhnev years was a Sisyphean effort to restructure the organization of the national economy to improve control and performance. Gertrude Schroeder aptly named this a 'treadmill' of reforms, all of which promised to exploit new information and management technologies to improve the economy, and all of which foundered on the shoals of the informal relationships that the bureaucracy had developed to keep things running to its satisfaction. Some in the West saw these efforts as signs of a struggle between market-oriented reformers and old-fashioned central planners; but others, including Schroeder, believed that the necessary structural changes that the economy demanded to reverse declining productivity and extravagant environmental waste were not within the range of policy debate.[17]

As with the Khrushchev reforms, one might tie the regime's legal policy to Cold-War competition with the West, but the position that they were largely unrelated is stronger. US blunders in Southeast Asia and the triumph of Soviet allies in Africa, Latin America and Asia might have given the Soviet leadership freer rein to impose its will on domestic dissidents and restless democrats and nationalists in Central and Eastern Europe. The formalization and legalization of the domestic order might have helped the Soviet Union present itself as a more acceptable model for non-aligned countries to emulate and as a less threatening partner for its friends and supporters in the West. One could depict the attempts to reform economic administration as indicating responsiveness to the economic dimension of Cold-War competition, and in particular to the emergence of new information technologies. All this is true but attenuated in the extreme.

On balance, it seems impossible to ignore the important domestic imperatives—unrelated to the Cold War—that shaped these policies. The leaders that replaced Khrushchev confronted an increasingly unruly political and

16 On the linguistic infelicities, see Stanislaw Pomorski, "The Language of the Soviet Constitution of 1977: A Note", 7 *Review of Socialist Law* (1981), 331.

17 See, *e.g.*, Gertrude E. Schroeder, "The Soviet Economy on a Treadmill of Reforms", in 1 *US Congress Joint Economic Committee. Soviet Economy in a Time of Change* (1970), 312.

economic administrative system, where informal accommodations undercut the formal chain of command. Those at the very top felt frustrated by their inability to exercise the kinds of authority that a centralized system should permit, but faced widespread opposition within the political élite to any fundamental change. The crackdown on dissidents reassured the élite; the reorganizations challenged them but also gave them an opportunity to renegotiate their patronage ties in ways that further insulated them from centralized control. The closer one looks at these events, the less important the Cold War seems to have been. At the time there was nothing comparable to Vietnam—a Cold-War event that transformed the United States—to cast a shadow over Soviet politics or law.[18]

Final Soviet Reforms and US Resurgence (1982-1991)

The last decade of the Soviet Union framed a period experienced in the United States as one of renaissance and triumph. Political divisions remained sharp and heated, but the ascendant position combined celebration of the leading international role of the United States with advocacy of tax cuts, privatization, and reduced government regulation.[19] Some part of the impetus for deregulation in turn came from the negative example of the Soviet Union, which had come to give command-and-control economic policies a bad name. Successful military interventions in Grenada, Panama and Iraq, depicted as responses to incursions by the Soviet Union and its allies in Angola, Mozambique, and Afghanistan as well as to its earlier victory in Southeast Asia, reinforced the sense that the superpower competition had turned in the United States' favor.

Looking closely at legal changes during this period, one is hard pressed to find specific steps that reflected the general sense of optimism and accomplishment. Deregulation had begun earlier, during the Carter Administration. In the field of international law, perhaps the most significant development was the emergence of human rights as a concrete and important project. At least in the United States, however, lawyers invoked international human rights largely to oppose particular actions of the government, rather than to bolster it. In the United States, the rise of the human-rights project constituted a significant step toward the privatization of international lawmaking at the expense of the Executive.

The decade also was heady in the Soviet Union. In terms of legal institutions and doctrine, the most momentous period in Soviet history was the last. The changes began under Iurii Andropov, who instituted potentially important economic reforms (although not political ones) in the brief period before illness

18 One might cite to Afghanistan, but this unhappy adventure belongs mostly to the last period of Soviet history, which I discuss in the next section.

19 Not, let me be clear, great fiscal probity. These years may have witnessed impressive growth of the domestic US economy, but also a remarkable increase in the overall claim of the federal government on the product of that economy.

overtook him. After the parentheses that was the Chernenko regime, General Secretary (from 1990, President) Gorbachev and his supporters sought to dismantle the vestiges of the repressive apparatus, to open up Soviet political organs to genuine democratic accountability through multicandidate elections, and to introduce elements of private property and market relations to the creaky command-and-control economic system, all while maintaining the fundamental institutions of the Soviet system. The task proved impossible, but many people in the West (although few in Russia today) gave these reformers high marks both for their aspirations and for their success in largely avoiding bloodshed during a traumatic transitional period.

To be sure, the 'rule-of-law state' (*pravovoe gosudarstvo*) of which the reformers spoke sounded much more like a *Rechtsstaat*; that is, a principle of executive accountability to the legislature, and not so much like a system of negative liberty protecting the subject from the state. The commitment to political and economic liberalism often was greater in the eyes of Western beholders than on the ground. And the events surrounding the *denouement* of the Gorbachev regime, in particular the August 1991 coup, remain a subject of intense speculation and controversy. But no one can deny that the Gorbachev team took important steps that made the Soviet Union a more decent society—including opening up the political process, releasing political prisoners from both the camps and mental hospitals, cutting back on the use of capital punishment, and laying out the rudiments of a legal private economy.

The question that confronts us is the extent to which these reforms reflected the dynamic of the Cold War. Of course, no one can give a definitive answer. As part of *détente*, large numbers of people within the Soviet Union's political, intellectual and technocratic élites had received some exposure to Western ideas, images, and people. A kind of cultural competition ensued. It seems fair to assume that the Gorbachev team understood that to win the support of the Soviet Union's *intelligentsia* they had to discard some of the more obvious absurdities in their public life, including the broad ban on public criticism of the *status quo*. Hence *glasnost'*, the one unqualified success among the reforms. But the other parts of the program reflected forces that had emerged in the 1950s—especially the increasing inability of the central administrative organs to maintain control over the local bodies that conducted economic activity.

Some in the West have argued that United States-led efforts to improve the NATO military capability forced the Soviet Union to launch broad reforms, because the command-and-control system could not compete technologically. Others have suggested that the liberal values of decency and respect for the individual, if you will the undeniable appeal of basic human rights, ultimately swayed the Soviet people. Reasons exist to doubt both these claims, at least as comprehensive explanations for what happened.[20] *First*, it remains unclear why

20 See Paul B. Stephan, "The Fall: Understanding the Collapse of Soviet Communism", 29 *Suffolk University Law Review* (1995), 17.

weapons procurement in the West, which has large elements of central planning and command-and-control, worked so much better than did the Soviet approach. *Second*, the liberal and humane values that the West identifies with itself had been on offer well before the 1980s. More to the point, neither story takes into account the fundamental administrative and organizational problems that confronted the Soviet leadership at the beginning of the 1980s, which had bubbled up even during the later Stalin period. The weight of the evidence suggests that the 1980s reforms of the Soviet system, in large measure, resulted from a breakdown in the command system that had frustrated those at the top who had expected to reap the benefits of being in charge, and not a liberal effort to improve the lot of the average Soviet citizen.[21]

The End of the Cold War?

For the United States, the first decade following the collapse of the Warsaw Pact and the death of the Soviet Union saw the birth of a new international order based on democracy, the rule of law, economic liberalism, and strong international institutions to promote the aforementioned values.[22] Great resources (although nothing like those deployed by the Marshall Plan) went to promote these values in the former socialist countries, Russia above all others. The legacy of this aid was mixed: the states of Central and Eastern Europe eventually adopted the *acquis communautaire* of the European Union as their legal structure, while Russia came to identify Western intervention with the economic and social nightmares of the 1990s.

After September 2001, the United States went in another, darker direction, winning itself no friends in the process. New arguments about international law, as well as greater awareness of its relevance to contemporary problems, arose, but without the creation of a new synthesis.[23] The financial crisis of 2008 put an exclamation mark on the obituary of the 'Washington consensus'.

In Russia, symmetrical transformations proceeded. In the immediate aftermath of the collapse of the Soviet Union, a new generation seized the formal reins of power in Russia, buttressed by holdovers from the old *nomenklatura* such as President El'tsin. With Moscow seemingly co-opted into the Washington consensus and a wide range of arms control agreements and economic pacts

21 Paul B. Stephan, "Toward a Positive Theory of Privatization: Lessons from Soviet-type Economies", in Jagdeep S. Bhandari and Alan O. Sykes (eds.), *Economic Dimensions in International Law* (Cambridge University Press, Cambridge, 1997), 324.

22 See Paul B. Stephan, "The New International Law: Legitimacy, Accountability, Authority, and Freedom in the New Global Order", 70 *University of Colorado Law Review* (1999), 1555.

23 See Paul B. Stephan, "Symmetry and Selectivity: What Happens in International Law When the World Changes", 10 *Chicago Journal of International Law* (2009), 91.

indicating closer ties between West and East, the great competition between the two superpowers seemingly had come to an end.

Yet even in the early years one heard dissonant notes. As the economic reforms of the 1990s unfolded, the criticism became more widespread. By the end of the decade, the large majority of Russians had come to see the disintegration of the Soviet Union and its planned economy as a disaster comparable psychologically, if not materially, to the seventeenth century's 'time of troubles'.[24]

With troubles came a search for scapegoats. Rather than look at the mistakes and misery as an inevitable consequence of decades of Soviet misrule, influential voices began to pin the blame squarely on the West. In 1999 Sergey Kortunov—a prominent foreign policy intellectual and a member of the Russian international relations establishment—published an article in a leading Russian foreign relations journal that reassessed the Cold War.[25] The struggle, he asserted, never was between capitalism and socialism, because neither society truly embodied either of those ideals. Rather, the United States had stepped into the shoes of Nazi Germany in its rejection of the historical legitimacy and moral worth of the Russian idea, as manifested in a multinational state. Many of those who initially came to power at the end of 1991, he claimed, failed to appreciate the extent to which they had served the interest of the West in its effort to destroy Russia. He perceived a dawning recognition on the part of the Russian leadership that the 'long twilight struggle' between Russia and the West had not come to an end, and would continue until the Russian idea and Russia's historic destiny finally had been realized.

Within a year, a man sharing Kortunov's world view became Russia's leader. Although cautious at first, President Putin seized the twin opportunities fate had dealt him—lush oil revenues and the United States' disastrous entanglement in a second Iraq war—to stake out a position that bemoaned the collapse of the Soviet Union and blamed the United States for its losses. In his state of the nation speech to the Federal Assembly in April 2005, he declared:

> "First of all, it is necessary to admit—I have already spoken about it—that the Soviet Union's collapse was the biggest geopolitical catastrophe of the century. For the Russian people, it was a true drama. Tens of millions of our compatriots and co-citizens found themselves outside Russian territory. The epidemic of disintegration spread to Russia itself. The savings of our citizens were depreciated and old ideals were ruined. Many institutions were disbanded or reformed hastily. The country's integrity was impaired by terrorist intervention and the Khasavyurt capitulation that followed. Oligarch groups, while having unlimited control over information flows, served exclusively their own, corporate, interests. Large-scale poverty was regarded as a norm. And this was happening against the background of a grave economic

24 See Allen C. Lynch, *How Russia Is Not Ruled: Reflections on Russian Political Development* (Cambridge University Press, Cambridge, 2005).

25 S.V. Kortunov, "Kholodnaia voina: paradoksy odnoi strategii", *Mezhdunarodnaia Zhizn'* (1998) No.5, 23, translated as "Is the Cold War Really Over?", *International Affairs* (1998), No.5, 141.

> decline, unstable finances and paralysis of the social sphere. Many believed at the time that our fledgling democracy was not a continuation of Russian statehood, but its total collapse, that it was a protracted agony of the Soviet system. Those who thought this way were wrong."[26]

Although he did not speak as explicitly as did Kortunov about the role of the United States, Putin did not hesitate to single out the country's former adversary for new and forceful criticism:

> "Today we are witnessing an almost unrestrained hyper-use of force—military force—in international relations, a force that is plunging the world into an abyss of permanent conflicts. As a result we do not have sufficient strength to find a comprehensive solution to any one of these conflicts. Finding a political settlement also becomes impossible. We are seeing a greater and greater disdain for the basic principles of international law. One country, the United States, has overstepped its national borders in every way. This is visible in the economic, political, cultural and educational policies it imposes on other nations.
>
> This force's dominance inevitably encourages a number of countries to acquire weapons of mass destruction. Moreover, threats such as terrorism have now taken on a global character. I am convinced that we have reached that decisive moment when we must seriously think about the architecture of global security. And we must proceed by searching for a reasonable balance between the interests of all participants in the international dialogue. Especially since the international landscape is so varied and is changing so quickly."[27]

As Putin saw it, grave security threats—terrorism and nuclear blackmail—arose not because the United States was too weak but because it was too strong. A strong Russia acting in opposition to US hegemony was the prescription.

To complete the irony undergirding these reversals, a kind of nostalgia for the Soviet *weltanschauung* recently has popped up in western legal academic circles. To be fair, nothing like a critical mass of legal scholars seeking meaning and legitimation in the Soviet past exists. But, as Dr. Johnson said about dancing dogs, what is remarkable is not how well they do it, but that they do it at all.[28]

Conclusions

The tendency of observers, whether historians, social scientists, or law professors, to see the 'other' in terms of their own issues and problems should be familiar to everyone. Alexander Dallin observed long ago that even the closest and most knowledgeable students of Soviet politics saw their judgments change in the face

26 Federal News Service, Official Kremlin International News Broadcast (25 April 2005), President Vladimir Putin's Annual Address to the Federal Assembly.

27 Vladimir Putin, "Unilateral Force Has Nothing To Do with Global Democracy", *The Guardian* (13 February 2007).

28 For instances of this nostalgia, see Bill Bowring, "Positivism v. Self-determination: The Contradictions of Soviet International Law", in Susan Marks (ed.), *International Law on the Left: Re-examining Marxist Legacies* (Cambridge University Press, Cambridge, 2008), 133 (defending Lenin and Stalin's approaches to international relations); and Eric A. Engle, "Socialist Legalism in the Early USSR: A Formal Rule of Law State?", 3 *Journal of East Asian and International Law* (forthcoming) (defending early Soviet conceptions of legality).

of, and apparently in response to, shifting Western foreign policy imperatives.[29] Thus, when we set out to review the complex history of the Cold War and its impact on legal institutions, those of us grounded in the US experience struggle with a natural inclination to tell the story in terms of what seems striking from the US side, namely newness and transformation.

A contrarian by nature, I have tried instead to emphasize the elements of continuity in Soviet and Russian legal culture in the years since World War II. I do not mean to deny the importance of the ongoing struggle with the West as a force shaping Soviet life. I maintain, however, that the daunting—and ultimately impossible—task of taming and rationalizing the Stalinist legacy, both administrative and cultural, mattered at least as much to those who made Soviet legal policy and organized the Soviet legal system. If we want to learn about ourselves by studying Soviet society, we must try hard not to impose the assumptions and norms we have acquired at home on this strange, terrible and inspiring history.

29 Alexander Dallin, "Bias and Blunders in American Studies on the USSR", 32 *Slavic Review* (1973), 560.

Cold-War Personal Interactions: Selected Amateur Photographs of Professionals in the Field

Some of the attractions of Russia (at the end of *perestroika*)
for the British eye.

Tatiana Borisova and William Simons, eds.
The Legal Dimension in Cold-War Interactions: Some Notes from the Field 159-165

Englishmen in the Baltic

Glasnost' in the water: Galina Shinkaretskaia and Maurice Mendelson

Bridge over the Moskva: Kremlin palace in background.
Cento, Slinn and Michael from Kiev

Cento, Michael and Duffy

Moscow from Lenin Hills. Professor Mark Boguslavskii.
Back of Vaughan Lowe

Museum of Economic Achievements, Riga. Vaughan Lowe, the guide, and Bill Butler

Gorkii Park: Cento and Danilenko

This group photo was taken in the period 14-16 May 1990.
The individual subjects have not been identified except that this photograph is annotated: "Section USSR ILA [International Law Association] branch".

1987 Bridgeport Soviet-Law Symposium: The Group

Front Row (left to right): Susan Finder (Harvard), Louise Shelley (American University), F.J.M. Feldbrugge (Leiden & NATO), Peter Maggs (Illinois), Wim Timmermans (Leiden), and Yuri Luryi (Western Ontario).

Second Row (left to right): A.J. Schmidt (Bridgeport), Susan Heuman (Lehman, CUNY), Robert Sharlet (Union College), Hiroshi Oda (University of Tokyo), and William Simons (formerly of Leiden, presently corporate attorney).

Third Row (left to right): Peter Juviler (Barnard and Columbia), Christine Genis (US Embassy, Moscow), Randy Bregman (Institute of International Law, Washington, DC) Zigurds Zile (Wisconsin), Vladimir Entin (Institute of State and Law, Moscow), Svetlana Polenina (Institute of State and Law, Moscow), William Butler (University of London), and George Ginsburgs (Rutgers, Camden).

Fourth Row (left to right): Jeff Kopstein (University of California, Berkeley), Malcolm Russell-Einhard (Boston College), Stash Pomorski (Rutgers, Camden), Andre Loeber (University of Kiel, Germany), Leon Lipson (Yale), Serge Levitsky (Leiden), and Jane Giddings (University of London).

Top Row (left to right): John Quigley (Ohio State), Stanislaw Soltysinski (Pennsylvania & University of Poznan), next unknown (not participant in program), and Thomas Hoya (US Dept of Commerce).

Missing from photograph:
George Armstrong (Louisiana State University), Harold Berman (Harvard and Emory), Albert Boiter (Georgetown), Gabriele Crespi-Reghizzi (U of Pavia, Italy), Marshall Goldman (Wellesley), Henry Morton (Queens, CUNY), Peter Solomon (Toronto), Ger van den Berg (Leiden), Gianmaria Ajani (University of Trento, Italy), Alan Sherr (Brown), and Lowry Wyman (DePaul).

1987 Bridgeport Soviet-Law Symposium: The Brochure

List of Contributors

Zlata Engel'sinovna Benevolenskaya graduated in 1994 from the Saint-Petersburg State University (*SPbGU*) Faculty of Law. After her graduation, she continued her studies at the graduate level focusing on the doctrine of trust law. In 1997, she was awarded the "Candidate of Jurisprudence" degree (at the *SPbGU* Law Faculty, Department of Commercial Law); her candidate dissertation was entitled "Problemy pravovogo regulirovaniia doveritel'nogo upravleniia imushchestvom v sfere predprinimatel'stva"—the first dissertation on the topic of trust management successfully defended in Russia.

Dr. Benevolenskaya has been a lecturer at *SPbGU* and, also, at the Novgorod State University. In her early practice of law, she was a consultant to a subsidiary of "Gazprom JSC". She has authored more than fifty publications in the sphere of commercial law, investments law and trust law including works published under the aegis of Moscow State University and St. Petersburg State University.

Her most-recent published works include: "Prospects for Trust in Russia: The Perspective as Seen from 2010 and 2011 Draft Amendments to the Russian Civil Code", 37(1) *Review of Central and East European Law* (2012), 31-52; "Perspektivy doveritel'noi sobstvennosti v Rossii s tochki zreniia proektov izmenenii v Grazhdanskii Kodeks RF", *Predprinimatel'skoe pravo* (2012) No.1; "Doveritel'noe upravlenie imushchestvom: istoriia i sovremennost'", *Predprinimatel'skoe pravo* (2011) No.3; and "Opredelenie, klassifikatsiia vidov i kvalifikatsionnye priznaki doveritel'noi sobstvennosti po pravu Velikobritanii", *Zhurnal Rossiiskogo prava* (2008) No.9.

Dr. Benevolenskaya also has authored a monograph entitled *Doveritel'noe upravlenie imushchestvom v sfere predprinimatel'stva* (Akademikerverlag GmbH & Co. KG., Lambert Academic Publishing, Saarbrucken, 3rd rev. ed. 2012).

For the last several years, she has practiced law as in-house counsel for a Russian industrial company headquartered in St. Petersburg.

Tatiana Iu. Borisova is an Assistant Professor at the National Research University Higher School of Economics (*Natsional'nyi issledovatel'skii universitet Vysshaia shkola ekonomiki*). Currently, she is working on a monograph provisionally entitled: *Codified Law and Legality in 19th and 20th Century Russia*. Her most recent articles—abstracts available at SSRN—include: "The Digest of Laws of the Russian Empire: The Phenomenon of Autocratic Legality", 31 *Law and History Review* (forthcoming 2012); "Legislation as a Source of Law in Late Imperial Russia", in Lindsay Farmer, Markus Dubber *et al.* (eds.), *From the Judge's Arbitrium to the Legality Principle: Legislation as a Source of Law in Criminal Trial* (Duncker & Humblot, Berlin, forthcoming 2012).

In light of her interest in 'contemporary legal history', she is a member of the "Circulation of Knowledge through the Iron Curtain" research project (hosted by the Centre for Historical Research, National Research University Higher School

Tatiana Borisova and William Simons, eds.
The Legal Dimension in Cold-War Interactions: Some Notes from the Field 167-172

of Economics) and, also, of the research project "Flexibility in Contracts" (hosted by the University of Eastern Finland). During the course of 2012, Dr. Borisova was awarded fellowships from the Köne Foundation and the Higher School of Economics to engage in research at the Helsinki Collegium for Advanced Studies and at the Centre for Socio-Legal Research, Oxford University.

Jane Henderson is an academic lawyer with a long-standing interest in foreign and comparative law, and particularly the Russian legal system. She graduated from University College London (1973), having been awarded the Joseph Hume Scholarship for Jurisprudence. She went on to postgraduate study, specializing in Socialist legal systems and English legal history, and having completed her Master's degree at London University was directly appointed (1974) as Lecturer in the Laws of Eastern Europe in the newly established Centre of European Law at King's College London. In the autumn of 1976, she established a course in Soviet Law for the first time at King's—since 1993 revised as 'Soviet and Post-Soviet Legal Systems', and now 'Russian Legal System'. Since 1986-1987, Ms. Henderson has also been an Adjunct Professor at the University of Notre Dame London Law School, where she runs a post-graduate seminar series on the Russian Legal System for the Concannon Programme of International Law. As well as her teaching expertise, Ms. Henderson also has considerable administrative experience, having served three-year placements successively as undergraduate welfare coordinator and undergraduate admissions tutor. She currently holds the post of Senior Lecturer in the Laws of Eastern Europe.

Ms. Henderson's main research interests and publications have been concerned with public and administrative law issues in the Soviet and Russian legal systems—including the development of the Russian Constitutional Court. She is the rapporteur on Russia for the journal *European Public Law*. Her book on *The Constitution of the Russian Federation* was published by Hart (2011) as part of the series of constitutions of the world in context.

Leena Lehtinen graduated in law from the University of Turku, Finland (1992) and defended her PhD at the University of Vaasa, Finland (1996); the topic of her doctoral dissertation was the privatization of state enterprises and company law in post-Soviet Russia.

Dr. Lehtinen has been a researcher in a number of international projects organized by Finnish universities and ministries and, also, a legal expert in several EU projects involving Russia and other CIS countries. Most of these projects have been devoted to further developing market economies and rule-of-law states in post-Soviet countries.

She is the author of more than seventy articles and the editor of several books. Dr. Lehtinen's most-recent article (in Russian) deals with institutions for registering enterprises in Finland in R.A. Adel'khanian (ed.), *Registratsiia sub"ektov predprinimatel'skoi deiatel'nosti: zarubezhnyi opyt* (Statut, Moscow, 2012), 173-183. She regularly lectures in Russian, English and Finnish in universities and at conferences.

A special focus of Dr. Lehtinen's work involves international commercial arbitration; she is included in the lists of arbitrators in several arbitration institutions, including Moscow and Kiev, and often appears as an arbitrator in international commercial disputes.

Boris N. Mamlyuk teaches comparative law and public international law at the University of Memphis, School of Law. Professsor Mamlyuk obtained his JD from the University of California (Hastings) in 2005 and, upon graduation, practiced as a civil litigator at a US firm. He defended his PhD at the Universitá degli Studi di Torino, Centre for the Comparative Analysis of Law and Economics in 2011. Professor Mamlyuk's doctoral work focused on reimagining Russian approaches to international law in the early Soviet and post-Soviet periods. His current research project focuses on Russia's attempts to harmonize domestic legal structures in light of WTO accession, as well as the effect of WTO accession on regional economic integration treaties in the post-Soviet space. His recent article "Russia & Legal Harmonization: An Historical Inquiry into IP Reform as Global Convergence and Resistance" appears in 10(3) *Washington University Global Studies Law Review* (2011), 535-592.

William Partlett is a lecturer and senior researcher at Columbia Law School. He also has a joint position as a nonresident fellow in the Global Economy and Development Program, Foreign Policy Program, and Center for the United States and Europe at The Brookings Institution. Dr. Partlett holds a law degree from Stanford Law School as well as a Master's in comparative politics and a doctorate in Russian history from Oxford University. He combines his background in comparative politics, history, and law to study the role of law (particularly constitutional law) in authoritarian and post-authoritarian political development.

Dr. Partlett's selected publications include: "Making Constitutions Matter: The Dangers of Constitutional Politics in Post-Authoritarian Constitution-Making", *Brooklyn Journal of International Law* (forthcoming); "Liberal Revolution, Legality, and the Russian Founding Period", *Review of Central and East European Law* (forthcoming); "Enforcing Oil and Gas Contracts Without Courts: Reputational Constraints on Resource Nationalism in Russia and Azerbaijan", 18 *Demokratizatsiya: Journal of Post-Soviet Democratization* (2010); and "Reclassifying

Russian Law: Mechanisms, Outcomes, and Solutions for an Overly Politicized Field", 2 *Columbia Journal of East European Law* (2008) (republished in Chinese by Tsinghua University Press, 2011).

Albert J. Schmidt was born in Louisville, KY in 1925 and grew up during the Depression years and World War II. During that conflict, he served in the Army Air Forces in the Philippines and New Guinea. In 1949, he received his AB degree from DePauw University and his AM and PhD in 1950 and 1953, respectively, in English and European history from the University of Pennsylvania (which included a Fulbright year at the University of London and an internship at the UN at Lake Success in 1950). Subsequently, he did post-doctoral work at the Russian and East European Institute, Indiana, Moscow University, Harvard Business School, and New York University Law School. His writings include articles and reviews regarding Russian architectural history, English legal history, and Soviet law. He authored *The Architecture and Planning of Classical Moscow* (American Philosophical Society, Philadelphia, PA, 1989) and edited *The Impact of Perestroika on Soviet Law*, in F.J.M. Feldbrugge (ed.), *Law in Eastern Europe*, No.41 (Martinus Nijhoff Publishers, Dordrecht, The Netherlands, 1990). At the University of Bridgeport (later Quinnipiac) School of Law, Professor Schmidt taught English legal history, Soviet law, and European legal history, organized workshops in European legal history, and lectured on the Cold War at the University of Lviv. After his retirement, he has been (since 1992) Visiting Scholar in The Institute for European, Russian and Eurasian Studies at The George Washington University and (since 1997) a docent of the National Portrait Gallery in Washington, DC.

William B. Simons received his undergraduate inspiration in Russian Area Studies at Carleton College (Northfield, MN: 1971) from the late Joe Shepard and in law at the University of Wisconsin-Madison Law School (Madison, WI: 1974) from the late Zigurds Zile. He also has a Master's Degree from the Russian School (Northfield, VT: 1974) and obtained his PhD under the careful guidance of Ferdinand Feldbrugge (Leiden, NL: 1997). Simons is Visiting Professor at the Institute of Constitutional and International Law, Faculty of Law, University of Tartu and Tartu's Centre for EU-Russian Studies (Estonia). His chair is in East European Law at Leiden University (Netherlands) and has been a Visiting Professor at the University of Trento (2004-2008). He has published in the area of Russian, East European and comparative law. His research interests include the tools of public policy, reasonableness and good faith as devices to strengthen the 'social character' of Russian law, the harmonization of law *versus* regulatory competition in the CIS region, and access to justice in the state and private sectors. Dr. Simons is Editor of the quarterly *Review of Central and East European Law* and the monograph series *Law in Eastern Europe*. He also has experience as a legal advisor and is a partner—along with Dr. Wim Timmermans—in the law firm Timmermans and Simons International Business Lawyers (Leiden, Netherlands) and has been an arbitrator and expert in lawsuits involving Russian law in Russia (and other jurisdictions). Together with his predecessor Leiden Professor Emeritus Ferdinand Feldbrugge, Simons also has been involved in the nearly two-decade-long collaboration among Russian and Dutch lawyers in work on the new Russian Civil Code (and on CIS model legislation in the private-law field).

Publications which Simons has authored/edited include: *East European Faces of Law and Society: Values and Practices*, in *Law in Eastern Europe*, No.63 (Leiden, Boston, forthcoming 2013); "Sblizhenie chastnogo prava SNG: Vzgliad na protsess", in the anniversary volume celebrating the founding of the Research Center for Private Law attached to the Office of the President of the Russian Federation, *Liudi. Etapy puti. Fakty* (Research Center for Private Law, Moscow, 2011); Zdeněk Kühn, *The Judiciary in Central and Eastern Europe: Mechanical Jurisprudence in Transformation?*, in *Law in Eastern Europe*, No.61 (Leiden, Boston, 2011); and *Private and Civil Law in the Russian Federation*, in *Law in Eastern Europe*, No.60 (Leiden, Boston, 2009).

Paul B. Stephan is the John C. Jeffries, Jr., Distinguished Professor, the David H. Ibbeken '71 Research Professor, and Director of the Graduate Studies Program at the University of Virginia School of Law. He received bachelor and master's degrees in history and Russian studies from Yale University in 1973 and 1974 and a JD from the University of Virginia in 1977. During the two-year period between his graduation and return to Virginia as a law professor, he clerked for Judge Levin Campbell of the US Court of Appeals for the First Circuit and for US Supreme Court Justice Lewis F. Powell, Jr. He taught at the Moscow State Institute for International Relations in the summer of 1991; spent the winter and spring of 1998 as a guest professor at the University of Vienna; the summers of 2000 and 2005 as a guest professor at Münster University; the fall of 2001 as a guest professor at Lausanne University; the summers of 2002, 2004 and 2006 as a visiting lecturer at Melbourne University; the fall of 2004 as a guest professor on the law faculty of University of Pantheon-Assas, Paris, and at Sciences Po; the winters of 2008-2009 and 2011-2012 as a visiting professor at the Interdisciplinary Centre, Herzliya; the fall of 2010 as the Justin D'Atri Visiting Professor of Law, Business and Society at Columbia University; the spring of 2010 and 2011 as a guest lecturer at Sydney University; and the spring of 2011 teaching at Peking University School of Transnational Law in Shenzhen, China.

An expert on international business and Soviet and post-Soviet legal systems, Professor Stephan has advised governments and international organizations, organized conferences, edited books and lectured in many venues on a variety of issues raised by the globalization of the world economy and the transition away from Soviet-style socialism. From 1993 to 1998, he served as an adviser to the US Department of Treasury with respect to its effort to assist Russia and other former socialist countries in designing modern tax systems. During 2006-2007, he served as Counselor on International Law in the Office of the Legal Adviser of the US Department of State. He also has participated as counsel or an expert witness in various lawsuits and arbitrations involving Russian investments and transactions, most particularly in the multiple claims brought by the Yukos oil and gas company and its investors in connection with the company's liquidation.

Professor Stephan has published numerous textbooks, monographs and articles. His casebook on international business in particular is used at law schools both in the United States and abroad. He has written extensively on international law, corruption and the history of the Cold War. He is the co-author (with Robert Scott) of *The Limits of Leviathan: Contract Theory and the Enforcement of International Law* (Cambridge University Press, Cambridge, 2006). Among his recent work is "Privatizing International Law", 97 *Virginia Law Review* (November 2011), 1573-1664; and a chapter on "Treaties, 1946-2000", in *International Law in the Supreme Court: Continuity and Change* (2011). He currently is involved in plans by the American Law Institute to produce a new Restatement of the Foreign Relations Law of the United States.

Subject-Matter Index

T

U

V

W

Name Index

T

www.ingramcontent.com/pod-product-compliance
Lightning Source LLC
LaVergne TN
LVHW020652300926
849161LV00004B/919